SAINTS AND SINNERS IN THE
CRISTERO WAR

JAMES MURPHY

Saints and Sinners in the Cristero War

Stories of Martyrdom from Mexico

IGNATIUS PRESS   SAN FRANCISCO

Front cover photograph
from the Cristero War in Mexico (1926–1929)
Provenance unknown

Cover design by Enrique J. Aguilar

© 2019 by Ignatius Press, San Francisco
All rights reserved
ISBN 978-1-62164-262-6 (PB)
ISBN 978-1-64229-065-3 (eBook)
Library of Congress Control Number 2018949822
Printed in the United States of America ∞

CONTENTS

FOREWORD

Historical memory is the soul of every nation. What we choose to remember helps define who we are. How we remember where we have been in the past shapes how we understand where we are in the present and our hopes for the future. Therefore, it is important to recognize who gets to decide what we remember and how we remember it—because these people control both the present and the future. It is said that the "winner names the age". That means history is always written by those who come out on top.

However, we need to realize that the story the victors tell is sometimes not the truth—but a narrative written to serve their own purposes. For instance, in this country, what we know about Christopher Columbus and Spanish missionaries like Saint Junípero Serra has been deeply colored by "la legenda negra" ("the black legend") which was anti-Hispanic propaganda invented by the colonial British and later "mainstreamed" by the Ku Klux Klan and anti-Catholic nativists for the 1920s. As Monsignor James Murphy points out in this fine book, the KKK was among the many elites in this country who lent support to the brutal anti-Catholic persecutions in Mexico in the 1920s.

This period in the history of the United States and Mexico is now largely forgotten in both countries. It is hardly mentioned in many contemporary histories of Mexico and Latin America. Even Mexico's renowned public intellectuals and men of letters, Carlos Fuentes and Octavio

Paz, have never had much to say about this dark stain on Mexico's conscience. Yet the history of the Americas has never witnessed persecution on such an epic scale as that waged against the Catholic Church in the years after the Mexican Revolution.

The post-revolutionary regime adopted a constitution in 1917 that outlawed the public practice of the Catholic faith. The decade that followed was a reign of terror—priests were killed at the altar and strung from poles along the highways; and believers were tortured and killed in the most horrible ways. Hundreds of thousands fled across the border seeking refuge and were welcomed by the Church in Los Angeles and elsewhere throughout the United States. This was a time of martyrs and saints and countless hidden heroes for the faith.

I learned the names of these heroes as a young boy growing up in Monterrey, just a generation after the persecution—Blessed Miguel Pro may be the only martyr in the history of the Church whose execution was photographed; Saint José Sánchez del Río, the child-martyr; Blessed Salvador Huerta Gutiérrez, the only auto mechanic in the communion of saints; Saint Toribio Romo González, the martyred priest who has become the patron of immigrants and refugees from Mexico; and Servant of God María de la Luz Camacho, the beautiful catechist who gave her life to prevent her church from being desecrated.

When I became an archbishop, first in San Antonio and later in Los Angeles, I began to see firsthand how the faith of the Church in this country has been shaped by the witness of the many refugees from the persecution. I learned the name of Saint Rafael Guízar Valencia, a bishop who ran a clandestine seminary in Mexico during the early years of the persecution. Later he was driven into exile, and he even spent some time preaching and teaching in San

Antonio, Texas. I was always humbled to know that this heroic priest once preached in the same pulpit in which I used to preach in every Sunday at San Fernando Cathedral. In Los Angeles, I learned of Venerable Mother Luisita, María Luisa de la Peña y Navarro, who founded one of the most vital religious orders here, the Carmelite Sisters of the Most Sacred Heart of Los Angeles. The litany of Mexican saints and martyrs is long, and we should know their names and their stories and the history of the times in which they lived. Monsignor Murphy tells this story well. His chapter on Miguel Pro should be required reading in every seminary.

These stories matter. We are living in a secular age and a globalized society that more and more functions with indifference or hostility toward religion. We need to remember that proclaiming Jesus Christ can lead to violence and persecution. This was true in the time of the apostles, it was true in Mexico in the 1920s, and it is true today. We should never forget that today, all across the world, Christians are still suffering and dying for Jesus.

In our time, the Church in the United States knows the "soft" persecution of those who would deny us our rights to live our faith in freedom. Increasingly, we face pressures to compromise and abandon our beliefs as "the price" for living in our society. It is especially in these times that we need to recover these lost stories of our recent history. We should be grateful to Monsignor Murphy for making this possible.

These stories are important because they remind us that there has always been a strong spiritual bond between the Church in Mexico and the United States. In fact, it was Hispanic missionaries from Mexico who first evangelized this country, and our country continues to be renewed by the spiritual contributions of men and women from Mexico and Latin America.

We need to remember this history and especially the saints—known and unknown—who laid down their lives to keep the Christian faith alive in many dark and faithless times. Because of their witness and courage, this beautiful faith, the truth of the living God, has been handed on to us.

In this way, may the blood of the martyrs continue to be the seed of the Church of the Americas.

Most Reverend José H. Gómez
Archbishop of Los Angeles
July 1, 2018
Memorial of Saint Junípero Serra

INTRODUCTION

In the late 1920s, a violent conflict over religious freedom broke out in Mexico between a large segment of the Catholic population and the government of President Plutarco Elías Calles. Called the Cristero War or Cristero Rebellion, also known as *La Cristiada*, the conflict began as a spontaneous rebellion by ragtag bands of rural Catholics whose machetes and homemade slings were no match for the armed forces of the Mexican Republic. It was a minor disturbance that the army should have crushed in a matter of days, but it didn't. The conflict went on for three years, and by the time it ended, the Mexican army had lost twelve generals, seventy colonels, and eighteen hundred officers. Over two hundred thousand people, combatants and civilians alike, were killed, and many more fled the country. It was during this time that significant numbers of immigrants from Mexico began coming to the United States.

Surprisingly little is known in Mexico about this religious conflict because for decades following the war the subject was too sensitive to teach in schools or to talk about in public discourse. There was a kind of conspiracy of silence both in the Church and the state, as Mexicans lived under what one Vatican official called the most anti-Catholic constitution on the planet.[1] Surprisingly little is known about it on

---

[1] Monsignor Girolamo Prigione, papal envoy to Mexico, interview with Tim Golden, "Mexico Ending Church Restraints after 70 Years of Official Hostility", *New York Times*, December 20, 1991, https://www.nytimes.com /1991/12/20/world/mexico-ending-church-restraints-after-70-years-of-official -hostility.html.

this side of the border either, despite the critical involvement of American Catholics in the crisis at the time. The Archdiocese of San Antonio, for example, had to host practically all of the Mexican bishops (who had been exiled) for several years during that period, and the Knights of Columbus provided financial assistance for the hundreds of priests, nuns, and laity who were fleeing the persecution. It was pressure from the American Catholic community that eventually caused President Calvin Coolidge to pay more attention to the crisis, and it was his ambassador to Mexico who eventually brokered an end to the conflict.

My interest in the subject began in the 1980s, when I met an old Cristero soldier in Mexico City whose eyes, at the age of eighty, would still fill up with tears at hearing the battle cry *Viva Cristo Rey!* (Long Live Christ the King!). It was my first time to hear stories about the Cristero War, and the hardships it visited on the Catholic rebels riveted my attention: the days with nothing to eat, the weeks without an opportunity to bathe, the constant fear of having to face an enemy who had vastly superior military hardware. A memoir that old soldier wrote for his children and grandchildren describes, among other things, the day he defecated in his pants as he faced the withering machine gun fire of the federal forces in the hills of central Mexico. When he returned home to Morelia for a break with his hair full of lice, the family had to burn his clothes rather than wash them—much to his disappointment. He wanted to keep the old *gabán* (overcoat) because, he said, it had been his faithful friend, the only thing he had had to keep him warm in those high elevations for so many months.

I have been studying that period in Mexican history ever since, in particular, the scholarship that has been done in recent decades by historians like Jean Meyer, Father Fidel

González Fernández, David Bailey, and others. I am particularly indebted to the even-handed approach to history found in the writings of Enrique Krauze (a secular historian) and Kevin Starr (a Catholic historian). Much of that research, however, leaves out many of the pivotal players in the crisis, in particular, the twenty-five priests and lay people who were canonized by Pope John Paul II in 2000 and others who are now in the canonization process. The one work that does deal with those personalities—the two-volume history by Father Fidel González Fernández—is not available in English.[2] My book fills that gap. It brings to an English-speaking readership the stories of these little-known heroes, Catholics who died for their faith just south of our border less than a hundred years ago.

The structure of the book is simple. In the first chapter, I deal with the obvious question: How could a Catholic country like Mexico end up persecuting the religion that was practiced by the vast majority of its people? The answer to that question takes us back to Mexico's colonial roots in Spain; that is where this problem has its origins. In the following chapters, I choose a representative group of martyrs using biographical reflections to tell each one's story. I also reflect on the accomplices in this persecution, people I call "sinners", although that characterization is for writing purposes more than for making a judgment on the state of their souls. Without including those "sinners", this epic story of Mexico would not be complete.

To understand the relevance of this story for American readers, one need only look at U.S. population figures. There are close to thirty-six million people of Mexican descent in the U.S., the second-largest Mexican-origin

---

[2] Fidel González Fernández, *Sangre y Corazón de Un Pueblo* (Guadalajara: Arzobispado de Guadalajara, 2008).

population in the world after Mexico itself.[3] The destinies
of our two nations are inextricably bound, as are the destinies of the Catholic Church in both countries. The majority of Mexicans are Catholic, and their numbers are having
a significant impact on the Catholic Church in America
at all levels. Moreover, studies have shown that Mexican
Catholics are less likely to drop out of the Church than
their American coreligionists are. Their impact comes not
only from their numerical strength, but from their deeper
faith. The reason for that is their history of persecution.
Mexican Catholics have seen suffering—the kind of suffering that makes the faith stronger for subsequent genera-
tions, who are inspired by it. Thus has it been throughout
the history of the Church. Since the days of the Roman
Empire, the stories that are told on the feasts of the martyrs
have inspired Catholics to embrace the Cross and live a
better life. The otherworldly peace on the face of Father
Miguel Pro as he was about to face a firing squad in Mexico City (detailed in chapter 8) is a good example. Rather
than being paralyzed by the terror most of us would feel
in that position, Pro was carefree and more than happy to
forgive the soldiers who were leading him to his death. "A
strange exultation shone in his face," one journalist wrote
at the time, "as if he already felt himself shaded by the
mighty wings of his patron, San Miguel the Angel."[4]

It reminds me of a similar scene in Tudor England in the
sixteenth century when the Carthusian monks were about
to be hanged, drawn, and quartered by the henchmen of

[3] Antonio Flores, "How the U.S. Hispanic Population Is Changing", Pew
Research Center Fact Tank, September 18, 2017, http://www.pewresearch.org
/fact-tank/2017/09/18/how-the-u-s-hispanic-population-is-changing/.

[4] Captain Francis McCullagh, *Red Mexico: A Reign of Terror in America* (New
York: Louis Carrier, 1928), quoted in Mrs. George Norman, *The Life and Martyrdom of Father Michael Pro, S.J.* (London: Catholic Book Club, 1938), 199.

King Henry VIII. Commenting on the joy he saw on the faces of those monks, Thomas More (who would soon be martyred himself) famously commented to his daughter: "Lo, dost thou not see, Meg, these blessed fathers be now as cheerfully going to their deaths as bridegrooms to their marriage?"[5]

Images like that help all of us feel a little less fearful of death.

---

[5] Quoted in Gerard B. Wegermen and Stephen W. Smith, *Thomas More Source Book* (Washington, D.C.: Catholic University of America Press, 2004), 54.

Chapter 1

Melchor Ocampo and the Enlightenment

In 1851, a newspaper debate took place in Mexico between two men with very different views on religion. On the one side was Melchor Ocampo, the highly cultured governor of Michoacán who (in addition to politics) practiced scientific farming on his hacienda, studied Indian languages, and assembled one of the best private libraries in all of Mexico. He was also a world traveler who came under the influence of the European Enlightenment, and at a young age concluded that religion was a waste of time at best. On the other side was an "anonymous priest" from a town near Ocampo's hacienda who never revealed his identity, but historians are confident it was Clemente de Jesús Munguía, the bishop of Michoacán. Munguía was a well-read theologian and dedicated churchman who believed it was his responsibility to protect his flock from false teachings coming from Europe, especially the atheism of the French Revolution. He was particularly impatient with anyone who took it on himself to air the Church's dirty laundry in public, insisting that internal Church problems should be dealt with in private so as "not to alarm the faithful by stirring up the bitterest ill-feelings against their priests".[1]

---

[1] Clemente de Jesús Munguía, [article title], [*periodical*], [date], quoted in Enrique Krauze, *Mexico: Biography of Power* (New York: HarperCollins, 1998), 155.

It was an embarrassing in-house problem involving a worldly priest that led to the famous debate. A poor worker on Ocampo's hacienda asked the local priest to perform a funeral service for his son without charge because he could not afford to pay the usual stipend. The priest refused to do it, saying that those fees were what he depended on for a living. "What will I do with my dead son, then," the poor man asked. "Salt him and eat him," the priest said dismissively.[2]

Ocampo was so enraged that he decided to make a "representation" to the Congress of the state of Michoacán, requesting that the system of charging for the sacraments in the Catholic Church be reformed. His action was immediately attacked in print by the "anonymous priest", and the result was a fiery debate that became a cause célèbre all over Mexico, riveting the attention of thousands of readers for eight months. The arguments went far beyond the case of one bad priest, and before it was over it offended the sensibilities of many an old-fashioned Catholic.

"What use are so many churches in a country which can barely afford to maintain one," Ocampo wrote, "of harmfully multiplying the number of festivals ... of encouraging idleness, drunkenness and other vices ... and of giving priests a surplus of income without their having earned it through doing anything really useful? ... Unhappy Indians whose wealth goes up in the smoke of the candles, the censers and the fireworks."[3]

The "anonymous priest" was quick to respond. These "pestilential doctrines" are the offspring of Martin Luther and European atheism, he wrote, and so are the twin ideas: freedom of religion and freedom of conscience. "These

[2] Ibid., 154.
[3] Ibid., 153.

two concepts," he wrote, "as ungodly as they are fatal, currently serve the interests of European socialism, and if God should decide to punish us by spreading them among us, it is certain we would end in universal devastation."[4] Could it be, he wondered, that the French Revolution was finally reaching Mexico, with its godless philosophy and godless laws banishing priests and confiscating "the sacred property of the clergy"?[5]

His words were prophetic. The banishing of priests and the confiscation of Church property would indeed soon come to Mexico, and the exaggerated tone in his response only served to bring on that crisis sooner. The debate foreshadowed a much more ominous confrontation that would take place in Mexico a few years later: the brutal civil war known as the War of the Reform that was fought between 1858 and 1861. By then, an irreconcilable division had developed between the Conservatives (which included the Catholic Church and the military) on one side and the Liberals (those influenced by the French Enlightenment) on the other, and that division would haunt the Catholic Church into the next century. The civil war of the 1920s—known as the Cristero War—would be the offspring of that destructive chasm.

Mexico's Catholic Heritage
1524–1855

Melchor Ocampo was justified when he called attention to the worldly priest, but he went too far when he ridiculed the smoke and candles of the Catholic religion. For three hundred years, those religious symbols had been a comforting

[4] Ibid., 154.
[5] Ibid.

presence in the lives of the people of New Spain (that is what Mexico was called in those days), connecting them with a mystery that was greater than themselves.[6] People came to church to baptize their babies, to celebrate their marriages, and to mourn their dead. They came to educate their children, to get advice when in trouble, and to get help when they were hungry. Above all, they came to find meaning in life. The tolling of the church bells punctuated the hours of the day in every town and village, lifting people above the drudgery of daily existence and putting them in touch with the transcendent. Parish celebrations, with their pageantry and fireworks, were the main form of entertainment in every town, celebrating a patron saint or marking a feast in the liturgical calendar. Despite class distinctions, all strata of society participated in the parish processions: Creoles and Indians, priests and soldiers, wealthy hacienda owners and farmhands. The procession was a metaphor for the journey of life itself. The Indians in particular traveled long distances from the hills to be part of those processions, and their proudest boast was the opportunity to carry the patron saint shoulder high, while elaborately dressed altar boys walked in front with lanterns.

The missionaries furiously defended the Indians against the cruelty of the Spanish conquerors, and they were instrumental in convincing the Spanish Crown to issue comprehensive new laws addressing the abuses of the colonizers. The missionaries also worked tirelessly to improve the Indians' standard of living, teaching them new skills that came from Europe. The Augustinians brought artisans from Spain to instruct them in carpet weaving, pottery making, sculpture, painting, and wrought-iron work. The

---

[6] When the country finally won its independence from Spain in 1821, the revolutionaries changed the name from New Spain to Mexico.

Dominicans introduced the silk worm and taught them how to produce an expensive fabric that was unknown in their world. One visionary priest—Vasco de Quiroga— set up communes in Michoacán based on the egalitarian vision elaborated in Saint Thomas More's book *Utopia*. Another organized a group of Indian stonecutters and masons to build an aqueduct twenty-eight miles long, crossing two states (Hidalgo and México state), to bring fresh water to villages that didn't have it. The remarkable structure crosses three valleys on huge bridges, the largest one containing sixty-seven arches, one of which is 128 feet high with a span of 70 feet.[7]

But more important than these civic missions was the spiritual one, and the success of the religious orders (Augustinians, Dominicans, Franciscans, Carmelites) in this was phenomenal, with millions being baptized in the decades following the conquest. Historians have called it one of the most extraordinary chapters in the religious history of the West.[8] The key to their success was the missionaries' skill at using Indian myth and symbols to explain Catholic teaching. Celebrating the lives of the saints, for example, was easy for Indians when it was explained in the language

---

[7] Called the Aqueduct of Padre Tembleque, to honor the priest who organized the construction, it was listed as a UNESCO World Heritage Site in 2015.

[8] Some historians question the freedom of the natives of that time to refuse Baptism, citing a royal declaration called the *Requerimiento* (the Demand), which promised to treat the natives justly on condition that they converted and became subjects of the Spanish Crown. However, this document was used by the military not the missionaries, and its use was roundly condemned by the religious orders—with reason. When the colonizers first encountered a group of native peoples, they perfunctorily read the document to them, but often without any real effort to communicate with the natives. By law, they were supposed to use an interpreter, but frequently they read it in Spanish only, sometimes addressing an abandoned beach because the natives had already fled. The missionaries, who were appalled by the abuses of the *Requerimiento*, solved the problem by writing their own guidelines on when to baptize.

of house gods. Our Lady of Guadalupe became a particularly powerful symbol of the new faith because it portrayed the Blessed Mother as a dark-skinned Aztec princess whose image was meaningful to both indigenous peoples and Europeans.

The explosion in architectural creativity is another measure of the missionaries' success. As previously suggested, approximately 11,800 cathedrals, churches, and chapels were built in New Spain from the middle of the sixteenth century to the middle of the seventeenth century, most of the work being done by native artisans under Spanish supervision. Add to that hundreds of hospitals, orphanages, and convents. The Jesuits joined the enterprise, shortly after their foundation in 1541, and took up the building of universities. By the middle of the seventeenth century, they were running thirty-two colleges and universities all over New Spain, providing the nation with a professional class that was well versed in the social gospel and dedicated to the common good. This all happened at a time when the United States was still an unexplored wilderness. The first university in North America was not Harvard, established in 1636, but the Royal and Pontifical University of Mexico, established in 1551. William Shakespeare was not yet born when the first library appeared in the capital of New Spain in the early sixteenth century.

Regretfully, this world of art, high learning, and social justice also had a dark side: the Inquisition. That judicial process, which had its roots in the Middle Ages, was used to keep out the dangerous ideas of the European Enlightenment by controlling the availability of books and printed material. It also put dissenters and suspected heretics on trial, sometimes handing them over to the state for execution. Church and state—some called them the "Two

Majesties"—worked together in this enterprise because both had a vested interest in protecting religious truth and the unity of belief in the body politic. The Inquisition was part of a worldview that saw the Two Majesties as a single indivisible unit.[9]

Such was the world the Spanish Crown and its missionaries created in New Spain, a world of confident faith and continuous prayer that seemed like it could never change. In fact it didn't for three hundred years, not until the new thinking from Europe finally reached Mexico in the early nineteenth century. (The Inquisition was dissolved in 1834.) At that point, a generation of intellectuals appeared on the scene that was keenly aware of empirical science, modern philosophy, and economics—in particular the economics of Spain and the Crown's unquenchable thirst for silver and gold. Melchor Ocampo was one of those intellectuals. A mestizo (mixed race) who was orphaned as a baby, he was lucky enough to be dropped off at the door of a wealthy woman who adopted him, raised him as her own, and eventually left her hacienda to him. She also saw to it that he got a good education, which (after a short time in the seminary in Morelia) included study in France, where he was influenced by the anticlericalism of the French Revolution. He became convinced that the religion he grew up with was not only a waste of time, but was at the root of all of Mexico's problems.

[9] The vast majority of the sentences consisted of penances such as wearing a cross or going on a pilgrimage, but someone convicted of "unrepentant heresy" could be handed over to a state magistrate for more serious sentencing. The Inquisition is out of step with the civil tolerance that has characterized the Catholic Church for centuries, and the Second Vatican Council confirmed that tolerance. Nevertheless, the Inquisition is one of the blots on the Catholic Church's past record, and stands as a cautionary tale for anyone who is tempted to indulge in blind religious zeal.

Polarized into Liberals and Conservatives
1855–1910

Regrettably, by this time in history there were reasons to criticize the practices of the Catholic Church, if one were so inclined. Diocesan priests (who don't have a vow of poverty) had taken the place of the religious orders, and it could indeed be said, as Ocampo said, that some of them were more interested in making money than in serving the people. Country pastors were often the owners of sizeable farms or sugar mills, in addition to their positions in the Church, and some were accused of having mistresses on the quiet. Moreover, the Church as an institution had become wealthy, so much so that its financial decisions could have an impact on the economy of the entire nation. The religious orders were among the largest landowners in the colony, mostly through donations and bequests from pious Catholics. By 1700, according to some estimates, as much as 50 percent of the usable land in Mexico was owned by the Catholic Church.[10]

Of course, one could argue that the money was usually put to good use. Religious orders and diocesan offices made money available on loan, in effect functioning as banks that fueled some economic growth at low interest rates. Moreover, the Church was the only institution in the colony providing services for the poor through its enviable network of hospitals, schools, and orphanages. Nonetheless, thinkers like Ocampo believed the Church was like a dead hand putting a damper on economic progress, and they increasingly resented it. They also resented the system of tithing, which placed heavy burdens on the poor

---

[10] Lesley Byrd Simpson, *Many Mexicos* (Los Angeles: University of California Press, 1974), 173.

to support the priests. Another source of deep resentment was the tradition of *fueros*, a body of laws that exempted clergy and military personnel from having to stand trial in civil courts, even if they were charged with a violation of civil law. This was precisely the kind of inherited privilege that fired the anger of the Enlightenment revolutionists in Europe and got swept away by the French Revolution. In addition, there was the question of the Two Majesties, the close alliance between the church and the state in the Spanish system. As soon as Mexico won its freedom from Spain, that issue would haunt the Church, and it would continue to be a problem into modern times.

Church-state relations under Spain's Catholic monarchs were rooted in the medieval concept of an ideal society, which saw the Catholic religion as a leaven permeating every aspect of life, civil as well as religious, from cradle to grave. What this meant in practice was that the state shared with the Church the responsibility of evangelizing the people of the New World. This power sharing (called the "Patronato Real" and approved by the Vatican) gave the Spanish Crown the right to nominate bishops and other ecclesiastical offices, control Church taxation, and give approval for the building of new churches and the establishment of diocesan boundaries. The Crown could also control the number of priests coming from Europe to the New World and could even veto the publication and execution of papal edicts in the colonies.[11] In return, the monarchs had the responsibility of assisting the Church in her mission to evangelize, and sometimes the civic officials doing this were themselves bishops. Nearly a dozen

---

[11] A vestige of this system can be seen in the United Kingdom, where the monarch is the head of the Church of England and makes episcopal appointments with the advice of the prime minister.

archbishops and bishops served in the government post of viceroy (a kind of "vice-king" whose job it was to oversee the colony) in New Spain between 1535 and 1821, and in Spain itself a cardinal (Giulio Alberoni) served as prime minister from 1716 to 1719. The typical town square in New Spain symbolized this interdependent relationship of church and state, with a large church or cathedral on one side, flanked on two sides by government buildings, reminders that the Two Majesties worked together to guarantee everyone a meaningful place in this world and a ticket to everlasting happiness in the next.

The arrangement worked well as long as the Two Majesties were on speaking terms, but if a problem developed between them the Church could be at the mercy of raw state power. The expulsion of the Jesuits in 1767 was the most dramatic example of this. That year the Crown ordered all members of the Society of Jesus, whom they saw as too powerful and too independent, to leave Spanish territories, and the state confiscated all their properties: universities, seminaries, churches. It was an ominous precedent, one that would not be lost on the Mexican revolutionists of the next century, when they finally won independence from Spain. Those insurgents would eventually demand the same control over the Church and her many properties. But not right away. In fact, the movement for independence from Spain was at first deeply religious, inspired by a Catholic priest, Miguel Hidalgo y Costilla, who had some four hundred priests actively supporting him and many more in sympathy with his cause; his troops marched behind the banner of Our Lady of Guadalupe. That connection to the Church would continue for some time. When General Agustín de Iturbide emerged victorious from the War of Independence and made himself the emperor of a free Mexico in 1822, the archbishop of México anointed him in a special High Mass. Moreover, the first constitution of independent Mexico, written in 1824,[12] continued to recognize Catholicism as the official religion, and the *fueros* were left untouched. But the church-state issue continued to smolder beneath the surface with questions such as, why does the Catholic Church continue to have special status and privileges in Mexico? Why can't the state curtail the power of the Church like the Spanish Crown did in 1767? Surprisingly, radicals were not the only ones asking these questions. Some of the most prominent proponents of this new thinking were liberal priests.

In the early 1830s, the Liberals found themselves in control for a brief period and immediately took advantage of it. They passed a host of anticlerical laws, stipulating, among other things, that future clerical appointments would be made by the government, not the local bishop. (Remember the Patronato Real!) These laws went nowhere, however, because within a year the Conservative Antonio López de Santa Anna got back into power, abolished the anti-Catholic laws, and expelled the politicians who authored them.[13] The Church had dodged a bullet, but it would not be for long because the Liberals threw Santa Anna out of power for good in 1855 and got their revenge. By that time, both sides had hardened, with the Liberals more determined than ever to curtail the power of the Church, and the Conservatives more determined than ever to fight the unholy ideas coming from the French Revolution. The Liberals were in power, however, and

---

[12] Mexico had three constitutions: 1824, 1857, and 1917.

[13] Santa Anna was the first of three towering figures in nineteenth-century Mexican history (the other two were Benito Juárez and Porfirio Díaz). He held the presidency for eleven terms. It was during his time that the disastrous Treaty of Guadalupe Hidalgo was signed (1848), ending the Mexican-American War and ceding half of Mexico's territory to the United States.

they used that power to settle the religious question once and for all, passing a package of laws known as the Laws of the Reform. The package was a mixture of good and bad: it banished the *fueros*, which made everyone in Mexico equal before the law (a good idea), but it also barred the Church from owning property she did not need for day-to-day operations, which was analogous to stripping a Catholic university of its endowment fund (a bad idea). Those laws were soon followed by the Constitution of 1857, which was also a mixture of good and bad; it guaranteed freedom of conscience, freedom of speech, and freedom of the press, but it also incorporated the anti-Catholic Laws of the Reform in the text. It was a hybrid that reflected the polarized world in which it was born, a document that looked to the future but at the same time remained a prisoner of the past. Despite the fact that it guaranteed many civil rights, a "monarchy in republican clothing" is how Justo Sierra described it.[14]

To this day, people are divided on just how anticlerical the 1857 Constitution really was, and they still fall into two camps similar to those of the eighteenth century. In the eyes of traditional Catholics, the convention delegates who wrote the constitution were one-sided—made up of liberals and radicals—and the document they produced did not represent the sentiments of the people of Mexico, the majority of whom were practicing Catholics. Neither was it ever ratified by a vote of the people. It could never be because its aim was to attack the Catholic religion and de-catholicize the people of Mexico, whether the people wanted it or not.[15]

[14] Justo Sierra, quoted in Krauze, *Mexico*, 551.
[15] Joseph Schlarman, *Mexico: A Land of Volcanoes* (Milwaukee: Bruce Publishing, 1950), 295.

However, progressive Mexicans (some of whom are Catholic) see it very differently. In their minds, the 1857 Constitution simply reflected the difficult realities facing Mexico at that time. The newly formed state under Benito Juárez had found itself competing against a kind of parallel state—the Catholic Church—whose leaders (including the pope) opposed it at every turn and even called on Catholics not to accept its legitimacy. The infant republic had no option but to fight to the death for its very survival. People in this camp also disagree that the constitutional convention was all that radical. Yes, there were some radicals (like Ocampo) present, but a large number of the delegates were moderates who wanted to work out a reasonable accommodation with the Catholic Church. It was those moderate delegates who put the explicit (and surprising) sentence in the text to "care for and protect" the Catholic Church "with just and prudent laws".[16] And it was these delegates who turned to prayer between sessions of the convention, and even took an oath before a crucifix as they assented to the final version of the document. Their aim was not to destroy the Catholic Church, but rather to disentangle church and state. Melchor Ocampo's friend and political colleague, the soon-to-be president Benito Juárez, was one of those moderates.

Like Ocampo, Juárez had been a seminarian who later became a disciple of the Enlightenment, but unlike Ocampo he didn't absorb the radical elements of the French Revolution—at least not at first. In fact, in his earlier life as governor of Oaxaca, he worked well with the local clergy, knowing that this was the most effective way to get things done. "He never ceased to attend the solemn

---

[16] Krauze, *Mexico*, 168.

ceremonies of the Church," one observer commented, "and take his seat under the chancel, on a carpeted platform with a prie-dieu and cushions, and a chaplain would say the Confiteor and the Credo and then bless him."[17] When an epidemic of cholera broke out in Oaxaca, he and government officials joined in three days of public prayer for the purpose of "begging our God for forgiveness to free us from the terrible scourge of cholera". After walking in one religious procession, he fell on his knees before the tabernacle while the priests chanted the *Miserere Deus*.[18] Juárez was still displaying those old-fashioned Catholic sentiments seven years later as a delegate to the constitutional convention. When the new constitution was promulgated in February 1857, he talked the bishop in Oaxaca into marking the occasion with a special Mass, including the singing of the Te Deum.

However, that Oaxaca bishop was the exception. The Church hierarchy in general was appalled at the new constitution and responded accordingly, hurling anathemas and threats of excommunication at its authors and at any Catholic who dared to support them. There was no room for compromise, and Mexico became polarized into two increasingly hostile camps. "The Church accepted nothing; it discussed nothing; its position was all or nothing," says historian Enrique Krauze about this period.[19] One moderate historian of the time grieved as he thought about the lost opportunities for negotiation that could have found common ground: "The Church worked with tireless activity and its clandestine roles were countless.... They used every means possible to stir up hatred among

[17] Ibid., 164.
[18] Ibid.
[19] Ibid., 168.

the people for the government in power, to trouble consciences and inflame passions."[20]
The Liberals responded with equal vehemence. Juárez,
who had been so religious in his early life, now fought back
by hurling his own anathemas: a string of anti-Catholic
decrees that made the earlier Laws of the Reform look
tame. The new laws (mostly written by Melchor Ocampo,
who was taking a leaf from the handbook of the French
Revolution) nationalized all Church property without
compensation, barred government personnel from attending religious services in any official capacity, closed monasteries and convents, forbade female religious orders from
accepting any new members, curtailed the number of official religious holidays and processions in the streets, and
even restricted the ringing of church bells in some places.
The Patronato Real of colonial days was now back, but in
a very different form. While the original version was one
of cooperation between the Two Majesties, this new version was born of deep hostility to Catholicism. The upshot
of the crisis was a brutal civil war in Mexico—the War of
the Reform (1858–1861)—with President Benito Juárez
and his anticlerical supporters headquartered in the port
of Veracruz, and General Félix Zuloaga and his clerical
supporters headquartered in Mexico City. Enrique Krauze
describes the mayhem and sacrilege that ensued:

> Eminent Liberals literally picked up axes to destroy altars,
> church facades, pulpits, and confessionals. Scenes out of the
> French Revolution were reenacted. Images of saints were
> decapitated, shot full of holes, burned in public *autos-da-fe*;
> Church treasuries were robbed, archives were plundered,
> ecclesiastical libraries went up in flames. Bishops were

[20] Quoted in ibid.

stoned to death, and Church property was auctioned off. Nuns who had spent their whole lives cloistered were suddenly forced out of their convents. Ocampo ordered the expulsion of all Catholic bishops from the country with only two exceptions.[21]

One radical commented, the government banishes the bishops; it ought to hang them.

In the fog of war, both sides were committing unspeakable atrocities. As one American university textbook puts it: "The conservatives shot captured prisoners in the name of holy religion, and the liberals did the same in defense of freedom and democratic government."[22]

Near the end of the war, Melchor Ocampo himself became a victim of the Conservative extremes. He had resigned from the cabinet and was retired on his hacienda in Michoacán when a group of armed men showed up at his door and took him away. After traveling for three days, they stopped in a small village and told him to write his will. "I die believing I did what I thought was good for my country," he wrote, after bequeathing his property to his daughters. He noted that he was making his will "at the very place of my execution" and told his daughters where to find documents relevant to their inheritance: "in a notebook written in English, to be found between the living-room wall and the window of my dressing-room".[23] When he was finished writing, his captors shot him and hung him from a tree.

After three brutal years, the Liberals won the War of the Reform, and Juárez was back in power, but the

[21] Ibid., 170.
[22] Michael Meyer, William Sherman, and Susan Deeds, *The Course of Mexican History* (New York: Oxford University Press, 2007), 336.
[23] Krauze, *Mexico*, 171.

Conservatives were not ready to give up. They aligned themselves with Napoleon III (who was itching for an excuse to plant the French flag in Latin America) in a plot to import a Catholic archduke from Austria and make him the emperor of Mexico. It was a farcical idea, but in the eyes of the Conservatives this was the only hope for saving Mexico from the mayhem of the French Revolution. The plot began when the French army invaded Mexico, and after an initial defeat in the Battle of Puebla on Cinco de Mayo 1862, the French forces overcame all resistance and drove Juárez out of Mexico City. With the country now occupied by a foreign army, a light-haired archduke with a pale complexion and blue eyes was shipped in from Europe and was installed as emperor in a Solemn High Mass in the cathedral in Mexico City. His name was Ferdinand Maximilian, an ambitious royal who lived in the shadow of his older brother, Franz Joseph, who would eventually become the powerful ruler of the Austro-Hungarian Empire. At this time, Ferdinand was living in a romantic castle by the sea in Lombardy-Venetia in northern Italy and was the ruler of a tiny kingdom, with scant prospects of ever ruling anything bigger. It suited Franz Joseph's plans to get his frustrated younger brother out of the way as much as it suited Napoleon's to plant a puppet in the New World. Maximilian was thirty-two years old when he arrived in Mexico, and his wife, Carlota (a Belgian royal), was only twenty-four.

Ironically, the imported emperor turned out to be a big disappointment to the churchmen who had blessed him. He was a liberal who sympathized with the liberal goals of the 1857 Constitution, and he showed no interest in rolling back the draconian Laws of the Reform. Furthermore, he surprised everyone by opening up his palace once a week to the people and even learned Indian languages. He was hoping this policy would win the support of Juárez and the Liberals, but it didn't work. In their eyes, he was a usurper who had grabbed power with the help of foreign troops, and Juárez was determined to get rid of him. Two important developments at this time turned the tide in favor of Juárez and sealed Maximilian's fate. Napoleon suddenly withdrew his troops from Mexico, and the United States (which had just survived its own civil war) decided to send military assistance to Benito Juárez. Hopelessly outnumbered, Maximilian could easily have escaped back to Europe at this point (Napoleon actually advised him to get out), but his sense of duty would not let him do that. Farcical as his position was in the eyes of the Liberals, Maximilian took his duties as emperor very seriously, and he did not want to abandon his people in a time of crisis. The inevitable end came in the colonial city of Querétaro in May 1867, where he gracefully surrendered after a siege of three months. The well-meaning emperor was immediately court-marshaled on orders from Juárez and executed (along with a couple of generals) by firing squad on a hill outside the city. One of his last acts was a gift of gold to the firing squad with the request that they not shoot him in the head; he did not want his mother seeing a disfigured face. According to some accounts, he forgave everyone and asked for everyone's forgiveness, adding that he hoped his blood would be for the good of Mexico. His body was sent back to Austria, and today it is in the Imperial Crypt in Vienna with the incongruous title "Emperor of Mexico" under his name.[24] Luckily for her, the empress

---

[24]Maximilian, who was the victim of international intrigue, was falsely led to believe that a majority of the Mexican people wanted him as emperor. Ironically, he abhorred violence and war. When his brother, Franz Joseph, brutally crushed a rebellion in the Austro-Hungarian Empire in 1848, Maximilian was openly in sympathy with the rebels.

consort Carlota was already in Europe when her husband fell from power, appealing for more military help. She had a nervous breakdown there, from which she never recovered, and she stayed in Europe for the rest of her life. She died in 1927 at the age of eighty-seven.

One of the casualties of this farcical history would be the credibility of the Catholic Church. From now on, in the minds of Liberals, the Catholic Church would be identified with those who opposed Mexican independence and the modernization of the nation. The Conservatives would be known as "the Party of the Cassocks". What the Church was really fighting was the atheism and materialistic socialism of the Enlightenment, but what the Liberals saw was the Church's preference for despots and the discredited structures of the past. Tragically, that view of the Church would continue into the twentieth century, with disastrous consequences for both church and state, as we will see in later chapters.

Revolution: Renewed Anticlericalism
1910–1926

The year was 1910, and the government of Mexico organized an extravagant national party. There were two big reasons to celebrate that year: the centenary of the War of Independence from Spain, and the eightieth birthday of Porfirio Díaz, the president who had been governing Mexico for more than a quarter century. Patriotic ceremonies and colorful parades were organized in Mexico City and other major cities across the country, and crowds everywhere saluted Mexico's glorious past and its promising future. Many new buildings were inaugurated during the festivities—a group of hospitals, a penitentiary, a seismic station, a drainage system—all examples of Mexico's modernity, of which Porfirio was very proud. In the evenings, banquets and theatrical performances drew elegantly dressed crowds that included official representatives from most of the nations of the world, including the United States. Mexico was showing itself off at its best, and Don Porfirio (as he was respectfully known) was happy to take credit for it all.[25]

Not without reason, however. There were indeed significant achievements for which the president could take credit, not the least of which was political stability. Before Don Porfirio took office in 1876, the presidency had changed hands seventy-five times in fifty-five years. But that was thirty-four years ago, and Porfirio had been ruling Mexico continuously ever since, without any major struggles between Conservatives and Liberals. The resulting economic progress could be seen everywhere. Miles of new railroad tracks crisscrossed the entire country, up from four hundred miles when he took office to fifteen thousand miles by 1910. The ports were buzzing with activity. Telephone, telegraph, and postal services were functioning well, and Mexico's credit was rated good among other nations. "Peace and order" Porfirio's supporters called it. "Bread and the bludgeon" (*Pan y palo*) others preferred to call it, but they were careful not to express those views in public. For most people, the inconvenience of dictatorship was a worthwhile price to pay for stability and progress.

Even relations with the Catholic Church were peaceful. Porfirio was not an active Catholic himself, but he had relatives who were (his uncle was a bishop), and in his youth he had spent some time in the seminary. As president, he was not interested in getting into fights with the Church.

---

[25] Krauze, *Mexico*, 1.

Mexican history had already seen too much of that, he said, and he was determined to live in peaceful coexistence with the clergy. That was no small relief for Catholics, especially for the older folks who could remember the War of the Reform of the previous century and the destruction and division it visited upon the nation.

So the nation ate, drank, and celebrated, and Porfirio basked in the glory of it all. Mexico was in a golden era—or so it appeared. Few of the visitors to those celebrations foresaw that the good feeling and pretentious show was about to come to an abrupt end very soon. Just ten weeks after the centenary celebrations ended, in November 1910, the nation erupted in revolution, and the dictator of thirty-four years was toppled from power by an idealistic newcomer called Francisco Madero.

For those who were willing to look closer, the warning signs were indeed there, in the slums of the cities and in the Indian pueblos of the countryside. While the champagne was being poured for Porfirio's guests, significant numbers of Mexicans were suffering from malnutrition. Those on the bottom end of the economic ladder—day laborers, domestic workers, and street vendors—lived on an inadequate diet of corn and beans (they almost never ate meat), and the lack of adequate nourishment made them susceptible to a variety of diseases. A visit to a qualified doctor was practically unheard of, and life expectancy was about thirty years.[26] The quality and availability of schools was equally dismal. Somebody calculated that the cost of the centennial celebration of 1910 exceeded the entire education budget for that year.

The revolution, when it happened, looked hopeful at first. Francisco Madero believed sincerely in freedom and

[26] Meyer, Sherman, and Deeds, *Course of Mexican History*, 410.

democracy and wanted to do the right thing as president. But he was painfully inept as a politician, and his social reforms were much too slow for the more radical revolutionaries who supported him. Within two years he was gone from power, overthrown by a notorious general, Victoriano Huerta, who wasn't sincere and didn't worry much about doing the right thing. However, within seventeen months Huerta was out of power himself, ousted by an alliance of rival generals who wanted his job. What followed was the civil war known as the War of the Generals (*La Guerra de Los Caudillos*), with revolutionary strongmen fighting among themselves for control of the country while the people suffered. In addition to the destruction of war, there was the blatant persecution of the Catholic Church. What many of these warring generals had in common was a fanatical anticlericalism, something that had remained dormant during the dictatorship of Porfirio Díaz. That anticlericalism was now out in the open again, and it was made more intense by the mistaken impression that many prominent Catholics (including members of the Catholic hierarchy) sympathized with the Huerta coup.[27] Out-of-control armies ransacked churches and jailed Catholic priests, in scenes reminiscent of the War of the Reform of the previous century. This war would seriously disrupt the lives of the saints whose stories will be told in upcoming chapters.

The War of the Generals ended shortly after the Battle of Celaya (1915), which put Venustiano Carranza in control, but the religious persecution did not end. In fact it

---

[27] Marisol López-Menéndez, *Miguel Pro: Martyrdom, Politics, and Society in Twentieth-Century Mexico* (Lanham, Md.: Lexington Books, 2016), 161. López-Menéndez claims that Catholics welcomed the fall of Madero, and that Catholic intellectuals have obscured that fact. However, other historians, such as Enrique Krauze and Jean Meyer, dispute that.

got worse. As soon as he had a confident hold on power, Carranza called a constitutional convention in the city of Querétaro in 1917 to rewrite the 1857 Constitution and to institutionalize the Revolution. What was institutionalized was rampant anti-Catholicism because the extreme radicals took over the convention against Carranza's better judgment. It was this infamous document—the Constitution of 1917—that triggered the massive economic boycott organized by a saintly attorney (described in chapter 3), and the armed rebellion against the federal government that began in 1926 (detailed in chapter 4). Mexican Catholics were facing unprecedented persecution, but they were now fighting back with unprecedented vigor. A Catholic revival had blossomed in Mexico that the framers of the new constitution did not count on, a revival that was inspired by a papal encyclical published a quarter century earlier. The next chapter will tell the story of that encyclical, and the pope who wrote it.

Chapter 2

Leo XIII and the Catholic Revival

In 1878 Pope Pius IX died, ending a pontificate that lasted thirty-one years and saw several incursions into the turmoil of Mexican politics. Pius IX had joined the bishops of Mexico in publicly condemning the Mexican Constitution of 1857 and later had endorsed the plan to import an Austrian Catholic archduke and install him as emperor of Mexico. Maximilian and Carlota received a special blessing from him before departing for Mexico in 1864. Later that year, the pope issued the famous Syllabus of Errors document, in which he seemed to condemn things like freedom of conscience, freedom of the press, and separation of church and state. In the eyes of Mexican Liberals, that document was one more proof that the Catholic Church was the implacable enemy of modern science, social progress, and anything that threatened clerical privilege.[1]

[1] Pius IX had started out as a liberal but was changed by the turmoil that ended the Papal States. To be properly understood, the Syllabus of Errors must be read in the context of the previous papal documents from which each proposition was drawn. It condemned many things that are still worthy of condemnation today: atheism, indifferentism, and exaggerated rationalism, as well as the claim that the Catholic Church should be subject to the control of the state everywhere. However, those were not the propositions that the public focused on. What the public remembered was the section dealing with church-state relations, particularly the false impression that the pope was opposed to freedom of conscience and separation of church and state. Throughout the turmoil of his papacy, Pius IX lived an exemplary life of simplicity. He was beatified by Pope John Paul II in the year 2000.

As the cardinals met to elect a new pope, church-state problems were on their minds, but not the problems in Mexico; things were relatively peaceful in that part of the world. What worried the cardinals was the situation in Italy, where relations between the government and the Vatican had been tense since the loss of the Papal States some years before, and now the security of the conclave that would elect the new pope was under threat. Some members of the press were hinting that the Italian government should occupy the Vatican and directly oversee the deliberations of the cardinals. Under these conditions, it didn't take the cardinals long to make a decision. After only three ballots, they elected Pope Leo XIII, a sixty-eight-year-old Italian intellectual who would go on to have a long pontificate also (he died at age ninety-three) and would dramatically change the direction set by his long-serving predecessor.

A master diplomat, Pope Leo did much to improve relations with several European states that had soured under the policies of the previous pope. He also went to great lengths to assure the world that the Catholic Church was not opposed to science, and he reestablished the Vatican Observatory, just to underline the point. Most famously, he published the encyclical *Rerum Novarum* (1891), which would reconcile the Church with the working classes around the world and set the course for modern papal teaching on Catholic social justice.[2] The encyclical had a transforming impact in many parts of the Catholic world, not the least of which was Mexico, where it sparked a veritable Catholic renaissance.

---

[2] Leo XIII, encyclical *Rerum Novarum* (May 15, 1891), http://w2.vatican.va /content/leo-xiii/en/encyclicals/documents/hf_l-xiii_enc_15051891_rerum -novarum.html.

In the encyclical, Leo called on all Catholics to apply Christian principles to the problem of the world's working class, and he was specific in his listing of the evils of capitalistic exploitation: the inhumanly long hours and exhausting work performed by laborers in agriculture and industry, the practice of child labor, the impossible working conditions of many women.[3] The ancient guilds no longer protected workers, the pope said, and the radical solution proposed by the Marxists would only dehumanize workers further. He stressed the right of workers to organize and called on Catholic workers to form their own unions.[4] The state had a special duty to protect workers from greedy men, he said, and he pledged that the Catholic Church would work with governments to improve the conditions of workers everywhere.[5]

Mexico was certainly fertile ground for this call to social reform. During the Porfiriato, the country had seen significant modernization and economic growth, but the benefits of that growth went to a select few. By the end of Porfirio Díaz's long dictatorship, Mexico was still a mostly rural country, with much of the land concentrated in a small number of large haciendas. Fifteen of the richest Mexican landowners owned haciendas totaling more than three hundred thousand acres each. One famous hacendado in Chihuahua had holdings that were eight times that of the famous King Ranch in Texas—which itself is bigger than the state of Rhode Island.[6] A poorly written land law, enacted by Porfirio in 1883, allowed this concentration of land to happen. The legislation had been designed to

[3] Ibid., no. 42.
[4] Ibid., no. 49.
[5] Ibid., no. 63.
[6] Michael Meyer, William Sherman, and Susan Deeds, *The Course of Mexican History* (New York: Oxford University Press, 2007), 399.

encourage foreign land companies to invest in Mexico's public lands for subdivision and development, but a loophole in the law allowed the shameless exploitation of small farmers. If a poor farmer or peasant on a traditional ejido[7] could not produce legal title to the land he was farming, that land could be declared public and would be subject to sale. Many peasants in fact could not. All they knew was that their parents and grandparents had worked that same plot of land, going back as far as anyone could remember, and nobody had ever questioned it before. Even boundary lines on these tiny farms were informal: from a certain tree, to a certain stream, to the crest of a hill.[8] Ruthless land speculators took advantage of this law, and the result was that by 1894 one-fifth of Mexico's total land mass had been bought up by a few land companies at bargain prices. More than one-half of all rural Mexicans lived and worked on those huge haciendas by 1910, and their lot was little better than slavery. They worked from dawn to dusk, six days a week—in some places, seven—and were paid not in currency but in vouchers or metal disks that were redeemable only at the hacienda store. That store routinely charged more than the stores in the nearby village, even as the purchasing power of the peon's wages gradually declined. Throughout the nineteenth century, the price of necessities like corn and chili more than doubled while the average daily pay of the peon did not change. Moreover, the hacienda manager was more than willing to extend credit to the peon because debt only benefited the owner. By law the peon could not leave the hacienda while he

---

[7] An ejido was a section of agricultural land that was held in common by a number of small farmers, with each family working a designated parcel of land. With roots in the Aztec culture, the ejido system was used as a way of breaking up large haciendas and giving the land back to the poor.

[8] Meyer, Sherman, and Deeds, *Course of Mexican History*, 398.

owed anything, and his debt did not cease with his death; it passed on to his children. Conditions in industry (the pride of the Porfirio regime) were no better. In the cities, the workweek for the vast majority of laborers was seven days, and workdays were eleven or twelve hours, with grossly inadequate pay. As if to add insult to injury, workers had to pay for the normal depreciation of the machinery they used in some textile mills, and insurance for accidents on the job was nonexistent, as was a pension program. When the world price of copper suddenly dropped in the early 1900s, the resulting wave of layoffs was the straw that broke the camel's back. Strikes began to break out in the mining industry, a development that was met with no mercy by industrialists and government officials alike. A strike at an American-owned mine in the border state of Sonora in 1906, for example, was quickly ended when the ringleaders were escorted out of town and hanged from trees. A volunteer force of Americans from Arizona crossed the border, with the permission of Mexican authorities, to help put down the strike—a dramatic example of Porfirio's willingness to favor foreign companies at the expense of his own people. A strike in a textile mill in Veracruz, some months later, was even worse. Federal troops and local militia fired into the crowd of demonstrators twice, killing over a hundred people, including several wives and children of the workers. These were dramatic examples of what Pope Leo was talking about in the encyclical *Rerum Novarum*, and they marked the beginning of the end for the Porfirio regime.

The Mexican bishops' reaction to the new encyclical was at first muted because it had to be; Porfirio Díaz was still in power. The old dictator did not look kindly on anything that smacked of agitating the masses, especially coming from the Catholic Church, and an assertive labor union movement would have been out of the question. So the bishops and other Church leaders did what they could. Instead of unions, voluntary mutual aid societies began to spring up that provided some security for their members in times of illness, injury, unemployment, and death. That in turn led to a series of Catholic congresses around the nation—four of them between 1903 and 1909—that gradually developed a list of progressive policies about the right of every worker to a just wage and benefits. On a parallel track, agricultural congresses were held that dealt specifically with the appalling working conditions of campesinos and sought to better the material and moral life of the rural population. Traditional organizations like the St. Vincent de Paul Society and the Sodalities of the Blessed Virgin Mary also played their part. Pope Leo XIII had also called for the founding of more Catholic newspapers to educate Catholics on the social teaching of the Church, and five regional weeklies were founded at this time. Mexico City saw a socially progressive daily Catholic newspaper with a circulation of two hundred thousand. There were dailies also in Guadalajara and Puebla.

Then in 1908 there was a surprising change on the political front. That year the aging dictator announced that it was time for Mexico to have an opposition party, and he personally guaranteed the freedom of that party to function. The timing was perfect for Catholics, thanks to Pope Leo XIII. Grassroots labor organizations were already in place, with membership in the thousands, and now the president was inviting Catholics to form something overtly political. Within months, two new organizations appeared—the National Catholic Circle and the Operarios Guadalupanos—for the specific purpose of answering the president's invitation. A short time later, in 1911, the leaders of those two organizations joined forces (with the mediation of the archbishop of Mexico City) to form an officially recognized political party called the National Catholic Party. At that party's convention a couple of months later, the members voted to support Francisco Madero for president, and they adopted a body of socially liberal policies that followed the lead of the pope. The platform appealed to Christian principles as a way to solve the problems between labor and management and pledged to work for reforms that would make religious freedom and democratic institutions part of Mexican everyday life. The Church had come a long way since the War of the Reform of the previous century, when Mexican bishops were calling for the importation of a foreign emperor to rule Mexico. The National Catholic Party went on to enjoy remarkable success during its brief existence of two years: it elected twenty-nine federal deputies, senators, and governors in four states including Jalisco, and it won control of the legislatures in Jalisco and Zacatecas. The National Catholic Party was well on its way to enacting historic social legislation when it suddenly disappeared, a victim of the chaos that gripped the nation during the War of the Generals.[9] However, by now the Catholic union movement was strong where it mattered—in membership—and the movement continued to be a significant force.

It was around this time that a new lay organization for youth, the ACJM (Asociación Católica de la Juventud Mexicana), also began to make its presence felt. Founded by a Jesuit priest who was also inspired by *Rerum Novarum*, this organization challenged young people to get involved in public service and infuse Catholic values into every level of

---

[9] A few years later, the 1917 Constitution would ban all political parties with a religious name or affiliation.

public life in Mexico. In the following decade, the ACJM would provide critical leadership for the successful boycott of the government in Jalisco and for the Catholic rebellion against the government known as the Cristero War. The famous Diet of Zamora in 1913 brought many of these strands of Catholic social action together, and the program adopted at that national meeting was strikingly similar to that of the revolutionists themselves. Among the things it called for were an adequate minimum wage; a ban on the exploitation of married women and children; the establishment of unemployment, accident, sickness, and old-age insurance; profit sharing and part ownership of the company for workers; obligatory arbitration councils for labor disputes; and gradual return of the land to farm workers with legitimate reimbursements to owners. Francisco Orozco, who had just been appointed archbishop of Guadalajara, was an enthusiastic proponent of Leo XIII's vision and was probably a prime mover in this meeting. Ten years later he would host a massive Catholic workers' congress in Guadalajara with the same progressive policies. The other martyrs described in this book would also be deeply influenced by *Rerum Novarum*, but in 1913 they were still in school. Toribio Romo was in the seminary in San Juan de los Lagos, Jalisco; Miguel Pro was in the seminary in El Llano, Michoacán; Anacleto González Flores was in the process of leaving the seminary of San Juan de Los Lagos to pursue a career in law and nonviolent protest in Guadalajara.

Dr. Charles Macfarland, an American Protestant minister and general secretary emeritus of the Federal Council of Churches (predecessor of the present-day National Council of Churches), studied the social gospel in Mexico at this time, and he came to a noteworthy conclusion. "In all honesty," he said in a talk in 1913, "the movement for real social Christianity in the US did not begin very much earlier than these procedures of the Catholic Church in Mexico." Social thought in Mexican Catholic study groups, he said, was ahead of that of similar religious groups in the United States.[10] The Church and government were now on the same page in Mexico, but you would never know it. Far from supporting this vision of social justice, the revolutionary generals of Mexico were contemptuous of the new Catholicism and repeated the old mantra that the Catholic Church was the enemy of social progress. As soon as Plutarco Elías Calles came to power in 1924, that contempt was translated into action. Calles set about putting the Catholic union movement out of business, using Luis Morones, the head of the notoriously anti-Catholic labor federation called CROM (Confederación Regional Obrera Mexicana), as his hatchet man. Morones was a ruthless political operator who was singularly lacking in both education and refinement of conscience, but that did not stop Calles from rewarding him with a position in his cabinet as secretary of the Department of Industry, Commerce, and Labor. A former staff member once made this sarcastic comment about Morones: "He is a marvelous man, lordly, princely! Why, I have seen him receive an enemy in his office, talk with him calmly and politely, and then, when the man turned to leave, whip out his revolver and shoot him dead, and go on with his work at his desk as if nothing had happened."[11]

Morones' way of dealing with the thirty-thousand-member Confederation of Catholic Workers was an example

---

[10] Wilfrid Parsons, *Mexican Martyrdom* (Rockford, Ill.: Tan Books and Publishers, 1987), 211.
[11] Ibid., 130.

of how he operated. That particular union had a significant number of female members, especially in Mexico City, where some five thousand women from more than fifteen factories had been organized into a highly effective Catholic force. The benefits enjoyed by the union members included free schools for children, night school for adults, a cooperative purchasing guild, a credit union, and a savings bank. In 1926, that all came to an end when Morones' agents ordered the Catholic union members to march in the anti-Catholic CROM procession in the capital. Many members refused, and the revenge was fast and ruthless. Their bank was confiscated, and employers were coerced into firing anyone who refused to join CROM. Soldiers manned the entrances of factories to take the names of those who were not cooperating. In one textile factory, the eight hundred skilled Catholic workers who refused to join were immediately replaced with CROM members who did not have proper training for the work in question. The factory ended in bankruptcy.

However, it wasn't those labor tactics, raw as they were, that finally killed the Catholic revival inspired by *Rerum Novarum*. The 1917 Constitution did. The draconian measures in that constitution changed the course of Catholic action in Mexico because they forced the Church to defend a much more fundamental right—the right to exist in Mexican society. When an institution is fighting for its very survival, recruiting members for a labor union is not the top priority.

One of those leading that fight for the survival of Catholicism was a saintly attorney from Guadalajara whose activism became the stuff of legend in Jalisco. In the end he would pay the ultimate price, as we will see in the next chapter.

Chapter 3

The Maestro and the
1917 Constitution

On April 1, 1927, an important arrest took place in Guadalajara. Anacleto González Flores, the famous attorney and Catholic activist, was picked up by the police at the house of some friends where he had been hiding, and he was taken to the barracks known as the *Cuartel Colorado*, the large red brick building that Catholics later called the "Colosseum of the Martyrs". All the occupants in the house were arrested with him.

Word of the arrests quickly passed around the city, and people waited and worried about what would happen to the Maestro; that is the nickname everybody used when referring to him. They knew it was unlikely that the authorities would just question him and let him go. General Jesús Maria Ferreira's agents, who were known for their barbaric methods of interrogation, had been looking for the Maestro for some months, and the general himself took charge of the interrogation that day. The chief of police was also present as was the former governor of the state—a remarkable display of interest. Clearly, a lot of important people were concerned about the outcome of this case.

Soon crowds gathered outside the *Cuartel Colorado*, waiting anxiously for news. The influential uncle of one of those detained succeeded in getting a "writ of *amparo*

52   SAINTS AND SINNERS IN THE CRISTERO WAR

judicial" (a court order to block the proceedings), but Ferreira ignored it! Around three o'clock, word reached the crowd outside that some of those retained had been released, but the Maestro and three of his companions had already been shot by firing squad.[1] Before being killed, the Maestro had been brutally tortured; they hung him by his thumbs and forced him to walk across a sandy courtyard after a soldier peeled the skin from the soles of his feet. Ferreira wanted information from him about the whereabouts of the archbishop of Guadalajara, who was also in hiding, but the Maestro refused to talk. "No se olvide" (Don't forget), he told the general, "que aquí fui abogado y allá puedo ser abogado para usted.... Yo seré tu major intecesor" (that here on earth I was an attorney and up above I can be your attorney.... I will be your best advocate).[2] Then, as if to add to Ferreira's frustration, the soldiers assigned to shoot him refused to pull their triggers, and a second firing squad had to be brought in to do the job. The soldiers in the first squad were immediately executed for insubordination.

This was a brutal ending for a man who had spent his life fighting state brutality, and for the crowd on the street it was another shocking reminder of the times in which Catholics were living. Anacleto González Flores had been a particularly prominent voice of protest against the insane policies of the Mexican revolutionaries. He had been a prolific writer; a brilliant attorney; an enthusiastic exponent of the encyclical *Rerum Novarum*; a convinced pacifist who once organized a successful boycott in Jalisco that

[1] The three people shot with Anacleto were Luis Padilla, Jorge Vargas González, and Ramón Vargas González. The González brothers were living in the house where Anacleto was arrested.
[2] Fidel González Fernández, *Sangre y Corazón de un Pueblo* (Guadalajara: Arzobispado de Guadalajara, 2008), 1224, my translation. All quotations were translated by the authors whose works I am citing unless otherwise indicated.

brought the economy of Jalisco to a standstill. Neither he nor his companions had been carrying arms that day. They had offered no resistance when arrested, and they had not been formally charged with anything. General Ferreira was not interested in formal charges. His plan was to make an example of González Flores and to teach the Catholics of Jalisco a lesson they would not forget.

Later that evening, when the family of Anacleto finally got the body back to prepare it for burial, they discovered that the torture had been even worse than they had feared. His clothes were soaked in blood up to his neck, and there were multiple bayonet wounds on the body, including one large one in the back that punctured his lung. His mouth was full of blood, his fingers badly dislocated, and his left arm had been practically severed from his body. Family members looked at the body in horror, afraid to imagine what he had gone through in those hours before he died. But they found consolation in a remarkable coincidence. It was Friday, and the killing took place at three in the afternoon, the hour of Jesus' death on the Cross.

The Maestro's home immediately became a center of pilgrimage, with crowds inside and outside praying the Rosary and learning new details about his death. The Maestro, they learned, had requested that he be killed last so that he could be a comfort to his companions. Before the shooting, he forgave his executioners and bequeathed his pocket watch to one of the soldiers (who later sold it back to Anacleto's wife). "Yo muero, pero Dios no muere. Viva Cristo Rey!" (I die, but God does not die. Long live Christ the King!) were his last words, as blood splattered from his mouth.[3] Now people touched his body with their rosaries, and some cut pieces of his clothing to take home

[3] Ibid. Some witnesses said his tongue was cut also.

with them. In life they had nicknamed him the Maestro. Now they were calling him the Martyr. Even bigger
crowds came to the funeral the following day, defying the
menacing presence of the police who kept watch from a
distance, unable to stop the huge public demonstration of
grief. The entire city of Guadalajara was shocked by their
deaths, one witness wrote. If General Ferreira wanted to
teach the Catholics of Jalisco a lesson, he was not succeeding. They were teaching him one.

A few years later, General Ferreira's military record
caught up with him. He made the fatal mistake of aligning
himself with a failed coup against the then president of
Mexico, and he was prosecuted in a scandalous trial that
highlighted the methods of torture he used against innocent people. During the proceedings he attempted suicide.
In the end, the authorities spared his life, but reduced him
to penury and disgrace for the rest of his life.

A Childhood of Poverty and Struggle

Who was this man everyone knew as the Maestro, this olive-
skinned lawyer some called the Mahatma Gandhi of Mexico? He was born on July 13, 1888, in Tepatitlán, a small
town some fifty miles from Guadalajara, the second son of
twelve children, whom his parents raised on a small business, making women's shawls. They lived in a one-room
house, and in that tiny space the family ate, slept, and made
their product, which the children tried to sell in the neighboring ranches. Anacleto learned the meaning of hardship
in that home, and the hunched back he had all his life may
have been the result of the labor of those early days. The
kids in school nicknamed him *el Camello* (the Camel).[4]

---

[4] Ibid., 1141.

The family was always struggling, one neighbor recalled, and knew firsthand the meaning of misery and deprivation. At one point, the father got a two-year jail sentence for joining a demonstration against the dictatorship of Porfirio Díaz, which didn't help the family budget. But these harsh conditions did nothing to dampen the young Anacleto's curiosity and zest for life. He was a voracious reader from a young age, devouring every book he could get his hands on, but he also loved music and dancing. He could keep up with the best when it came to whistling harmlessly at pretty girls, for which Tepatitlán was famous. In the interior of today's city hall, there is a large mural portraying the history of Tepatitlán, including a large image of Anacleto González Flores. It also has a section on the "beautiful women of the city".

Anacleto's parents couldn't afford the one Catholic school in the town, and the public schools were blatantly anti-Catholic, which didn't bother the young Anacleto because he had little interest in religion anyway. When he was seventeen, however, a missionary visited the parish to give a retreat, and the experience changed Anacleto's life. He became more reflective, and his taste now changed to the kinds of books most young people would not read: philosophy, social morality, and ethics. Finally, the local priest recommended him to the high school seminary in San Juan de los Lagos to get a good education, if not to become a priest.

Anacleto took the usual courses in the seminary in San Juan de los Lagos and later the seminary in Guadalajara, and he also deepened his appreciation for the Eucharist, something that would stay with him for the rest of his life. He got his first taste of Catholic activism at this time. Inspired by Pope Leo XIII's *Rerum Novarum*, he volunteered with the newly founded National Catholic Party, which came into existence following the long dictatorship of Porfirio Díaz. While on vacation from the seminary, Anacleto vigorously promoted this new party in his hometown of Tepatitlán and in San Juan de los Lagos. At the time, the party was at the zenith of its short-lived success with election successes in four states.

After four years in the seminary, Anacleto decided that the priesthood was not for him and, in July 1913, he left the seminary to pursue a career in law in Guadalajara. But he was still a man on a mission, devoting significant time to prayer each day and nourishing the interior life he had begun as a seminarian. He and a group of five like-minded young men rented a house in a poor neighborhood of Guadalajara, there to form a community in which they could pray together and satisfy their common thirst for knowledge and reflection. They hired a lady named *Geronima* to cook and do household chores for thirty cents a day, and they called the house *La Gironda* in honor of her; the members of the community became *Los Girondinos*. For financial support, they took jobs wherever they could find them, but frequently the work was not sufficient to support their needs. There were days when they didn't have enough to eat. But nobody complained, and a spirit of cheerfulness marked the tiny lay community under the dynamic personality of the Maestro.

He possessed the gift of gregariousness; he was a teacher and a friend, one student wrote. "His spirit of camaraderie, his jovial approach to work, his profound piety, his humility, and his love of others, his wisdom which he knew how to share without showing off, and his capacity to advise, captivated me from the beginning," he wrote.[5] The house had only three rooms, and the walls "did not know the meaning of paint", this student wrote. The first

5 Ibid., 1147.

THE MAESTRO AND THE 1917 CONSTITUTION   57

and biggest one served as a living room, dining room, bedroom, and kitchen. Three *Girondinos* slept there, and three more slept in the second smaller room, which was connected to it. Further down the untiled passageway was a bathroom and washbasin without running water. The small room at the end "was for the unselfish housekeeper, who demanded nothing except that pigsty and the meal she cooked, which was divided equally among all".[6] The house was open to all and sundry, especially to young people whom the Maestro organized into study circles. They discussed the encyclical *Rerum Novarum*, but also other subjects: sociology, history, public speaking, and essays on oratory. The Maestro also found time for his many commitments outside the house. Sleeping little, he taught catechism to kids in the neighborhood, and visited the sick. On top of it all, he never missed daily Mass, and he was frequently seen praying silently in a dark corner in Holy Name Church. When asked once what he enjoyed doing most, he replied: "Receiving Communion! The day I don't receive Communion, I am nothing; my life and equilibrium are missing."[7]

Meanwhile, outside the peace of the *Girondino* community, the country was in turmoil. Mexico had just survived the War of the Generals with all its destruction and sacrilege, and now a constitutional convention was meeting in Querétaro (1917) to target the Catholic Church once again. The Maestro and his *Girondinos* were horrified at the reports they were receiving. One particularly outspoken leader in that convention, Francisco Múgica, who had been expelled from the seminary in Zamora some years before, set the tone when he called the Catholic clergy

[6] Ibid.
[7] Ibid., 1154.

"the most dismal, the most perverse enemy of the father-land".[8] It was he who ended up writing large parts of the final document—what would become the famous Consti-tution of 1917—and the text reflected the full force of his anticlerical agenda. It targeted two institutions in particular that were at the heart of every functioning Catholic parish: Catholic schools and the Catholic priesthood.

"No religious corporation and no minister of any cult shall establish or direct schools of primary education," the new constitution stated. In that one sentence, all Cath-olic primary schools were declared illegal. Furthermore, Catholic secondary schools and universities would only be legal if the curriculum was changed to reflect the new anti-Catholic agenda.

From now on priests could not vote, or hold public office, or comment on political issues, or wear religious garb in public. Neither could they inherit property.[9] "Religious institutions known as churches" were not legal bodies anymore and could not hold, acquire, or administer real property. All religious buildings—churches, seminar-ies, convents, residences, schools, hospitals, orphanages—were declared to be the property of the state, and if new churches were built they would immediately become the property of the state also. Public worship outside the con-fines of the church was banned.[10] So were all monastic orders, and foreign-born priests were banished from the country. Most ominous of all, state legislatures were given

[8] Enrique Krauze, *Mexico: Biography of Power* (New York: HarperCollins, 1998), 361.

[9] I remember my Spanish professor in the seventies telling me about her uncle who had inherited property from the family. Because he was a bishop, her father (the bishop's brother) had to be the nominal owner of the property.

[10] This law was still on the books when Pope John Paul II visited Mexico in 1979. His outdoor Masses were technically against the law, but by then nobody cared.

the power to decide how many priests would minister in each state.

Actually, some of these new laws, such as the one on monastic orders and the one on Church property, rehashed ones from the old constitution that had been ignored, but others pushed the anticlericalism of the revolutionists to unprecedented extremes. The old constitution had provided for the separation of church and state; this new one made it a nonissue by declaring that the Church had no existence in the eyes of the law. The old constitution had allowed Catholic schools to exist alongside public schools; the new one declared the entire Catholic primary school system illegal. The old constitution had barred clergy from criticizing state or federal laws from the pulpit; the new one barred them from having any voice whatsoever in the public life of Mexico.[11]

When the shell-shocked Mexican bishops read the full text, they issued a blistering protest calling the document tyrannical. It blatantly sanctioned religious persecution, they said, and violated the most fundamental rights of the Church and individual Catholics. However, their voice was muted because it was issued from outside the country. By the time the bishops' statement was issued, most Mexican bishops had been exiled to the United States by the revolutionists. It would fall to a new generation of Catholic laymen who had been influenced by *Rerum Novarum* to take up the fight for Catholic rights. The most famous of those was Anacleto González Flores.

It was the provision giving state legislators the power to limit the number of priests that riveted the attention of the twenty-eight-year-old Anacleto and earned him

---

[11] David Bailey, *¡Viva Cristo Rey!: The Cristero Rebellion and the Church-State Conflict in Mexico* (Austin: University of Texas Press, 1974), 25.

the nickname Maestro. At first, most governors and legislators had the common sense to ignore that draconian
provision, but not the legislators in Jalisco. They immediately passed a law stating that from now on only one priest
for every five thousand people would be allowed in their
state. Priests would have to apply to the state for a license
to work by filling out a long questionnaire and submitting
two passport photos, and there was no guarantee that they
would be granted the license. In effect, the state registry
office, not the bishop, would now make the decision about
which priest or bishop could or could not celebrate Mass
and administer the sacraments. The penalties for infraction
of the law included time in jail and a heavy fine.

Anacleto González Flores had seen enough. With the
help of many friends, he organized a statewide boycott to
protest this new law, and the campaign was so successful
that it brought the state's economic and social life to a halt
in a matter of weeks. The strike was launched on several
fronts. Catholics were asked to buy only the bare essentials
for life, avoiding luxuries like candy, lottery tickets, and
tickets to the theatre and cinema. They were also asked to
keep their children home from public schools. Some people packed the gallery of the legislature, disrupting sessions
with animal noises, while others joined massive demonstrations in the streets in spite of a warning from the police.
Hundreds of demonstrators happily filled the jails in Guadalajara, and, as one witness said, their prayers and singing
converted those filthy dungeons into oratories of faith and
joy.[12] After only eight months of nonviolent protest, the
government caved in and abolished the new law. It was a
stunning victory for the Maestro and his supporters.

Two factors account for the remarkable success of
this nonviolent action. One was the Maestro's magnetic

[12] Fernández, *Sangre y Corazón*, 1152.

personality and skill as a communicator. "His words could move a multitude of people," one witness wrote. "Just a word from him was enough to stuff any courtroom."[13] He was also a talented journalist who wrote regular columns in several Catholic publications, some of which he helped found, encouraging participation in the boycott and nonviolent demonstrations on the streets. (Not surprisingly, he was put on the watch list by the authorities.) The women were usually the first to answer his call to action, and they in turn prodded their husbands and brothers to get involved. Catholic women were the driving force behind the Maestro's nonviolent campaigns, he said many times.

The other key to his success was the powerful ACJM (Asociación Católica de la Juventud Mexicana), an activist organization for Catholic youth who were also inspired by *Rerum Novarum*. This organization had been founded by a French Jesuit in 1913 in Mexico City, but it was particularly strong in Jalisco due to the organizational skills of the Maestro. Idealistic, well educated, and militant, these ACJM members led demonstrations in the streets against the new constitution, and they frequently fought pitched battles with the police. The support of the Maestro's archbishop, Francisco Orozco, was also important. He authorized the suspension of all public Masses in the archdiocese as part of the protest.

State Harassment

Through all of this time, Anacleto continued his studies, and in April 1922, he graduated at the top of his class with a law degree. With his career now secured, he immediately turned his attention to more personal matters. Eight

[13] Ibid., 1158.

months later, he married Concha Guerrero Figueroa in the ACJM chapel in Guadalajara with his friend and admirer Archbishop Francisco Orozco, performing the ceremony. He was thirty-four years old and she twenty-seven. The couple moved to a lower middle class part of Guadalajara and subsequently had three children (one of whom died of fever). However, while the marriage was outwardly harmonious and self-sacrificing, it was not especially happy. His wife was an orphan whose upbringing left emotional scars, and she was not an ideal partner for the intellectual and religiously committed Maestro. "I am married to a book,"[14] she once said, and she complained bitterly about his lack of interest in improving the family's standard of living. One reads the literature on this part of Anacleto's life with sympathy for two people who were not well suited for one another.

To make things worse, something shocking happened shortly after they began their life together. One day, Anacleto read in the newspapers that the government had issued a new regulation stating that studies done in Catholic seminaries should no longer be recognized by the state. In other words, Anacleto's high school graduation no longer counted for anything. The news of this state harassment came down on him like an ax, one of his friends wrote later, but the shocked Maestro soon pulled himself together and rolled up his sleeves.[15] At the age of thirty-five, he enrolled at a state-run high school, picked up the course material, and did the coursework at home. In a short time, he was back to the authorities demanding the exam, which he easily passed. But then they came up with a new angle. They told him he would have to

---

[14] Ibid., 1164.
[15] Ibid., 1162.

repeat his law studies also, because the original law studies were built on an illegitimate high school record! Not to be bested, the Maestro signed up to repeat the law courses and after some months demanded another exam. This time his scores were so high (he got an unprecedented perfect score) that the panel of hostile instructors had no recourse but to grant him his law degree. It was a remarkable example of tenacity and intellectual brilliance from a man who was determined to fight state tyranny head-on. It was also a dress rehearsal for fights that were to come.

The Enlightenment

Meanwhile, the Maestro continued his life's mission: fighting the revolutionists who were in control of his country. Those usurpers, he wrote, were determined to destroy Mexico's ancient Catholic foundations by imposing a militantly atheistic philosophy on the people of Mexico whether the people wanted it or not. In reality, what the Maestro was fighting was the philosophy of the European Enlightenment, in particular, the atheistic philosophy of the French Revolution.

Not all Enlightenment philosophy was bad, of course. In fact, the originators of the movement embraced an insight that we take for granted today: that the observable world can be figured out by pure reason, just as Isaac Newton had figured out the laws of nature and the universe by pure reason.[16] Parallel with this insight was the quest for individual liberty, tolerance, social progress, and the separation of church and state—all laudable goals in themselves. But when those parallel movements evolved into a revolution

---

[16] The early founders of the Enlightenment movement included thinkers like John Locke, Voltaire, Jean-Jacques Rousseau, and Immanuel Kant.

in France and culminated in the execution of King Louis XVI, the movement became as much a fight against the influence of the Catholic clergy as against the absolutism of the French monarchs. Man will never be free, Denis Diderot famously said, until the last king is strangled with the entrails of the last priest. A fanatical anticlericalism had taken over the French Enlightenment movement, one that ridiculed the most fundamental Christian doctrines taught by the Catholic Church—by all Christian churches for that matter. Human beings don't need redemption, the French radicals said. On the contrary, they are born good, and they would stay that way if it weren't for the influence of society and its institutions—in particular the "unnatural" practices of the Catholic clergy. Living a celibate life in a monastery was against human nature, the radicals said, and should be banned. Religious fasting was a waste of time, and priests should be forbidden to mislead parishioners into practicing it. Clerical titles and Church hierarchy were an obstacle to progress and should be abolished. People should stop seeking an imaginary world in the next life, they said, and concentrate on making a better world in this life. This was the philosophy adopted by the Mexican revolutionaries going back to the days of Melchor Ocampo, and it would continue to be their philosophy long after the Maestro's death. "Every moment spent on one's knees is a moment stolen from humanity," presidential candidate Lázaro Cárdenas said in a speech in 1933.[17]

At its core, this movement denied the Christian doctrine of original sin—the belief that human nature is broken and prone to selfishness and corruption. It focused rather on the "innate nobility" in every human being, and put man rather than God at the center of the universe. It

[17] Michael Meyer, William Sherman, and Susan Deeds, *The Course of Mexican History* (New York: Oxford University Press, 2007), 529.

was not surprising then that Catholic idealists like Anacleto González Flores would fight the movement, nor was it surprising that Catholic priests would be vilified as the principal obstacles to rational thinking and social progress. Examples of this anticlericalism can be found in surprising places. Thomas Jefferson once said: "In every country and in every age, the priest has been hostile to liberty. He is always in alliance with the despot, abetting his abuses in return for protection of his own."[18]

To fight this philosophy, the Maestro and his closest friends founded a Catholic organization called the Unión Popular, a group that would work alongside the ACJM but would be for adults. The new organization was an immediate success among peasants and laborers because it had a simple structure (no bureaucracy or formalities) and the five-member directory included two women. Its founding officers were all future martyrs: Anacleto González Flores, president; Luis Padilla Gómez, secretary; and Miguel Gómez Loza, treasurer. The Union Popular grew to more than a hundred thousand members in a short time, and to extend its reach the Maestro founded a weekly publication called *Gladium* (the Latin word for "sword") that reached a hundred thousand in readership. Most daily newspapers of the day would have loved to boast that kind of circulation.[19] He also founded a publication called *La Palabra*,

---

[18] Thomas Jefferson to Horatio G. Spafford, March 17, 1814, in Founders Online, https://founders.archives.gov/documents/Jefferson/03-07-02-0167.

[19] Anacleto was also involved in a third organization called the "U", whose purpose was to encourage Catholic involvement in Mexican political life. It had the support of many Mexican bishops, but its leaders often clashed with the leaders of the National League for the Defense of Religious Liberty (the League is described below). Because it was a secret organization and kept no records, not much is known about it. It ceased to exist in 1930 when Pope Pius XI banned secret organizations. The leaders of the League petitioned Rome to have the "U" (which it considered a rival) suppressed.

to which he contributed regularly. His columns preached a single plan of action: nonviolent protest through collective civil disobedience.

Anacleto admired Mahatma Gandhi, who had led India to independence from Britain in the twentieth century by using nonviolent civil disobedience. He also admired Daniel O'Connell, the civil rights attorney who organized nonviolent "monster meetings" all over Ireland in the previous century to protest anti-Catholic laws put in place by the British government. Using nonviolent strategies, O'Connell won Catholic emancipation for Irish Catholics in 1829 without ever firing a shot. The Maestro liked these examples of nonviolent action, but he added two specifically Catholic components for the Mexican context: personal sacrifice and prayer. It worked. The 1918 economic boycott in Jalisco was successful because people were willing to sacrifice everything except the bare essentials, and they stormed Heaven with their prayers. What they were practicing was in effect a bloodless martyrdom, a radical dying to self, the Maestro told them, echoing the words of Jesus in John's Gospel: "Unless a grain of wheat falls into the earth and dies, it remains alone; but if it dies, it bears much fruit" (12:24). But the other kind of martyrdom— the bloody kind—would be the Maestro's personal fate. And when it finally came on April 1, 1927, it could not have been a complete surprise. At the height of the 1918 boycott, the authorities had warned him: "If you keep this up, you will end up being shot!"[20]

By 1927, however, something ominous had developed that troubled the Maestro and challenged his most cherished convictions about nonviolence. With a new and more violent president in power, Catholic intellectuals

[20] Fernández, *Sangre y Corazón*, 1152.

had come to the conclusion that nonviolent protest was no longer enough to bring about change in Mexico. In fact, a nationwide rebellion had broken out—the Cristero War—led by a coalition of organizations called the National League for the Defense of Religious Liberty, known simply as the League and also referred to as the National League for the Defense of Religious Freedom.[21] Actually this organization was founded as a nonviolent movement in 1926 in Mexico City, and within weeks of its foundation it had launched a national boycott along the lines of the one Anacleto successfully carried out in 1918 in Jalisco. The campaign was a failure everywhere (except in Jalisco), and the frustrated League directors made a radical decision to change course. Instead of wasting their time with boycotts, they said, they would take over the scattered rebellions that were irrupting in different parts of the country and turn them into a coordinated national rebellion against the government of Plutarco Elías Calles.

The League's leaders took this step fully aware that their action would put them on a collision course with the famous lawyer of Guadalajara, Anacleto González Flores. His opposition to violence was well known, as was his power and influence in his own state, one of the most Catholic parts of Mexico. Going ahead with the rebellion without the Maestro's support would have been unthinkable. So a representative from League headquarters in Mexico City traveled to Guadalajara to talk to him personally and plead for his support. The details of that discussion are not known, but what is known is that Anacleto in the end did reluctantly agree not to stand in the way of those who were willing to

[21] The coalition included the ACJM, the Congregación Mariana de Jóvenes, the Knights of Columbus, the Labor Federation of the Archdiocese of Mexico, the Mexican Nocturnal Adoration Society, the National Catholic Confederation of Labor, and the Union of Mexican Women.

take up arms. Many of the Maestro's followers eventually did take up arms. The hundred thousand members of the Unión Popular would eventually be a rich source for volunteers in the Cristero army and in the civil administrations that the Cristeros would set up in the areas they controlled. By then the Maestro would be dead.

A lot of ink has been spilled debating why the Maestro went along with the Cristero War, against his deepest convictions, but one reason seems to be the need for unity. Anacleto knew that the rebellion could not succeed without the help of Jalisco. He also knew that many members in his own organization in Jalisco were becoming more militant (despite his efforts to the contrary) and to oppose the rebellion would split his organizations down the middle. Furthermore, he knew that a theological case could be made for saying that armed rebellion was indeed justified given the atrocities of the Calles state.

According to the Catholic just war theory, dating back to the writings of Saint Augustine in the fourth century or earlier, people have a right to defend themselves with armed rebellion if certain conditions have been fulfilled: nonviolent means of resistance must have failed; the rebellion must have a reasonable chance of success; the good to be achieved must outweigh the destruction and loss of life the rebellion would bring. The Maestro had to admit that the nonviolent option had been tried and had failed at the national level. And who was to say that armed rebellion would not succeed?

From today's perspective, this issue looks very different, because the moral reasoning about war has changed in the Catholic Church. Today there is a growing conviction that the just war theory is out of date, because modern weapons of war are much more destructive and civilian casualties are far more numerous. Back in World

War I, for example, civilian deaths were 10 percent of the death toll; in recent wars, such as the conflict in Syria and the U.S. invasion of Iraq, civilian deaths have been in the 80 percent range.[22] Those kinds of statistics make it more difficult to argue that the good to be achieved outweighs the destruction and loss of life that is inevitable in modern warfare.

Another argument against the just war theory comes from the success nonviolent resistance has had in the twentieth century. There are numerous examples: the civil rights struggle in the United States; the struggle for equality in South Africa; the struggle against Communism in Poland; the People's Power movement in the Philippines. Ironically, Anacleto was one of the early thinkers to see the value in this nonviolent approach, as is apparent from his admiration for Mahatma Gandhi and Daniel O'Connell. But in his day, the just war theory was still the accepted formula for evaluating wars, and it became a key factor in his reasoning. In the end, his decision was not to take up arms himself, but to allow others to do so. He made that painful choice despite receiving a letter from his beloved archbishop (who was in hiding) strongly advising him to stay away from armed resistance.[23] For the Maestro, this was martyrdom for the motherland: the Way of the Cross. Here are his words to his followers in announcing his decision:

[22] Terrence Rynne, "Why Is the Catholic Church Moving Away from Just War Theory?", *National Catholic Reporter*, 9 April 2016, https://www.ncronline.org/news/world/why-catholic-church-moving-away-just-war-theory.

[23] Bailey, *¡Viva Cristo Rey!*, 109. In a subsequent memorandum, Orozco expressed disappointment at Anacleto's decision and said that if he were not in hiding he would have been more effective in heading off the decision the Maestro made.

I know only too well that what is beginning now for us is Calvary. We must be ready to take up arms and carry our crosses. . . . I who am responsible for the decision of all, feel a sacred obligation not to deceive anyone. If one should ask me what sacrifice I am asking of you in order to seal the pact we are going to celebrate, I will tell you in two words: your blood.

If you want to proceed, stop dreaming of places of honor, military triumphs, braid, luster, victories, and authority over others. Mexico needs a tradition of blood in order to ensure its free life of tomorrow. For that work, my life is available, and for that tradition I ask yours.[24]

Stop dreaming of braid and places of honor indeed! Many of those who listened to the Maestro that day would soon die in the squalor and deprivation of a guerilla war that was fought in the central-western highlands of Mexico between 1926 and 1929 and would claim the lives of some two hundred thousand Mexicans when you include civilians. The Maestro himself never fought in that war, but his torture and death in the *Cuartel Colorado* on April 1, 1927, was more painful than the death of most soldiers on the battlefield. In November 2005, Pope Benedict XVI declared him "Blessed", one of the principal milestones on the road to canonization.

The war the Maestro endorsed so reluctantly would go on for three long years and would pit ragtag bands of rural Catholics against the well-trained forces of the Mexican Republic. It was an uneven fight, but despite the odds, the losses suffered by the federal troops were stunning. How did the Cristeros do it? The next chapter will answer that question.

---

[24] Ibid., 109.

Chapter 4

The Cristeros and the Dilemma of Violence

José Reyes Vega was one of the most successful generals in the Cristero War, but what made this man extraordinary among his troops was what he did before he became a soldier. Vega was a Catholic priest, from the Archdiocese of Guadalajara, who joined the rebels in spite of the explicit orders of his archbishop and rose to the rank of general in a short time. Only five priests took up arms in the Cristero War, but Father Vega was the most famous and the most controversial.[1] Known as "Pancho Villa in a cassock" he was among the toughest of soldiers, and his ruthlessness in shooting federal prisoners, apparently on a whim, raised quite a few eyebrows, as did his personal life. "A black-hearted man, a murderer, a skirt chaser" is how historian Jean Meyer has described him.[2]

Born in Tuxpan, Jalisco, of Indian parents, Vega spoke Nahuatl (the language of the Aztecs) growing up. In the seminary, he already stood out as a leader, winning the admiration of his classmates for his skill as a horseman and a

[1] Another of the five, Father Aristeo Pedroza, also became a general but was very different from Father Vega. Personally austere and disciplined, he imposed strict discipline on his troops; he was known as the "pure man".

[2] Jean Meyer, *The Cristero Rebellion* (London: Cambridge University Press, 1976), 74.

chess player. Nobody at that early stage, however, could have foreseen how the tides of history would sweep up this young man nor could they have foreseen the troubling mixture of virtues and vices those tides would uncover. As a Cristero soldier, Vega was said to have Pancho Villa's military genius, something that won the loyalty of his troops, despite his unpriestly behavior. (Officers in the Cristero army were elected by their men and could lose their jobs on a whim.[3]) It didn't hurt his standing with the troops that his siblings were just as tough as he was. Two of his brothers fought alongside him in battle, and his sister was part of the underground female network that kept the rebels supplied with ammunition. His mother carried a dagger with her at all times.

It was an attack on a train from Guadalajara to Mexico City on April 19, 1927, that earned Vega the name of murderer. The train, which was transporting a large amount of cash, came to a halt some miles outside Guadalajara when it hit a section of track that had been torn up by the Cristeros. A large force of the rebels immediately opened fire on the train, which drew return fire from the military escort on the train itself. The Cristeros soon overwhelmed the train's defenses, took a hundred thousand pesos from the baggage car, and set fire to the train before departing. In all, about 150 people were killed in the action, over 50 of them civilian. Not surprisingly, the world press picked up the story immediately, and the role of the Catholic priest ensured that it got prominent space.

A war of words followed in the news, with both sides accusing the other of atrocities. A government spokesman

[3] Ibid., 128. Jean Meyer is the most prolific author on the Cristero War and its causes. His exhaustive three-volume work, *La Cristiada: La Guerra de Los Cristeros* (Mexico City: Siglo XXI Editores, 1974) was first published in Spanish in 1973 and 1974.

pointed to the attack as clear proof that "a clerical gang" was behind the Cristero Rebellion, adding that this barbarous behavior was typical of the methods the Catholic Church had used ever since the Inquisition. The National League for Religious Defense, which was leading the Cristero War, responded that the government's reaction was like the kettle calling the pot black. It pointed to the torture and murder of Anacleto González Flores days earlier as an example of government atrocities, adding that during the train attack the federal troops had used the passengers as shields, a claim that seemed to get confirmation from the *New York Times*. The high loss of life, the *Times* reported, was due to the federal troops entering the passenger cars and staging their defense from there.[4]

Archbishop Leopoldo Ruiz y Flóres of Morelia, speaking for the hierarchy, denied that the bishops had anything to do with the rebellion or the attack on the train. He said the alleged atrocity by Father Vega, if true, was deplorable, but that the real culpability lay with "those who have provoked this situation".[5] The response of the government was immediate. Archbishop José Mora y del Rio of Mexico City, Archbishop Ruiz, and four other bishops were abducted from their homes and brought before Interior Minister Adalberto Tejeda, who again accused them of directing the rebellion. The aging Mora flatly rejected that accusation, but added that the armed movement by the nation's Catholics was justified and had the sympathy of the Mexican bishops. Tejeda had heard enough. By nightfall, all six prelates found themselves on a train bound for the U.S. border, escorted by federal agents.[6] Archbishop

[4] *New York Times*, April 21, 1927, and April 22, 1927, quoted in David Bailey, *¡Viva Cristo Rey!* (Austin: University of Texas Press, 1974), 142.
[5] Bailey, *¡Viva Cristo Rey!*, 143.
[6] Ibid.

Mora would never see his homeland again; he died in San Antonio, Texas.

More expulsions soon followed. By early summer there were few bishops left anywhere in Mexico. Francisco Orozco was still in Guadalajara running his diocese from hiding, and Bishop José Amador Velasco y Peña was in a similar situation in Colima. A few others were living in private homes in Mexico City. But the members of the episcopal committee on church-state relations[7] were all in exile, and from now on would have to meet in San Antonio, Texas.[8] Even the apostolic delegate was gone.[9] He had been expelled the previous year, and the Vatican had asked the U.S. apostolic delegate in Washington to include Mexican affairs in his portfolio.

Meanwhile, the priest who triggered the recent clashes between church and state, Father José Reyes Vega, was continuing to fight with the gun. His most famous action in the war was the Battle of Tepatitlán in Jalisco, two years after the train attack. Six regiments of federal soldiers had been advancing across the state in three columns, the

[7] The special episcopal committee was established the previous year on the suggestion of the apostolic delegate, Archbishop George Caruana. It was chaired by the archbishop of Mexico and included the archbishops of Morelia, Guadalajara, and Puebla.

[8] The Catholic Church in Mexico had to survive with no bishops, or almost no bishops, four times in her history. After the declaration of independence in 1822, the bishops gradually died out and were not replaced by Rome for more than a decade. In 1863, the bishops were expelled by Benito Juárez because they opposed the 1857 Constitution. Between 1913 and 1917, during the War of the Generals, the bishops left the country or went into hiding because of threats to their lives. In 1927, President Plutarco Calles expelled all the bishops from Mexico again, falsely accusing them of being the masterminds of the Cristero Rebellion.

[9] Archbishop George Caruana lasted only two months as apostolic delegate before being expelled by President Calles. The apostolic delegate before him, Archbishop Serafino Cimino, O.F.M., lasted five months!

center one of which numbered twenty-five hundred. The federal troops had passed through Jalos and were advancing toward Tepatitlán when Vega, who had only three regiments, decided to lure them into a trap. He positioned about seventy of his men on top of tall buildings and church towers in the town and led the rest (over fifty) to positions of hiding some miles from the town. As soon as the feds entered the town, they were attacked by Vega's snipers, and before they could dislodge the snipers they found themselves under attack from more rebels who suddenly showed up from nowhere. The feds had to withdraw from the town immediately, back along the road to Jalos, but as they did they were ambushed by more of Vega's cavalry who had hidden along the road. Before long the panicked federal troops were in disorganized flight, and they would have been wiped out if the Cristeros had not (as usual!) run out of ammunition. Some 225 of the enemy were killed that day, according to reports from the jubilant rebels. But the rebels suffered a significant setback as well when Father José Reyes Vega himself was mortally shot by federal soldiers who had been cut off in the retreat.[10]

On his deathbed, a few hours later, Vega was reconciled to the Church and his priesthood. He made a general confession to the local parish priest and was buried at the parish church in Arandas, where he had served before he joined the Cristeros. Not surprisingly, Cristero sympathizers would remember him as a hero, despite his breach of Church discipline and personal morals. Some even compared him with Miguel Hidalgo y Costilla, the famous priest who faced Church sanctions when he took up arms against Spain in the previous century. One of Vega's lifelong defenders was fellow Cristero Heriberto Navarrete, who said this about

[10] Bailey, ¡Viva Cristo Rey!, 251.

him years later: "No matter how great his faults, it is certain that no one can doubt the rectitude of his intentions in the undertakings he carried out."[11]

A Moral Dilemma

So, was José Reyes Vega a saint or a sinner? As far as our human judgment can tell, he was the latter. Certainly, his ruthlessness in combat was extreme, if not murderous, and his womanizing caused more than a little scandal to those around him. General Enrique Gorostieta, who eventually took over command of the entire Cristero army, said once that the reason he could never go to Confession to a priest was the scandalous behavior he saw in the life of Father Vega. Besides, Vega ignored the wise directive from his Church that priests should never pick up a gun, no matter how horrific the injustice being faced.

However, Vega's admirers defend his decision to take up arms despite the marching orders of his archbishop. The 1986 movie classic *The Mission* deals well with this issue, albeit in another part of Latin America (an area called the Iguazu Falls between Argentina and Paraguay) in the 1750s. As the movie plot unfolds, a Vatican envoy is visiting the Jesuit missions there to settle a dispute between the local Jesuits, who have been preaching against the atrocities of the slave trade, and the Portuguese and Spanish authorities, who want these meddling priests silenced and their missions (which were much too independent) shut down. After much agonizing and prayer, the Vatican envoy rules in favor of the colonizers and orders the Jesuit missions closed. On the face of it, it seems like a shocking

[11] Ibid.

decision, but the envoy is trying to head off a worse tragedy in Europe, where the Jesuits have also made themselves unpopular for the same reasons. He was afraid that
the entire Jesuit order would be suppressed by European
powers if he did not make concessions in Latin America.
(As it turned out, the Jesuits were eventually suppressed in
Europe anyway.) In the movie plot, however, the priests
are not impressed by the plight of their fellow Jesuits in
Europe. Their concern is the plight of the Guaraní Indians
in their charge, and they are appalled at the Vatican decision to close the missions.

Sensing that trouble is coming, the envoy warns the
Jesuits to accept his decision obediently and do nothing to
encourage the Guaraní to rebel—a warning that falls on
deaf ears. Two of the Jesuits take up arms to fight alongside
the Guaraní, while the third one (the superior) refuses to
go that far. He decides to help the Guaraní by nonviolent
means only. The Jesuit community is now divided on the
question of using violence to defend the innocent.

In a dramatic scene right before fighting breaks out, one
of the Jesuits who had chosen violence (Robert De Niro)
goes in to see his superior (Jeremy Irons) whom he is about
to disobey and asks for his blessing. Not surprisingly, the
superior says no. "If God is on your side," he says, "you
will not need my blessing; if he is not, my blessing will not
make any difference." But the superior does embrace his
fellow Jesuit and gives him his personal crucifix to wear. In
the ensuing destruction, both priests die with their people,
one fighting with a gun and the other carrying the Blessed
Sacrament in a monstrance. It is a heart-wrenching scene
that portrays two sincere priests who disagree on the use of
violence to fight injustice.

José Reyes Vega's life was more controversial than that
of Robert De Niro's character, of course, but it could be

said that, although Vega would never survive the canonization process, he was sincere in giving his life for the faith
at a time when most other priests went to live with their
rich friends in the city. (Some priests even preached against
the Cristeros, calling them "cattle thieves".) According to
historian Jean Meyer, on the day that Father Miguel Pro,
S.J., was shot in Mexico City, Chief of Police Roberto
Cruz (who ordered the execution) had a priest dining
at his table.[12] This bred bitterness in the hearts of many
who risked their lives for the cause, as can be seen in this
comment from a Valparaiso priest: "The overwhelming
majority of the bishops and priests, displaying a criminal
degree of conformism, wallowed in the accursed inertia,
all expecting sheer miracles from Heaven to give liberty to
the Church. They were content to give exhortations and
say a few prayers. The priests, more strict than ever, mostly
had recourse to theology and without further consideration announced the illicit nature of the violent struggle
in defense of the Church."[13] That blanket condemnation
was probably unfair (the bishops ordered the priests to
leave their parishes because so many priests were being
killed), but the Valparaiso priest's words illustrate the pain
of the dilemma.

In any case, the real heroes in this story are those priests
who volunteered to support the Cristeros actively *without*
taking up arms—about one hundred out of a total priest
population of some thirty-six hundred.[14] A significant
number of those volunteers were from the Archdiocese
of Guadalajara and were inspired by the actions of their
archbishop, Francisco Orozco. At great personal sacrifice,

[12] Meyer, *Cristero Rebellion*, 71.
[13] Ibid., 69.
[14] Ibid., 75.

Orozco ran his archdiocese from hiding rather than abandon his people in a time of such need, and many Guadalajaran priests made similar sacrifices at the risk of their lives.[15] Some administered the sacraments to the families of the rebels in secret locations, others went to the front lines to anoint dying soldiers, others collected donations to support the war effort; several paid the ultimate price, men like Father Toribio Romo, Father Miguel Pro, and Father Cristóbal Magallanes. In May 2000, Pope John Paul II canonized the first twenty-two of those martyrs, fifteen of whom were from Jalisco; the rest were from Aguascalientes, Chihuahua, Durango, Guerrero, Michoacán, and Zacatecas. (Three laymen were also canonized.) Others are in the process of canonization, including Anacleto González Flores, the famous Guadalajaran attorney, but it is unlikely that all the heroes of this era will be tracked down and canonized.

Historian Jean Meyer has compiled a list of 250 whose sacrifices, in his judgment, deserve official recognition of some kind, if not canonization. They are people who did acts of kindness that would be insignificant in normal circumstances, but under the Calles regime must be considered gestures of great courage—acts such as having a Mass in the home or keeping the Blessed Sacrament in the house or appealing to a federal soldier to spare someone's life or organizing the funeral of a Cristero soldier. These unsung heroes include old and young, rich and poor, married and single, men and women—all of them people who committed acts of heroism. A similar situation has prevailed in England going back to the persecution of the Church in the sixteenth and seventeenth centuries under Henry VIII and Elizabeth I. Forty-two of those English

---

[15] Bishop Amador Velasco of Colima also went into hiding.

martyrs have been canonized, and a further 242 have been declared blessed, but the full number of heroes will never be known.

David versus Goliath

How did this rebellion start? The Cristero War was not launched with a formal call to arms or symbolic action that the history books have recorded as the official beginning. It began with isolated uprisings here and there, some of which were successful and some not. People just grabbed whatever arms they could find—homemade slings, machetes, old guns—and joined groups of exasperated Catholics that were attacking barracks or municipal buildings in local towns. The date was August 1, 1926, and the unintended trigger was an order from the Mexican bishops that came into effect the previous day. "Since the conditions imposed render impossible the continuation of the sacred ministry," the bishops' statement read, "we have decided, in consultation with the Most Holy Father Pius XI, that from July 31 of the present year until we determine otherwise, all public worship requiring the participation of priests be suspended in all the churches of the Republic."[16] It was an unprecedented act of protest by the Catholic hierarchy of Mexico in the face of unprecedented religious persecution. Over the previous years there had been some local, short-lived suspensions of worship by individual bishops trying to put pressure on local governors, but nothing on this scale. For the first time in over four hundred years, all church sanctuaries

---

[16] Javier Navarro Rodríguez, *Tierra de Mártires: Diócesis de San Juan de los Lagos* (Guadalajara: Impre-Jal, 2002), 26.

in Mexico were dark and tabernacles were empty, while
parishioners stared in stunned disbelief not knowing what
to think. No more Masses or Confessions? No more
Baptisms or weddings? No more priests to visit the sick
and anoint the dying? No more sounds from the church
bells, those comforting timekeepers that had marked the
hours of the day in every town square for centuries? The
action sent shockwaves through the souls of millions of
Mexican Catholics.

Average parishioners, who did not understand the legal
niceties of the 1917 Constitution, had no problem understanding this. To them it was very simple. Plutarco Elías
Calles was taking away their priest. The man who had
expelled every priest from Sonora when he was governor there was now taking away the priest who celebrated
their Mass every Sunday.[17] To them, it was satanic! The
president of Mexico wanted to exterminate the Catholic
Church from the face of the land. That was why in June he
had signed the Calles Law, which gave legislatures unlim-
ited power to reduce (to zero if they chose!) the number of
priests in each parish. That was why he had tried to create
his own "Mexican pope" in the capital, a farcical scheme
to cut all links between the Catholic Church and the Holy
Father. And that was why the bishops were suspending all
worship. The people in the pew did not blame the bishops
because the bishops had no choice. Every other means of
protest against this insane policy had failed.

Parishioners had been warned ahead of time that this
cessation of public worship was coming, and thousands had
crammed into churches for days, trying to get Confession

---

[17] Most Catholics were sympathetic to the general aims of the revolution,
despite its anticlericalism. It was when their personal priest was taken away that
their opposition to the revolutionists crystalized.

one last time, or get married, or get confirmed, driving the clergy to the point of exhaustion.[18] But that did little to lessen the impact of the nightmare when it actually happened. Many a mother said to her husband on that fateful day of July 31 that enough was enough. Something must be done, even if it meant death. Better to die a martyr than to put up with this tyranny.

In the first month, there were six minor insurrections that had no connection or coordination. In September, there were thirteen more and still more in October.[19] Each time, the rebels took whatever guns and horses they could find in the barracks they overran, thus building up some resources for the next fight. In the eyes of the government, however, this was nothing more than a nuisance—local riots that called for severe punishment for those who took part.[20] Representatives in Congress even made jokes about it when they saw the military reports. But then a general was killed in Durango along with half of his regiment. Soon after, another general was killed in Jalisco, and this time the entire regiment was wiped out! By now it was no longer a joke.

The success of these isolated revolts soon came to the attention of the National League for the Defense of

[18] Jean Meyer, *La Cristiada* (Garden City Park, N.Y.: SquareOne Publishers, 2013), 24. *Time* magazine reported on the efforts of aging Archbishop José Mora y del Río to answer the pleas of so many people seeking Baptisms and Confirmations in Mexico City. "Weak, fainting, the Archbishop was all but carried from his cathedral on the first day of his heroic labors, having performed over 3,000 baptisms" (*Time*, August 2, 1926).

[19] Meyer, *Cristero Rebellion*, 49.

[20] In many places, the disturbances were riots more than intentional attacks on government facilities. Archbishop Francisco Orozco told the *New York Times* on August 13 that one riot in Guadalajara left forty-three federal troops killed and five Catholics dead (L. C. Speers, "Bishops Stand Firm against Calles Law", *New York Times*, August 14, 1926).

THE CRISTEROS AND THE DILEMMA OF VIOLENCE   83

Religious Freedom, the coalition of Catholic organizations whose directors were frustrated with the ineffectiveness of nonviolent protests and wanted to do something more. They decided to take over the isolated incidents of insurrection and turn them into a serious nationwide rebellion against the Calles government. This immediately raised the question, what would their bishops say? Would the bishops approve of a rebellion that was led by a high-profile Catholic organization, one that had as its goal the overthrow of the government of Mexico? League directors had no choice but to find out, and in November 1926, they asked to meet confidentially with members of the episcopal committee on church-state relations in Mexico City. Their strategy at that meeting was to hand the bishops a fait accompli rather than ask for their advice, and they brought along two Jesuit priests to help them make their case.[21] In a manifesto that one of them read, they reminded the bishops that the people were already in a state of rebellion, and that those grassroots rebellions were justified because peaceful means had been tried and had failed. Besides, this was a good opportunity to get rid of the Calles government once and for all, they said. They wanted the hierarchy to endorse the rebellion, adding bluntly that to fail to do so would seriously harm their credibility with the people.

The bishops asked for a couple of days to think about it, fully aware of the complications involved. They knew that to say no to the League would tear the Church apart, but to act without careful thought would be equally harmful. Their response would have to be carefully crafted. When

---

[21] The two Jesuit priests were Alfredo Méndez Medina and Rafael Martínez del Campo. See Fidel González Fernández, *Sangre y Corazón de un Pueblo* (Guadalajara: Arzobispado de Guadalajara, 2008), 1198.

they met again with the League directors, they confirmed in theory the League's general statement that Catholics have a right to rebel under certain conditions, but they declined to give an opinion on whether or not those conditions were actually fulfilled in this particular case. In effect, the bishops were being sympathetic to the cause without getting directly involved. With this wording, they could truthfully say that they did not initiate the rebellion or finance it, and their approval of what was already a fait accompli was implicit only.

Careful as the wording was, however, when news of the Mexican bishops' decision reached Rome it made people nervous. Pius XI had been carefully following the crisis, and he had even taken the unusual step earlier of ordering public prayers for Mexico in the churches of Rome. More importantly, he had already issued an apostolic letter, cautioning the Mexican bishops to avoid all violence and involvement in political activity. This warning, the pope added, applied to all Catholic lay organizations "so that you will not give the enemies of the Catholic faith the pretext to contend that your religion is bound up with any political party or faction".[22] What the League was now doing—leading an armed rebellion—was obviously in direct violation of his apostolic letter. However, the pope decided to remain silent at this juncture, saying nothing about the latest decision by the League, or about the latest decision by the bishops. He did this in part because he was receiving reports that the Mexican bishops were seriously divided on what to do about the crisis, and he did not want to make a complicated situation more complicated.

---

[22] Pius XI, Apostolic Letter *Paterna Solicitudo*, February 2, 1926, English translation in *New York Times*, April 20, 1926.

The Mexican bishops were indeed divided. Most of them felt Rome was too conciliatory with the Mexican government—and they had told Vatican officials just that during their *ad limina* visits two years before—but there was little agreement on how to fight the government. A very small group of bishops (about a half dozen out of thirty-eight) were in favor of the war. The most famous of those was Archbishop José Maria González y Valencia of Durango, who wrote a pastoral letter stating that he had consulted the best theologians in Rome, and that Catholics who took up arms should be tranquil in conscience.[23] Another twelve bishops believed violent revolution was not a good idea. The most articulate of those was Archbishop Francisco Orozco of Guadalajara, who preached nonviolent resistance in the face of tyranny, even to the point of martyrdom if necessary. The rest were undecided and simply ducked questions from parishioners about what to do. In effect, they let the people decide for themselves.[24]

The League directors, however, did not have to deal with that bewildering range of opinions. They dealt with the episcopal committee on church-state relations, and that committee did not condemn their decision to go to war. That was all they cared about. They were also happy about another answer they received from the episcopal committee—the one addressing the appointment of chaplains. The bishops would not officially assign chaplains to the Cristero army, they said, but they would grant permission to any priest who volunteered to risk his life in that role.

[23] Bishop José de Jesús Manríquez y Zárate of Huejutla went even further. In a letter to the League, he said: "I have resolved to send them (the Cristeros) each month at least a few thousand cartridges" (Bailey, ¡*Viva Cristo Rey!*, 215). He was eventually removed from his diocese by the Holy See.

[24] Meyer, *Cristero Rebellion*, 68.

The news of the League's decision came in late December 1926, when local League leaders throughout Mexico received copies of a document signed by René Capistrán Garza, one of the directors, that formally called for armed revolt against the Mexican government, based on "the sacred right of defense".[25] So began the Cristero War, the brutal religious rebellion that would eventually spread to thirteen states across the center and west of Mexico, from Durango to Tehuantepec, from Querétaro to the Pacific Ocean, and would last three years. The Mexican army had expected to put down the rising in a matter of weeks, while the rebels were hoping to topple the Calles government in that short time. Neither side expected the protracted struggle that materialized, costing over two hundred thousand lives and a huge disruption in the lives of millions of others. (The first significant immigration to California began during this time.)

The rebels would come to be called "Cristeros" (those who fought a war for Christ), a term that originally came from their enemies and was meant as a term of derision. It eventually became a term of pride, describing men who believed deeply they were fighting in the name of Christ the King. Their battle cry would be *Viva Cristo Rey* (Long Live Christ the King), words that have since become synonymous with Cristero martyrdom in the minds of Mexican Catholics. To this day those words can bring tears to the eyes of people whose grandfathers or great-grandfathers died in the countryside around Guadalajara or Guanajuato or Zacatecas. Devotion to Christ the King had been widespread in Mexico well before this time, but it was validated by Pope Pius XI when he instituted the Feast of Christ the King the year before (1925) in response

[25] Bailey, *¡Viva Cristo Rey!*, 108.

to the rise of secular governments that were trampling on religious freedom in Europe and Mexico. For the Cristeros, the fight was like David facing Goliath. A collection of inexperienced rebel bands was confronting a Mexican army that had recently been modernized by President Calles and was being supplied with up-to-date equipment from the United States. As the war advanced, the Cristeros became a more efficient guerilla force, but even at their peak only about half of them were organized in brigades and regiments with designated officers. And of those officers, only about a third were professional soldiers (veterans who had served in the Mexican army or during the War of the Generals). The rank-and-file Cristeros were mostly laborers and small land owners—60 percent of them had never been to any kind of school—who volunteered to fight on their own terms. They would not fight in places far from their families, and they insisted on going home each year for the harvest.[26]

Not surprisingly, communication was a constant problem, with orders from the League directors in Mexico City getting lost or arriving too late to the battlefield. Lack of resources was an even bigger problem because of the U.S. policy forbidding the supply of arms to rebel groups in Mexico. The Cristeros faced the machine guns, artillery, and planes of the federal army with whatever guns they were able to capture in previous battles, and a shortage of ammunition kept them in a constant state of crisis. Because they were not trained, they did not know how to hold their fire and use ammunition efficiently. In one case in Michoacán, a Cristero expeditionary column, consisting of new recruits, fled in panic before the superior forces of

---

[26] Meyer, *Cristero Rebellion*, 126.

the enemy. It was like shooting pigeons, the federal officer said in his report.[27]

"Poorly clad, filthy, their hair matted with sweat and dirt, the horses' equipment and their cartridge belts dirty, they spent most of the day stretched out under trees," Heriberto Navarrete wrote.[28] The members of one family from Michoacán interviewed by this writer remember their father, Francisco Lemus, coming home with a fellow soldier after months of fighting in urgent need of a shower. Both rebels had lice in their hair and ticks on their bodies, and their clothes were so filthy that their families just burned them. (The fellow soldier's name was Luis Calderón, the father of Felipe Calderón, who was president of Mexico from 2006 to 2012.)

For food, the Cristeros depended on the charity of people in the area, which was always unpredictable. Rebels sometimes went for days without food and often survived by looting food wherever they could find it. One unit got in trouble with superiors when the men stole two cows from a nearby hacienda; they had not eaten in two days. And it wasn't just food. "If you have any coats, send them, and also sandals," one officer wrote to his sister back in the city. "We are short of both, and the men are already walking barefoot. I've got a lot of men without clothing, and I need blankets." Other things he needed (in addition to cartridges and horseshoes): salt, tobacco, and soap.[29]

To make things worse, the *agraristas*, who had an intimate knowledge of the remote countryside, turned out to be a bitter disappointment to the Cristeros. These peasant farmers were deeply Catholic and should have been

[27] Ibid., 171.
[28] Quoted in Bailey, ¡Viva Cristo Rey!, 156.
[29] Meyer, Cristero Rebellion, 120.

natural allies of the cause, but because they were getting
small land parcels in the government land reform program,
they felt obliged to fight on the government side. The
issue caused bitter divisions within Catholic families. A
father would take the side of the Cristeros, and his son,
who had received free land, would take the side of the
enemy. Government officials accelerated the land program
with this advantage in mind, and some thirty thousand
agraristas swelled the ranks of the Mexican army at a time
when the government needed the extra auxiliaries.

Despite these disadvantages, however, the Cristero
army had as many as fifty thousand seasoned rebels in the
field by 1929, and they controlled vast areas of Jalisco,
Colima, Aguascalientes, Querétaro, Guanajuato, Michoacán, Zacatecas, and Nayarit. Incredibly, they set up fully
functioning municipal governments in those areas, which
included a judicial system, a department for taxes, and a
school department. They even had an underground press
to offset the propaganda of the government. Some munic-
ipalities even declared themselves autonomous republics,
independent of the federal government in Mexico City.
Jean Meyer gives striking examples of the phenomenal pace
of growth in this independence movement: In December
1927, there were fifty functioning Cristero municipali-
ties in Jalisco; by 1929 that number was ninety-two, plus
eleven in neighboring Guanajuato. In the municipality of
Valparaiso, Zacatecas, there were nineteen schools edu-
cating six hundred children in 1927; by 1929, those numbers had doubled. The five regiments of the brigade in
Zacatecas controlled one hundred thousand inhabitants
in a "liberated territory" 50 percent bigger than the state of
New York. A strict wartime code of conduct was enforced
in these areas, which meant drinking and gambling were
severely punished, and fiestas were banned. Not that the

Cristeros had anything against music and fun, but "where there was music, there was wine, and the enemy might surprise us when we were drunk."[30] It was an astonishing achievement, considering the ragtag bands of rebels that began this rebellion on August 1, 1926.

How did the Cristeros do it? There are four reasons.

1. *High morale*: The Cristeros believed intensely in their cause, and they charged into battle singing psalms and crying out, "Long live Christ the King!" For them the struggle was a religious movement more than a military operation. They were soldiers of a new army, and their enemies were persecutors of religion and allies of the devil. One former soldier who had seen the horrors of war under Pancho Villa as a teenager cried all night at the thought of leaving his family for life as a guerilla, but he had already made a promise. "I have an obligation to the Blessed Virgin," he said.[31] Another volunteer, Justo Ávila (later general), had developed a reputation as a marauder, killer, and rapist in his earlier life. As a Cristero officer, he became a reformed man who prohibited his soldiers from having women other than their legitimate wives. Some elderly Catholics saw the war as an easy way to the next world. "We need to earn our way to heaven now that it's cheaper," one said. "How much our grandparents would have appreciated earning thus the assurance of heaven, and now God provides it for us; I'm ready to leave."[32]

Contrast this spirit with conditions on the other side. The Mexican army at this time was dogged by morale problems because the soldiers were fighting a war they

[30] Ibid., 142.
[31] Ibid., 172.
[32] Jean Meyer, *La Cristiada* (2013 edition), 96.

did not much believe in, and living conditions in the barracks were not good. The end result: about twenty thousand federal troops a year were deserting out of a total force of seventy thousand. Interestingly, the man at the top of this demoralized chain of command, Minister of War Joaquín Amaro, became a Catholic some years later and left his valuable archives to the Jesuits. The seeds of conversion may already have been germinating in that soldier's soul, even as he ordered the Mexican army to kill its own citizens.

2. *Strong support of the rural population:*[33] One rural ironsmith called himself a Cristero, although he never fought in battle; his contribution to the cause was to make swords and knives secretly for the troops. They were the people who made the struggle possible, he would say, pointing out that you could not distinguish between the soldiers in the field and the soldiers who secretly worked in shops like his. The government troops tried to break this secret network of support by intensifying their acts of cruelty. They raped women, murdered civilians, and seized property at will. A priest in Leon told this writer about his grandfather's brother who gave shelter and food to Cristero soldiers passing through the town. When a federal officer demanded to know where those Cristeros were headed, he refused to talk and they hanged him from a tree. In Tecolotlán, Jalisco, they hanged a priest because he would not tell them where the pastor was hiding. They executed a priest in Zacatecas for not telling them what Cristeros had said in Confession. Another priest had a worse fate.

---

[33] There was some support among urban populations, but it was minimal. Most city Catholics, whether from indifference or from fear, simply watched the rebellion from the sidelines.

They suspended him for three days from the portico of his church, and then cut the soles of his feet and forced him to walk to the cemetery where they shot him. But nothing was able to break the determination of the people to support the Cristeros. In fact, these atrocities only deepened the anger of the people against the government.

In desperation, the government then tried an even more brutal tactic: the shifting of populations that were known to supply the Cristero army with food. Under this plan, called "reconcentration", the army forcibly moved entire communities out of rural areas into towns, thus leaving a million and a half hectares of rich agricultural land unpopulated and uncultivated. Some seventy-six thousand civilians were herded into reconcentration towns that were not equipped to handle the extra people. Tepatitlán, for example, grew from ten thousand to fifty thousand overnight, with the result that smallpox and typhoid devastated the town population. For those who didn't die from disease, the reconcentration program meant permanent exile from their hometowns and the loss of their property (which the government appropriated). The descendants of Santo Toribio's family still tell stories about how friends had to move from Santa Ana to Aguascalientes and were never able to go back. However, this reconcentration plan did not work any better than the murder of civilians and the torture of priests because the Cristeros found ways around it. They raided crops from the lands around the cities before the surprised federal troops had time to stop them and stored them in secret places—again with the unbreakable support of the people.

3. *Hit-and-run, guerilla-style war*: The Cristeros fought a hit-and-run, guerilla-style war, for which the Mexican army was not prepared. Hidden in remote parts of the

countryside in small units, they came together to launch surprise attacks and then scattered before the enemy had a chance to fight back. They attacked only when they were certain to win, which left the federal troops feeling helpless and frustrated and only added to their low morale. The Cristeros avoided the big cities where the military was based, but there were surprising exceptions to this. In May 1929, two Cristero officers walked into Aguascalientes in broad daylight and stole a hundred army horses from the railway station! It was an audacious act, and it secured a welcome bonanza for rebels who had plenty of use for a bunch of well-groomed horses.

4. *The Women's Brigade*: This was a clandestine military organization of teenagers and young women, founded near Guadalajara after the war started in order to supply badly needed ammunition as well as intelligence to the men in the field, and to take care of the wounded. They were simple shop girls, office workers, and seamstresses, but they moved mountains to find munitions and get them out to the front lines. They bribed (or charmed) corrupt federal officers into selling them supplies. They befriended the sympathetic wives of those officers, who undid at night what their husbands were doing during the day. They transported the supplies of bullets by hiding them in trucks carrying cement or in bags of coal or in cartloads of maize. If all else failed, they carried the ammunition under their dresses, wearing specially made shirts with large pockets that could carry up to seven hundred cartridges, which was triple the military allotment of each soldier at the time. Weighed down with all that lead under their clothes, they traveled by train from city to city, all the while dodging wartime police who were watching out for anything that looked suspicious. They even learned how to manufacture

explosives, blow up trains, and handle batteries and deto-
nators, and then they passed on that know-how to their
fathers and brothers. With female creativity, they used
every idea they could think of, and their accomplishments
were astonishing. They are among the unsung heroes of
the Cristero War.

The members of the Women's Brigade had to take oaths
of obedience and secrecy, and they were organized in military fashion with ranks all the way up to general. At their
peak, there were twenty-five thousand of them, mostly
young and unmarried, between fifteen and twenty-five
years of age, and they were led by female generals, none of
whom was over thirty-five. The efficiency of this organization was such that the government did not even know
that it existed until near the end of the war. Not a single
defection was ever recorded. "I was overcome with joy,"
one nurse and ammunitions purveyor said. "The willingness with which everybody worked. The silence that they
all kept."[34] Clearly, the Cristero rebels could not have
functioned as well as they did without these resourceful
young women. Unfortunately, historians have not written much about them because the secrecy oath meant that
records were not kept.

In all, the Women's Brigade had four generals, but the
best known was Maria Goyaz, the daughter of Francisco
Goyaz, the manager of a Guadalajaran newspaper called
El Cruzado. She is not listed as one of the founders of the
first Women's Brigade unit (called after the recently canonized Joan of Arc), but she must have joined soon after
its foundation because before long she was the supreme
commander of the entire organization and was using two
aliases ("Celia Gómez" and "Celia Ortiz"). Constantly

[34] Meyer, *Cristero Rebellion*, 137.

changing identity and location was standard procedure for the top brass in the Women's Brigade.

Under Goyaz's leadership, the Western Division became the largest, with eighteen brigades, each one consisting of 650 women. Guadalajara alone, which was in her division, had five brigades, and they ran an underground hospital for Cristero casualties and an underground press. Goyaz eventually moved to Mexico City, where all the ammunition was made, and organized a brigade there. The road from Mexico City to Guadalajara soon became a critical transport route, with small detachments of women in every town secretly passing on the ammunition to the next town as it made its way to the battlefield.

These heroic women had only one serious problem. The directors of the League were jealous of their growing power and tried to rein them in. It was the League directors who prevailed upon Rome to order an end of their secrecy, a decision that obligated Archbishop Orozco of Guadalajara to rescind their oath reluctantly. But that decision from Rome (near the end of the war) did not lessen Orozco's admiration for the organization, nor did it lessen the admiration of the generals in the field who knew the effectiveness of the Women's Brigade firsthand.

An Inspired Decision

These Cristero advantages would not have been as decisive if the Cristeros had not had a military commander who knew how to take advantage of them. His name was Enrique Gorostieta, and the directors of the League hired him when they realized that they knew nothing about how to win a war; they were making serious mistakes leading to unnecessary loss of life. The choice they made

for a military leader was inspired, one of the most important decisions in the three-year conflict. It was that decision more than anything that turned the tide in favor of
the Cristeros.

Gorostieta was a career military officer who was studying at the Heroico Colegio Militar in Chapultepec in
Mexico City when the 1910 Madero revolution broke
out. His self-discipline and talent as an artilleryman soon
came to the notice of his superiors, and in 1914, at the
age of twenty-seven, he became the youngest general in
the country. However, it was his misfortune to launch his
career during the War of the Generals, and he ended up on
the losing side; he was in the camp of General Victoriano
Huerta, who lasted only seventeen months as president. So
he abandoned his military career and went to live in Cuba
until the political winds improved. By 1920, things were
looking more hopeful with the assassination of Venustiano
Carranza, and Gorostieta decided to return to Mexico. He
didn't return to military service, however, instead taking a
job in an unlikely place—a soap factory. Apparently, that
line of work allowed him to use the scientific knowledge
he had gained as an artillery officer years before. But the
work was boring, and the longer he stayed the more he
hated it. His life was at a dead end and he was frustrated. It
was at this point that the League contacted him and offered
him a job, which he accepted without much hesitation. It
sounded more exciting than making soap. Besides, he was
a Catholic (although not very active at times), and he sympathized with the Cristero Rebellion. In fact, he detested
the regime of Plutarco Calles just as much as the Cristeros
did, and he was happy for an opportunity to take on Calles
on the battlefield.

Exactly how pious a Catholic Enrique Gorostieta was
has been debated ever since. It was said that he made critical remarks about bishops and the religious practices of

his soldiers, and complaints to that effect reached the ears of the League directors in the capital. But his commitment to his faith seems to have been genuine. A personal experience he had before the League ever contacted him had deepened his sympathy for the Catholic cause, he told friends. His wife had given birth to a son, but when he looked for a priest to baptize the child, he was shocked at how hard it was to find one. The experience apparently underlined for him the practical reality of living the faith under the Calles regime.[35]

In any case, his commitment to winning the Cristero War was never in question nor was his competence as a commander. He began work in July 1927, by assuming the post of chief of operation in Jalisco, and was soon in charge of six states and shortly thereafter became supreme commander of the entire insurrection. By then, he was getting to know his men, and he was "astounded by the miracle he was witnessing", Jean Meyer writes.

> Soldiers in sandals and dressed in white linen, still filled with the communal spirit of their villages ... held steady under fire, did not hesitate to respond to supreme demands.... He saw them stand up and march calmly to the battle, hurl themselves, machete in hand, on the Federal machine-guns, and scale heights at the summit of which simple peasants begin to appear to us as great warriors.[36]

Gorostieta set about honing the battle skills of these men, who were doing so much with so little, teaching them how to protect lives and conserve resources. "You will only fight where it suits you to do so, and never where it suits the enemy," he explained in one circular. "You must never tire of maneuvering until you tire the enemy

[35] Bailey, ¡Viva Cristo Rey!, 171.
[36] Meyer, Cristero Rebellion, 53.

and oblige him to fight a battle in conditions unfavorable to him."[37]

By spring 1929, Gorostieta was also knee-deep in politics, something that made a nervous President Calles even more nervous. He supported the rebellion by Federal General José Gonzalo Escobar against the Calles regime, extracting promises from Escobar about military help for the Cristeros if his coup succeeded. It didn't, but Gorostieta used the occasion to increase his attacks in the center and west of the country, while the federal forces were busy putting down Escobar's rebellion in the north. All the time, he was tightening his control on a large area of the Mexican Republic, and even the capture of major cities like Guadalajara was within his grasp if he chose to go that far. He decided not to. Caution held him back, but he did pull off his greatest success of the war at this time.

When the federal troops returned from the north, and turned their attention to the Cristeros again, Gorostieta defeated them in a confrontation that was not guerilla warfare anymore. His forces won a major battle head-on. The Cristeros were at the zenith of their combat readiness, and the Mexican army casualty list was reaching a thousand a month. A worried minister of war, Joaquín Amaro, warned the president that peace negotiations with the Church was the only way to end this nightmare. (By this time, Calles' four-year term had ended and Emilio Portes Gil was the new president.)

Despite his success on the battlefield, however, Gorostieta was worried. He knew the Mexican army was getting nowhere in its efforts to crush the rebellion, but he also knew that the Cristeros could not win without more money and ammunition, and finding those resources was

[37] Ibid., 170.

impossible while the U.S. embargo on arms continued. He had no intention of giving up the fight, but he could see that the war had reached a stalemate. General Gorostieta was killed soon after this in what was an unlucky circumstance. It was June 1, 1929, and he was on the road to Michoacán with some staff to attend to personnel issues when the group ran into federal troops in an area that would normally be safe. To make matters worse, the weather was unusually wet and cold. The mud clung to the horses' hooves in large clods, historian David Bailey wrote, and the animals could not go much further.[38] The party decided to spend the night at a friendly hacienda along the way, but federal troops were spotted there also and they had to move on, despite feeling tired and miserable. The group finally found a wood that was safe and stopped there in an effort to get some sleep. It was two o'clock in the morning. At dawn, they moved on again and arrived at another friendly hacienda where they thought they could eat, relax, and rest the horses.

After a breakfast of eggs and beans, Gorostieta lay down, but not for long. Suddenly a sentry on the roof shouted the alarm that federal cavalry was approaching the house. In an instant, the party was on its feet grabbing guns and rushing out to saddle the horses. Just as Gorostieta was mounting his horse, the federal troops burst through the gate of the hacienda, and a hail of gunfire ensued. Before he knew it, Gorostieta's horse was on the ground dead with the general's leg trapped under the animal. He pulled his leg loose and rushed back into the house, while the other members of the party ran in the opposite direction, away from the house. With the house now surrounded by federal troops, Gorostieta did not have many options. In desperation, he

[38] Bailey, ¡Viva Cristo Rey!, 264.

decided to shoot his way out of the building, but it didn't work; he was instantly cut down in a hail of bullets. One other member of the party was also killed, and the others were taken prisoners.[39]

It was not until sometime later that the federal troops realized how lucky they were. The officer in charge informed Minister of War Amaro that they had killed General Gorostieta, and warm congratulations flowed to all involved, including a word of thanks from the president Portes Gil himself. With smug satisfaction, the army embalmed the body and sent it to Gorostieta's sister in Mexico City, just to make sure everyone had proof that the "so called supreme chief of the fanatical rebellion" really had been killed.[40]

Plutarco Elías Calles, who was still running the country from behind the scenes, was pleased at the news, but he was deeply worried nonetheless. The rebellion he thought he could crush in a matter of weeks was still going on three years later, with no end in sight. In fact, the Cristeros had never been so strong.

Why did this president miscalculate his enemy so seriously? And what was behind his hatred of the Catholic Church? The next chapter will deal with that.

[39] Ibid., 265.
[40] Ibid.

Chapter 5

Plutarco Elías Calles and a Religious Obsession

On February 21, 1925, a bizarre incident unfolded in Mexico City that was supposed to change the history of the Catholic Church in Mexico. Around eight o'clock that evening, about a hundred armed men walked into La Soledad Church in the working class district and ordered the three astonished priests to get out. Soon afterward, an elderly clergyman arrived, accompanied by more armed men, and announced that he was the "patriarch" of a new church called the "Mexican Catholic Apostolic Church", and that this place was going to be his national headquarters. The elderly cleric in question was Joaquín Pérez, seventy-three, a former priest whose resume included membership in the Freemasons and time as an officer in the army of Venustiano Carranza. Another former priest, Manuel Monge, who had an equally controversial background, accompanied him.

The next day, a group of workers from the notoriously anti-Catholic CROM union (Confederación Regional Obrera Mexicana), who called themselves the "Knights of the Order of Guadalupe", formed an armed guard around the building; the curiosity of the parishioners grew from bewilderment to anger.[1] By the following morning, things

[1] The Knights of the Order of Guadalupe had nothing to do with Catholic organizations of that name.

were out of control. As Monge was preparing the altar to begin Mass, a group of parishioners rushed into the sanctuary and physically attacked him, forcing him to flee for his life to the sacristy, where he was joined by his companion "Patriarch" Pérez. Before long, a riot had broken out in the neighborhood involving over a thousand protestors, and it took mounted police and firemen with high-pressure hoses several hours to restore peace. One person died and several were injured in the melee. Meanwhile, the two renegade priests barricaded themselves in the rectory and sent an urgent appeal to the leaders of CROM, who were now forced to come up with alternative plans for "Patriarch" Pérez. They decided not to give him La Soledad Church after all, but instead to set him up in nearby Corpus Christi Church, a building that had not been used for religious services for several years. La Soledad was never again used for religious services; it was turned into a library.[2] By this time, Monge had had a change of heart. He published a statement in the newspaper *El Universal*, expressing regret for his involvement in the plot and pledging his submission to legitimate Catholic Church authority.[3]

Luis Morones, the founder of CROM and a close ally of President Plutarco Calles, carried out this plot with Calles' full support—if not more. Calles may have been the actual mastermind. Their plan was to start a schismatic church movement in Mexico that would eventually spread to all parts of the country and turn the Catholic Church into a state-controlled organization independent of Rome. This idea was not new. Following the example of the French Revolution, Melchor Ocampo and Benito Juárez had

---

[2] The churches were technically the property of the government, and most of them still are to this day.

[3] Manuel Monge statement in *El Universal*, March 2, 1925, quoted in Bailey, *¡Viva Cristo Rey!* (Austin: University of Texas Press, 1974), 53.

suggested the same thing in the previous century.[4] Juárez even sent a request to the American Episcopal Church to provide Mexico with a bishop who would function as a kind of Mexican pope, in charge of a national patriotic church.[5] And Plutarco Calles also had this idea in mind when, as governor of Sonora, he banished every Catholic priest from the state (an unprecedented act at the time), hoping to replace them with clergymen who would organize a locally controlled patriotic church of Mexico.

Calles failed in Sonora and he would fail here also, although this time the plot continued for a few weeks before it died. A half dozen other churches were taken over, with the same violent reaction from parishioners, and there was even discussion about taking over the Basilica of Our Lady of Guadalupe in Mexico City. The *New York Times* reported that the "Knights of Guadalupe" petitioned the state to turn over the famous basilica to "Patriarch" Pérez and make it "the Vatican of Mexico".[6] A glance at photos of the "patriarch" gives a hint of how bewildering the whole scheme must have appeared to Catholics in the pew. They show images of an old man, dressed in a rumpled white cassock, with a confused look on his face that belied his claim that he was the leader of an important new movement. However, the "Mexican pope" scheme,

[4] In 1790, during the French Revolution, a law was passed that attempted to turn the Catholic Church in France into a national church independent of the pope, and all priests and bishops were required to take an oath of allegiance to the new state-controlled church. Over half of the clergy refused to take the oath, however, and after a period of deep division in the country the law was abrogated. In 1801, a concordat between Napoleon and the Vatican restored the Church's full civil status as a religious institution under the authority of the pope.

[5] Jean Meyer, *The Cristero Rebellion* (London: Cambridge University Press, 1976), 35.

[6] Quoted in Jean Meyer, *La Cristiada* (Garden City Park, N.Y.: SquareOne Publishers, 2013), 15.

ill-advised as it was, did have lasting consequences. It set off alarm bells among Catholic leaders, both clerical and lay, and it set the stage for the ominous sequence of events that would follow in 1925 and 1926. Just two weeks after the attack on La Soledad, leaders of all major Catholic lay societies met in Mexico City to found the National League for the Defense of Religious Liberty, the organization that would lead to the Cristero Rebellion fifteen months later.

His Obsession with the Catholic Church

The man behind the attack on La Soledad Church (and so many other attacks on the Catholic Church) wasn't all bad. In fact, if it were not for the religion issue, Plutarco Calles might be considered one of the better presidents of Mexico. By the time he reached the presidency, he already had a long list of qualifications to his name: successful military general; governor of Sonora; two positions in Venustiano Carranza's cabinet; minister of the interior in the cabinet of his predecessor, Álvaro Obregon; a student of the governmental and economic order in social-democratic Germany. In the minds of many, he had all the qualities of a great statesman, and some continued to see him in that light up to his death. "Let me tell you something," the veteran Mexican politician Rubén Figueroa once said. "There has never been another man like Plutarco Elías Calles. And to this day, he has been denied the recognition he deserves."[7]

There are indeed accomplishments for which Calles deserves recognition as president of Mexico. It was he who set up the central banking system—the Bank of

[7] Ibid., 13.

Mexico—modeled after the Federal Reserve System, the central bank of the United States; while it went through growing pains at first, it turned out to be an institution that stood the test of time. He also made extensive improvements to the transportation system, constructing new railroads and highways. The Southern Pacific Railroad of Mexico, running from Nogales on the Arizona border all the way south to Guadalajara, was hailed as an historic achievement at the time. His social legislation was equally ambitious: vastly expanding the network of schools (he had been a teacher himself once), adding two thousand rural schools during his term; accelerating the breakup of large haciendas, including Church-owned lands; setting up a bank of agricultural credit to help small farmers (based on a program he saw in Germany); setting badly needed standards for sanitation in public markets and the food supply in general; launching vaccination campaigns—five million Mexicans were inoculated against smallpox in 1926 alone. He even conducted a program against alcoholism. It was all part of his ambitious vision for improving the standard of living among the Mexican people, especially the Mexican poor. "Who should be able to reach out a hand to the poor?" he asked a reporter once, then answered the question himself: "Only one agency—the government."[8] By American standards it would be considered socialism, but Calles made it work for the Mexico of his time.

Most importantly, he institutionalized the succession of power in Mexico. Up to that time, changes in office had been marked by violent revolutions and shaky coalitions, and the country had been run by military strongmen for a century. There were some eight thousand political parties

[8] Enrique Krauze, *Mexico: Biography of Power* (New York: HarperCollins, 1998), 416.

competing for attention, and their battles were physical as often as they were verbal. Not that their fights mattered. The really powerful figures in society were the generals, whose only creed was that might was right, and all of them wanted to grab the presidency if they could. Since 1884, every Mexican president had been assassinated or driven out of office by revolution. Put another way, when Calles took office in 1924, his term marked the first time in forty years that the presidency was handed over peacefully from one head of state to the next. It was an important milestone, and Calles understood that to make it last, Mexico needed a stronger political system. With that end in mind, he founded a political party called the National Revolutionary Party, which has endured into modern times as the Institutional Revolutionary Party—the PRI (Partido Revolucionario Institucional). It was at first a one-party system, of course—one that stayed in power through electoral fraud—but it was better than what the country had before. If nothing else, it meant that the succession of power in Mexico would now be determined by a group of leaders rather than individual strongmen. As Enrique Krauze puts it, the National Revolutionary Party provided "a civilized conclave of generals who resolved their differences without drawing their revolvers".[9] It brought to an end the militaristic history that continued to haunt many other Latin American countries—an achievement for which Calles could take credit.

His record in dealing with the U.S. oil companies was equally impressive. American citizens' property rights in Mexico had been a sore point since the wording of the 1917 Constitution that brought all oil and mineral findings under state control. As soon as that new constitution

[9] Ibid., 431.

passed, the American oil executives protested loudly, and Calles' predecessor (Álvaro Obregón) was forced to work out an agreement with President Warren G. Harding's administration in 1923, promising not to implement the new constitution retroactively for foreigners.[10] However, the issue heated up again two years later when two new presidents—Calvin Coolidge and Plutarco Elías Calles— took office, and a new U.S. ambassador to Mexico (James Sheffield) convinced his bosses at the U.S. State Department that the "Bolshevik" Calles was planning to seize U.S. oil company lands despite the agreement worked out by Obregón.[11] The issue brought relations between the two countries close to the breaking point and was diffused only by the appointment of a new ambassador to Mexico. President Coolidge replaced James Sheffield with the more affable Dwight Morrow and gave him specific marching orders: "Keep us out of war with Mexico."[12] Morrow did just that, and Mexican sovereignty began to get more respect in Washington.

However, that is not the side of Plutarco Calles that is remembered today. What has endured in the memory of the Mexican people is his dislike for the Catholic religion, and his reputation for executing priests without trial— ninety of them during his four years as president. He was an atheist, and he wore that as a badge of honor all his life; when he was an altar boy, he stole money from the

[10] The Harding administration was deeply influenced by big business, in particular the oil companies. The powerful oil lobby convinced President Harding to withhold recognition of Obregón's presidency until he gave the Americans assurances about property rights, which Obregón finally did in 1923. This excessive influence of the oil lobby was eventually exposed in the Teapot Dome Scandal.

[11] In fact Calles was a nationalist, not a Bolshevik.

[12] Krauze, *Mexico*, 419.

collection to buy candy, he once boasted. He was also a social engineer, a radical thinker who believed that the only way to help the Mexican people was to reform society from its roots. That meant getting rid of the institutions that he saw as an obstacle to social progress, the chief of which was the Catholic Church, and he attacked the Church with a fanaticism that often shocked foreign diplomats. U.S. Ambassador James Sheffield said this about him in a memo to the U.S. State Department: "This president has become so violent on the religious question that he has lost control of himself. When this topic has been dealt with in his presence, his face turns red, and he has hit the table to express his hate and profound hostility towards the practice of religion."[13] Historian Jean Meyer compares him to the Roman emperor Diocletian: both leaders were politicians with unusual talent and dedication to the state; both were deep thinkers with powerful self-control; and both were deeply threatened by the Christian religion. Why such talented men were so threatened is a mystery, Meyer concludes.[14]

Other historians see clues in his childhood. His father was an alcoholic who showed no interest in helping to raise his children; he died in a hotel in Sonora, trying to hide bottles of liquor under his pillow—and those memories left a mark on his son. When Plutarco was governor in Sonora, he once ordered the execution of a poor drunk to underscore his seriousness about a new law restricting access to alcohol. To make matters worse, he was born out of wedlock, and that stigma (which he blamed on the Catholic Church) followed him throughout his life. As president, he passed a law that abolished the distinction

[13] Ibid., 421.
[14] Jean Meyer, *La Cristiada* (Mexico City: Editorial Cleo, 2008), 21–23.

between legitimate and illegitimate children, normally a good idea but in his case one that was driven by "a blind and irrational passion" to deny the circumstances of his own birth.[15] That blind passion also drove his obsessive attempt to banish the Catholic Church from the land, never mind that the majority of the Mexican people were practicing Catholics. A coincidence in timing made that obsession even worse. As luck would have it, the threat of a U.S. invasion by the Coolidge administration over oil rights coincided with the rise of the Cristero Rebellion in the second half of 1926. There was no connection between the two issues, but in Calles' mind they were connected. At the very least, the timing was a reminder to him that Catholics had more allegiance to a foreign power (the Vatican) than to the revolution.

The Calles Law

When Plutarco Calles took over the presidency of Mexico on December 1, 1924, there were enough laws on the books to emasculate the Catholic Church as an institution. The articles of the 1917 Constitution had stripped the Church of all of her property, forbidden the Church to run schools or seminaries, and banned all religious services outside the confines of the church building. More ominously, it gave state legislatures the power to determine how many priests could serve in each state. Thankfully, these measures had never been enforced. Even Venustiano Carranza, who called the convention that wrote the constitution, was ambivalent about the final text, and he avoided a strict interpretation while he was president, as

---

[15] Krauze, *Mexico*, 424.

did his successor, Álvaro Obregón. Consequently, most of the governors and state legislators followed a kind of "gentlemen's agreement" policy that allowed them to turn a blind eye to the more extreme parts of the constitution.[16] That quickly changed as soon as Calles took office. The new president made no secret of his desire that every governor and state legislature interpret the constitution literally, and some governors—the most anticlerical ones—immediately began to act on that. A circular published in the state of Mexico reminded municipal authorities that Holy Week services in the open air were against the law and should not be tolerated. In the state of Tabasco, legislators passed a law limiting the number of priests in the state to six—one for every thirty thousand Catholics. Soon after, Tabasco legislators doubled down with a new law stating that priests in their state must be over forty years of age and be married! Meanwhile, Luis Morones and his CROM henchmen launched the plan to set up "Patriarch" Pérez in La Soledad Church. However, these examples were still the exception. Most governors continued to drag their feet in implementing a constitution that they considered extreme, and some of the newspapers supported them in that. "Are we perhaps so free of problems," the daily newspaper in Mexico City, *Excelsior*, asked in an editorial, "that we need to revive the religious warfare that has stained three-quarters of the past century with blood?"[17]

---

[16] According to historian Jean Meyer, a "gentleman's agreement" not to interpret the 1917 Constitution in the literal sense existed in Veracruz, Coahuila, Guerrero, Puebla, Oaxaca, Chihuahua, Campeche, Guanajuato, and Zacatecas. Ruthless application of the new constitution was pursued in Tabasco, Jalisco, and Colima. A few places, like Michoacán and San Luis Potosí, had a mixture of severity and laxity.

[17] *Excelsior*, February 18, 1925 quoted in Bailey, *¡Viva Cristo Rey!*, 50.

But Calles was determined, and eventually he got the excuse that he was looking for. On February 4, 1926, the newspaper *El Universal* published a ten-year-old interview with Archbishop Mora in which he said that Catholics did not recognize the anticlerical articles of the 1917 Constitution, but the reporter gave the impression that the interview was recent.[18] If the reporter was looking to stir up trouble, he certainly succeeded. "This is a challenge to the government and the Revolution," Calles thundered when he read it. "I am not prepared to tolerate it. Now that the priests are making these moves, we must apply the law as it stands."[19] He immediately closed more Catholic schools and convents, expelled more foreign-born clergy, and then unveiled a decree that shocked everyone—the Calles Law, the decree (among other things) that ordered every Catholic priest in the nation to register with the state immediately, if he intended to continue working as a priest. The clerical ministry, he said, was a public profession like medicine or the law, and priests would have to hold a license from the state to practice. The new law was to take effect in one month (July 31), and any priest or governor who continued to drag his feet in complying with the law would face penalties ranging from stiff fines to jail time.

Colonial history was now coming back to haunt Mexican Catholics. Church-state relations had come full circle: from the Patronato Real of the Spanish Crown (1524–1821); to a brief period of freedom from state control after independence from Spain (1822); to a nominal separation of church and state under Benito Juárez (1857); to a new church-state union that gave the Calles state the kind of control that the Spanish Crown used to have. But

18 Bailey, ¡*Viva Cristo Rey!*, 62.
19 Krauze, *Mexico*, 420.

this latest version was very different. The monarch was no longer the Catholic Queen Isabella who saw herself as a partner in preaching the Gospel in the New World. The monarch was a fanatical atheist who wanted to wipe the Catholic Church off the map.

An invitation of war, American journalist Walter Lippmann called the Calles Law in his newspaper columns, as more and more voices were raised in protest. Bishop Arthur Drossaerts of San Antonio, who was hosting some of the exiled Mexican bishops in his diocese, wondered aloud how the United States could keep an ambassador in "Soviet Mexico" when it did not recognize Soviet Russia. In Baltimore, Archbishop Michael Curley said that Plutarco Calles would not last a month if Washington would stop aiding this "Bolshevik regime", and he challenged the Knights of Columbus to use their considerable power to put pressure on the U.S. government. The Knights did just that. At their annual convention in Philadelphia a couple of months later, the Knights passed a high-profile resolution, protesting the atrocities being perpetuated against their fellow Catholics on the other side of the Rio Grande. Speaking to twenty-five thousand Knights, including representatives from Mexico, Grand Knight James Flaherty denounced the government of Plutarco Calles and criticized his own government's total silence in the face of blatant persecution of the Catholic Church.

A month later, President Calvin Coolidge met with Flaherty and his delegation, while rank-and-file Knights raised a million dollars to increase public awareness of the crisis and to assist the victims of the persecution who were fleeing to the United States. Meanwhile in Rome, Pope Pius XI called on Catholics throughout the world to pray for the Catholics of Mexico, and the apostolic delegate to the United States sent a follow-up letter to all American bishops, underlining the gravity of the situation. Archbishop

Edward Hanna of San Francisco, chairman of the administrative committee of the National Catholic Welfare Conference (that is what the U.S. bishops' conference was called in those days), issued a statement that translated the persecution into terms that Americans could understand. "Let us suppose," he wrote,

> that President Coolidge ordered the governors of every state in the Union to define the number of Catholic priests or Presbyterian ministers who would be permitted to hold religious services and that the governors, by virtue of the power invested in them by law, complied. What would the people of the United States do? Suppose the editor of the Christian Science Monitor were sentenced to jail for six years, because his journal criticized adversely, for example, the present federal immigration law. What would be the public sentiment of this country?[20]

Calles, however, was impervious to the storm of protest, both at home and abroad. "Every week without religious ceremonies will cost the Catholic Church two percent of its faithful," he predicted triumphantly to a French diplomat (Ernest Lagarde), after hearing about the suspension of all religious services, adding that it was time "to finish with the Church and to rid his country of it once and for all".[21] In a column for the *New York Times*, he flatly denied that his policy on religion was anti-Catholic, insisting that Mexican law applied to all religions equally.[22] (He

[20] Archbishop Hanna statement in "Archbishop Punctures Propaganda", *The Register*, Superior California edition, July 31, 1926. *The Register* and most diocesan newspapers followed the crisis in Mexico closely at this time.

[21] Meyer, *Cristero Rebellion*, 44.

[22] Dr. Antonio Castro-Leal, "Mexico Cannot Be Judged by the Standards of the Church in the United States," *New York Times*, August 1, 1926. *The Times* had requested an op-ed from President Calles and Castro-Leal, the acting head of the Mexican Embassy in Washington, wrote it on the president's behalf.

neglected to explain how a ban on celibacy and monastic life could apply to any religion other than Catholic.)
When a delegation of Mexican bishops went to plead with
him, he coldly repeated his warning that they must follow
the law, concluding with the menacing comment that if
they wanted to attempt the overthrow of the government,
he was fully prepared for that. The struggle to destroy the
Catholic Church had reached apocalyptic proportions in
his mind. "We are at the point when the lines will be
drawn forever across the fields," he said to the French diplomat. "The hour when we will unleash the final battle is
approaching; we are going to know if the Revolution has
defeated the reaction or if the triumph of the Revolution
has been ephemeral."[23]

Not surprisingly, Calles got strong encouragement from
the anticlerical faction that had gathered around him, in
particular his interior minister, Adalberto Tejeda. "The
Church has exceeded our wildest hopes in decreeing the
suspension of religious services," Tejeda told a foreign
diplomat. "We have got the clergy by the throat and we
will do everything to strangle it."[24] The Tijuana affiliate of
CROM wrote to Calles pledging to fight (with weapons
if necessary) to defend the principles of the revolution,
adding: "The people from this remote region of Mexico
wish to see a school erected on the site now occupied by
each church.... This is the will of a people who want
to bequeath instruction instead of fanaticism to its children."[25] He also received many letters of support from
anti-Catholic groups in the United States, groups such as
the Ku Klux Klan, the Masons, the Freethinkers Society,

---

[23] Krauze, *Mexico*, 421.

[24] Meyer, *Cristero Rebellion*, 44.

[25] Marisol López-Menéndez, *Miguel Pro: Martyrdom, Politics, and Society in Twentieth-Century Mexico* (Lanham, Md.: Lexington Books, 2016), 114.

the American Federation of Labor, and the Methodist Episcopal Church.[26]

The Women Heroes

It was the women who took the lead in rebelling against the atrocities of the Mexican government at this time. They did not fight on the front lines, of course, but they pushed their men to fight, and they would not take no for an answer. "A woman would tell a man that he was not a man if he accepted such atrocities committed against the faith without retaliating," Jean Meyer writes.

A sister would goad her fifteen-year-old brother by telling him that he lacked the worth possessed by the defenders of 'God's Cause.' Prodded by their wives, mothers, girl-friends, and sisters, the men left for combat until many townships were left practically without men, while the women worked the land to feed combatants or followed them into the mountains.[27]

The Women's Brigade, which assisted the Cristero troops, was one of their greatest contributions to the cause, but not much is known about the membership except that María Goyaz was the supreme commander, since it was a secret organization, and no records were kept. The wife of Secretary of War General Joaquin Amaro reportedly was one of the women working in that clandestine network, and a member of President Calles' own family was also involved, secretly lending her house in Mexico City to serve as a warehouse for ammunition. One would love to know more about those courageous volunteers.

[26] Meyer, *La Cruzada por México*, 106.
[27] Meyer, *La Cristiada* (2013 edition), 70.

But it was not just the Women's Brigade. A cloud of mystery also surrounds a group of women in the city of Colima who took to the streets to protest the Calles Law in 1926, distributing printed information about the persecution of the Church there. One day five of them were hanged from trees in the town square, but nothing is known about their identities except that they belonged to prominent Catholic families. If that had been a group of men, it is unlikely that they would have remained so anonymous in the history books. A cloud of mystery also surrounds a woman who was martyred in Ciudad Victoria, Tamaulipas, around this time. She is another nameless female hero.

That said, there are a few female heroes whose memories have come down to us. One is María del Carmen ("Carmelita") Robles, a brilliant young woman who led the resistance in Huejuquilla el Alto, Jalisco; the first major battle of the Cristero War was fought there. At the height of the religious crisis, Carmelita engaged the federal general of the region (Juan Bautista Vargas) in a public debate about religion and politics, and she roundly defeated him. She also founded a lay community of fifteen women who lived a life of prayer and poverty while doing charitable works for the poor and sick. However, the members of that community became the victims of the general she bested in debate, although the details of his motives are not known. "It is unclear whether the general was romantically interested in her, or simply wanted to seduce her," says Jean Meyer. "But what is clear is that one day he took the whole community as his prisoners and left Huejuquilla with the women."[28] That night Carmelita disappeared and wasn't heard from again. Some of the other women—we're not sure how many—were raped. Forty years later, Carmelita's

[28] Ibid., 75.

remains were found in a residence that was being demol-
ished by the city to make room for a street, and she was
finally given a funeral and appropriate resting place.
María de la Luz Camacho is another hero whose memory has stayed alive. She was shot in cold blood at Immaculate Conception Church in Coyoacán near Mexico City at
the end of December 1934. The *Rojinegros*, a paramilitary
force whose sole purpose was to harass Catholics, arrived
at the church that day and opened fire on the crowd, killing five people as they left the ten o'clock Mass.[29] María
de la Luz, who was a prominent catechist at the church,
opened her arms in the form of a cross and cried, "Viva
Cristo Rey", as she fell to the ground.

Some information also exists regarding the nuns who
struggled to keep the Catholic schools going during this
time despite constant invasions by inspectors and arrests by
the federal police. Jesuit Father Wilfred Parsons devotes a
chapter to them in his book *Mexican Martyrdom*, quoting
from "an official ecclesiastical report" about the hide-and-
seek games the sisters played as they outwitted government
inspectors with lighthearted humor. "Put them out of their
college or academy, and within two weeks they were back
in another, which they rented from somebody," Parsons
writes. "Or dressed in secular clothes, a group of them
would set up one school in five different places, with one
or two classes in each of them. In many cases, they had
finally to admit themselves beaten, and the community
was dissolved."[30]

Parsons cites the example of the Sisters of the Perpet-
ual Adoration whose college was raided by soldiers and

[29] More on the *Rojinegros* in the epilogue.
[30] Wilfrid Parsons, *Mexican Martyrdom* (Rockford, Ill.: Tan Books and Publishers, 1987), 73.

stripped of everything of value. The sisters dispersed and
lived with Catholic families, and when things calmed down
they applied as laywomen for authorization to found a
new college called Christopher Columbus. But the harass-
ing visits by inspectors continued, and during one raid the
sister in charge was arrested and imprisoned. The people
had to bribe the police to get her out. Finally in 1933,
the sisters had to close the institution, and they ended up
living with families or surviving on private charity. Another
example quoted by Parsons is more ominous. Five Fran-
ciscan sisters were taken away by troops who forced them
to ride (man-style) on galloping horses. The superior, who
had never ridden a horse (man-style or otherwise), fell off
the horse and broke her collarbone. Those nuns remained
prisoners of the soldiers for a month, and "the details are
silent about this terrible experience", Parsons writes.[31]

His Alliance with Obregón

As the Calles presidency progressed, one of the moderates who tried to hold him back from his extreme policies
was his predecessor and political ally, Álvaro Obregón.
Calles and Obregón were revolutionary heroes from the
War of the Generals—both from Sonora—who later supported each other in the war of Mexican politics. Obregón
became president in 1920 with the support of Calles,
and Calles became president in 1924 with the support of
Obregón. Obregón then declared his intention to seek a
second term (1928–1932), again with the support of Calles,
which gave Calles the option of repeating the routine at
the end of Obregón's second term. However, while the

[31] Ibid., 76.

two generals needed each other politically, their personalities could not be more different. Alvaro Obregón was the likeable extrovert who had a charming sense of humor, coupled with a surprising detachment from worldly success. As he piled up victories on the battlefield during the War of the Generals, he expressed himself in amateur poetry that had an almost Shakespearean sense of death to it. In one of those poems, his words soared in praise of the beauty of nature—the light of dawn, the flight of birds, the mountains that "meditate"—but then added a line about the transience of human life: "But man, the fool, does not even so much as notice how near to him is the eye of the rifle of death."[32]

During the War of the Generals, Obregón looked directly into the eye of that rifle and didn't blink. Shortly after the Battle of Celaya (in which he decisively beat Pancho Villa), he was conducting a military operation nearby and recklessly walked up to the front lines of battle where he was immediately surrounded by artillery shells. He took a direct hit that severed his right arm, but he remained conscious and was able to stand up without help. Let the general himself describe what happened next: "I was bleeding so much that I was sure that it was useless to prolong a situation from which all I could gain would be delayed and anguished dying, a painful spectacle for my comrades. . . . With the hand that was left to me, I drew my pistol . . . from my belt and shot at my left temple, trying to finish the work that the shrapnel had not."[33]

Obregón survived the suicide attempt because there was no bullet in the chamber, and he went on to live a successful life as a chickpea farmer—albeit with the nickname *el*

[32] Krauze, *Mexico*, 386.
[33] Ibid.

Manco de Celaya (the one-armed man of Celaya). "Every-body wanted to be with the brave and attractive visitor, the charming talker with the penetrating intelligence," says historian Enrique Krauze. "He had not lost his sense of the vanity of everything human but, blessed by fortune, he was living on the sunlit side of that conviction—with humor. He loved fun and jokes, even acting the fool."[34]

Plutarch Calles' personality was the very opposite. He was an introvert who rarely revealed his innermost thoughts to anyone and rarely laughed. When he looked at people, it was with an intensity that gave them the uncomfortable feeling that he was looking into their souls. The most outstanding characteristic of his temper-ament was silence. General Roberto Cruz remembered bringing a report to him and sitting in silence for twenty-five minutes while Calles read without ever lifting his eyes from the page. "He looked more like a statue than a man," Cruz said. "He never altered his posture; he did not move except to turn the pages."[35] While some were intimidated by these characteristics, others saw in them signs of greatness. When he visited Europe, right before taking office, the press described him as a rising star with an iron will, some comparing him to the Prussian Otto von Bismarck. After his death, a general who knew him well commented on his personality: "There was no one in the government, absolutely no one, who refused to obey him or would even so much as stand up to him on a matter of principle, not a single person who would resist any of his decisions."[36]

[34] Ibid., 388.

[35] López-Menéndez, *Miguel Pro*, 91. The report concerned the attempted assassination of Álvaro Obregón in November 1927, which is detailed in chap-ter 8 of this book.

[36] Krauze, *Mexico*, 426.

Calles and Obregón did share one personal trait. Both were anticlerical soldiers who were threatened by the Catholic Church's power and influence, and both had a record of brutality against the Church.[37] But unlike Calles, Obregón was a pragmatist, and his acts of brutality were usually accompanied by gestures of peace. While professing to implement the most extreme religious articles in the 1917 Constitution, President Obregón sent a letter of congratulations to Pope Pius XI on being elected pope in 1922. The following year, he expelled the apostolic delegate from the country for participating in an open-air religious ceremony, but at the same time he admitted that the social justice aims of the Catholic Church were similar to those of the revolution. After he left office, he tried to convince Calles to follow a similar policy of moderation, advising against the extreme policies Tejeda promoted. He even worked behind the scenes to find a way to end the Cristero War, arranging a private meeting in San Antonio, Texas, between members of the episcopal committee on church-state relations and Mexican officials. The initiative went nowhere because Calles was still unwilling to admit that the Cristeros represented more than a small minority of the population. By that time the Cristero army had close to fifty thousand men in the field, and the Mexican army's list of casualties was rising rapidly. Agricultural production was also showing serious losses: down 38 percent between 1926 and 1930. Under this pressure, Calles' health broke down, and he turned to a *curandero* (Mexican folk healer) for relief—a curious act for a rationalist who had expressed such disdain for all things superstitious.

[37] For example, when Obregón's victorious army entered Mexico City at the end of the War of the Generals, he imposed a heavy fine on the archdiocese and then banished 167 priests from the city because he had the mistaken notion that they supported Victoriano Huerta in the anti-Madero coup.

If the more moderate Obregón had become president in 1928 as planned, Mexican history would have been very different. That was not to be. In November 1927, a lone wolf Catholic assassinated the president-elect, mistakenly believing that he was a bigger threat to the Catholic Church than Calles was. In the national crisis that followed, Calles was the only strongman in the country with the political capital to fill the vacancy, so he did. He had Congress rubber stamp a lawyer friend, Emilio Portes Gil, as the temporary president until new elections could be held. Then his newly founded political party, the National Revolutionary Party, put forward a former governor of Michoacán, Pascual Ortiz Rubio, in the election and won by a suspiciously wide margin. However, as soon as Ortiz Rubio made a policy decision Calles did not like, he found himself out of a job. The hapless president learned about his dismissal in the morning newspapers, which simply stated that he had resigned. Calles replaced him with another puppet, a former military officer called Abelardo Rodríguez, a man with more ambition than ability. He was the third puppet in a row to fill the presidential chair while Calles continued to run the country from behind the scenes, earning for himself the nickname Jefe Máximo (Maximum Leader), a title that would follow him into the history books. That period in Mexican history is called the Maximato.

His Final Days

In 1934, Calles made a serious miscalculation when he backed Lázaro Cárdenas for president, assuming he would be another obedient puppet. "I love Cardenas like a son," he once said.[38] But Cárdenas had more backbone than

[38] Krauze, *Mexico*, 456.

his predecessors, and as soon as he established himself in power he broke with the Jefe Máximo and exiled him from the country. Calles spent the next five years away from the caldron of Mexican politics, in San Diego, California, where he had time to ponder the vicissitudes of his controversial career. One wonders what went through his mind during those quiet years by the sea in Southern California.

Plutarco Calles' greatest mistake was his failure to understand the loyalty of Mexicans to the faith of the Roman Catholic Church. Each week without religious services would cost the Catholic Church 2 percent of her faithful, he had boasted when the bishops suspended worship in 1926. He soon found out otherwise, as millions of Mexican Catholics continued to practice their faith under conditions that were reminiscent of the persecution of Christians by the Roman emperors. The images of those miscalculations (many of them in the capital itself) must have haunted his imagination: families risking everything to host secret Masses in their neighborhoods despite his anticlerical laws; uninterrupted streams of people flocking to the Basilica of Our Lady of Guadalupe on major feasts, even after the Masses had been suspended;[39] the funeral procession of a priest-martyr that brought out some twenty thousand people and five hundred cars in the capital.[40] It became obvious to everyone that the Church was not losing 2 percent of her people per week. Furthermore, it became obvious

[39] Mrs. George Norman, *The Life and Martyrdom of Father Michael Pro, S.J.* (London: Catholic Book Club, 1938), 134. Father Pro described the crowds at the Shrine of Our Lady of Guadalupe for the Feast of Christ the King in October 1926, months after worship had been suspended, in these words: "I was there from 9am to 11am and from 3pm to 9pm, impossible to tear myself away. Thousands and thousands of folk barefoot, others on their knees along the whole avenue of Peralvillo, all saying the Rosary and singing; poor and rich, workmen and gentlemen in groups" (ibid.).

[40] The funeral of Father Miguel Pro, which will be described in chapter 8.

that Mexican Catholics would not tolerate a scheme to set up a Mexican pope in the capital. That idea didn't work in France under the French Revolution or Napoleon, and it didn't work under Calles either. Plutarco Calles did eventually get invited home to Mexico. Cárdenas' successor, Ávila Camacho, allowed him to return in 1941, and he spent his remaining days on his hacienda in Cuernavaca, gardening and playing golf, sometimes alone. His archives (maintained lovingly by his daughter Hortensia, Enrique Krauze tells us) reveal some startling details about his frame of mind in those final days.[41] Two months before he died, he let it be known that he believed in a Supreme Being after all.[42] The old nineteenth-century rationalist, who had once turned briefly to a *curandero* for relief, was now beginning to talk like a believer. The archives also reveal something else. In the end, he and some old political friends (including the labor leader Luis Morones) were attending weekly spiritualist meetings in Cuernavaca and listening to a "spirit guide" tell their fortunes and "communicate" with people in the afterlife. Reflecting on this surprising change in Calles, historian Enrique Krauze makes the following comment: "He had wanted to banish faith and enthrone reason. At the end—in the darkness of the human condition—he found himself groping for some kind of faith, reaching for hands around a spiritualist table, trying to interrogate the dead."[43]

Indeed! Archbishop Francisco Orozco, if he had lived long enough, would have been surprised to see that change

---

[41] Krauze, *Mexico*, 436.

[42] There is a widespread rumor among Mexican Catholics that he confessed to a priest in the end. Because of the nature of the Sacrament of Penance, that rumor can never be confirmed or denied.

[43] Krauze, *Mexico*, 437.

in his old nemesis. Orozco was one of Calles' greatest threats, a towering figure in Guadalajara who spent his life fighting everything Calles stood for. He was the bishop Calles disliked most and feared most, and for that Orozco paid a heavy price. The next chapter will tell his unusual story.

Chapter 6

Francisco Orozco and the Trials of Exile

Somebody should make a movie on the life of Francisco Orozco y Jiménez, the bishop who guided the Archdiocese of Guadalajara during the persecution of the Catholic Church in the 1920s. He was expelled from his diocese five times but kept coming back, and while in Mexico he spent much of the time in hiding in the hills outside Guadalajara, playing cat and mouse with federal troops who kept letting him slip through their fingers. Of all the bishops in Mexico, Orozco was the one that the government disliked most and feared most, because of his brilliant mind and ability to command attention when he spoke. The more the government failed to catch him, the more the people lionized him.

His brush with the military in Atotonilco in 1918 is an example of the stuff that made him a legend. He was hiding in that remote area of the archdiocese at the time, disguised by a black beard, dirty ranchero clothes, heavy boots, and a ten-gallon hat. One day, he and a local priest were traveling on horseback to San Ignacio Cerro Gordo, when the two unexpectedly met a company of federal soldiers on the road. They had to think fast.

"Am I allowed to do what is necessary here?" the priest asked his boss.

"Of course," the archbishop said.

In a loud voice (so the soldiers could hear him) the priest ordered his companion to round up a bunch of cattle that were grazing nearby, which the archbishop went about doing as best he could. As the priest took out a lasso and spun it, he began swearing at his bearded companion who wasn't having much success with the cattle.

"Round up the cattle", he yelled. "The older you get the more stupid you get! What a pain in the ass it is working with this idiot." The soldiers were taken in by the performance and never knew how close they were to their prize.

"By any chance have you seen the archbishop around here?" one of the soldiers asked.

"I just left San Francisco," the priest answered, "and they told me he was there. If you hurry, you will find him."[1] The priest later apologized to the archbishop for his disrespectful language, and the two laughed about their close call.

The unkempt beard and ranchero dress were serving their purpose for this famous member of the Mexican hierarchy, but life on the run wasn't easy. The boots were uncomfortable (they affected his blood circulation), and the vest of animal skin, which covered his clerical collar and pectoral cross, was too hot in sunny weather. The food was also poor, the kind of monotonous fare that simple folk could afford; even eggs were a rare luxury.[2] It was a far cry from the lifestyle Orozco would have had in the episcopal palace in Guadalajara, or from the lifestyle in which he grew up, for that matter.

---

[1] Vicente Camberos Vizcaíno, *Francisco el Grande* (Mexico: Editorial Jus, 1966), 393, my translation.

[2] Ibid., 370–71.

Controversy from an Early Age

Francisco Orozco y Jiménez was born in Zamora, one of the most Catholic regions of Mexico, to a wealthy family in November 1864, and he seems to have been groomed for higher office from his first days in seminary. He did all his studies in Rome, which included a doctorate degree in philosophy from the prestigious Gregorian University, before being ordained there in 1887. On returning to Mexico, he taught in the diocesan seminary in Zamora and before long became rector of that seminary. At the same time, he earned another doctorate, this time in theology, at the Pontifical University in Mexico City, where he also taught for a while. In 1902, when Orozco was thirty-eight years old, Pope Leo XIII appointed him bishop of Chiapas, a mountainous tropical state in the southernmost part of Mexico that was known for its poverty. It was home to one of the largest indigenous populations in the country, and it had a history of rebelling against the government in Mexico City, a history that continued throughout the twentieth century.[3] Orozco's ten years of service there would turn out to be more controversial than he ever imagined.

The first couple of years were somewhat routine, with Orozco doing the kinds of things you might expect a young energetic bishop to do in a remote diocese that had been neglected. He built a number of new churches, a diocesan seminary, a Catholic college, an orphanage, and a Catholic hospital. Education of the young was also a high priority. There was only one Catholic school in the

[3] The rebellion by the Zapatista Army of National Liberation in 1994 was finally settled through the mediation of Samuel Ruiz, another famous bishop of Chiapas. He was bishop there from 1959 to 1999. Pope Francis prayed at Ruiz's tomb when he visited Mexico in 2016 (Patrick J. McDonnell and Cecilia Sanchez, "Pope Francis Prays at Tomb of Controversial Bishop", *Los Angeles Times*, February 14, 2016).

diocese when he arrived, and the public schools were not only poor quality but corrupt. The teachers made the students do manual labor in the fields and fined them when they did not show up for work. Orozco built six new Catholic schools and helped pay for them from money he had inherited from his family. He brought in several religious orders from Europe to staff the parishes and schools.[4] He also arranged the installation of an electric generator in San Cristóbal, and another in remote Comitán, despite the warning from advisors that it could not be done. At his own expense, he carted the enormous German-made boilers, motors, and dynamos over inaccessible mountains and rivers, bringing modern conveniences to towns that had never known them. Also at his own expense, he erected a marble statue in San Cristóbal to honor Bartolomé de las Casas, a former bishop of that diocese whom Orozco deeply admired and emulated, as did many priests and bishops of the time.

Las Casas (1484–1566) was the son of a slave owner who began his life as a typical colonizer, participating fully in the ambitious plans of his financially strapped family to make a fortune in the New World. After landing on the island of Santo Domingo (present-day Haiti and the Dominican Republic) in 1503, he gladly joined in an official campaign against rebellious Indians, but the slaughter of natives he saw on that campaign shocked his conscience. (Called the "Massacre of Xaragua", he would write about it forty years later.) However, he put that atrocity out of his mind for the present and plunged himself into the business of making money in mining and agriculture. Ten years later, he found himself being haunted by feelings of guilt as he

---

[4] Alfredo Ochoa, ed., *Homenaje a la Memoria de Francisco Orozco y Jiménez* (Guadalajara: Imprenta y Libreria Font, 1936), 11.

struggled with the realization that the business in which he was engaged depended on slave labor to produce a profit. Without that free labor, he admitted, there would be nothing of value in the Indies for him or his family. Nothing! And so it was that in June 1514, Bartolomé de Las Casas renounced his properties and told his friends that from now on he would pour his energy into defending the Indians rather than exploiting them. It turned out to be a genuine commitment. A few years later he was ordained a diocesan priest, eventually becoming a Dominican friar, and he spent the rest of his life on a crusade, preaching about the dignity and beauty of the pre-Columbian culture and exposing the lies of the colonizers who claimed that the Indians were subhuman cannibals and sodomites. Eight times he braved the ocean to testify before the Spanish Crown. Speaking from personal experience, he was particularly eloquent when describing the evils of the encomienda system, that body of rights and privileges whereby Spanish colonizers could "own" entire villages and could use the free labor of the Indians in those villages in return for a commitment to protect them and oversee their welfare. In theory it was a bad idea and in practice it was worse. It was slavery by another name. The Indians were overworked, separated from their families, cheated, and physically assaulted by their owners. When Las Casas spoke to the Spanish authorities about this scandal (he was a brilliant debater with a magnetic personality), he had the appalling results of this system at his fingertips: a native population of over three million on the island of Santo Domingo alone, he said, was reduced to less than eighteen thousand in two decades. That wasn't an exaggeration. In fact, historian Kevin Starr says that recent scholarship has tended to make those figures even more shocking: as many as six million Indians in the entire Caribbean were reduced to a tiny population (much less than eighteen thousand) by the end of thirty years of Spanish occupation.[5]

Not surprisingly, Las Casas met with fierce opposition in Spain. In attacking the encomienda system, he was striking at the heart of the Spanish colonial system, and one of his fiercest enemies was Archbishop Juan Rodríguez Fonseca, president of the Council of the Indies and the king's principal adviser in all matters involving the colonies. Fonseca reacted to the stories of enslavement and genocide with indifference, saying he could not see why the Crown should get into the nuts and bolts of Spanish economic activity in the colonies. But there were other powerful churchmen on the side of Las Casas, in particular Francisco Jiménez de Cisneros, the ascetical archbishop of Toledo, and the equally admirable Archbishop Adriaan Florensz Dedel, a Dutchman who later became the reforming Pope Adrian VI.[6] With friends like these, Las Casas managed to outmaneuver people like Fonseca, and even enlisted the help of the Inquisition. A panel of Dominican theologians produced signed affidavits stating that, in their opinion, denying the humanity of the Indians constituted heresy. These efforts eventually had a direct influence on the wording of an edict published by the Crown in 1542 called "New Laws of the Indies for the Good Treatment and Preservation of the Indians", which addressed the kinds of abuses Las Casas had brought to light.[7]

[5] Kevin Starr, *Continental Ambitions: Roman Catholics in North America* (San Francisco: Ignatius Press, 2016), 31.

[6] Dedel was the last non-Italian pope before John Paul II.

[7] The edict turned out to be a disappointment to Las Casas because the colonists found ways around it or just ignored it. The debate continued after his death in 1566, with his fellow Dominicans leading the fight for spiritual and economic reform in New Spain. In 1573, both Spain and the papacy unambiguously condemned the notion that the Indians were a species of subhuman beings. By then millions of Indians had died from enslavement and slaughter.

Bartolomé de Las Casas did make one serious mistake that must be mentioned here, one that has haunted his reputation in the history books ever since. In his efforts to win support for an end to slave labor in the Indies, he had to face an important question: Where would the workers come from if New Spain were deprived of free labor? His answer to that question (in a memorandum) suggested the subsidized immigration of free Spaniards and their families, but then he added a surprising idea. The slave trade from Africa could also be used to supply the labor needs, he wrote.[8] The suggestion was out of character, coming from a man who had given up everything of this world's goods to end genocide in the Indies, and it has tarnished his reputation ever since.

Why did Las Casas make that suggestion? Did he really mean to promote African slavery in order to save his beloved Indians? Historian Kevin Starr thinks the answer is no. Las Casas was merely resorting to an existing institution in the heat of argument, and he spent the rest of his life regretting those rash words, as did another famous apostle in history. "Like Saint Peter," says Starr, "Las Casas wept in the years to come when the cock of his hasty suggestion crowed."[9]

This is the man who ended up heading the Chiapas diocese (he was appointed there in 1544), bringing his disgust for the encomiendas to a place in Mexico that had plenty of them. He immediately challenged the wealthy landowners of the state to give their haciendas back to the Indians and even denied the sacraments to hacendados who were especially cruel, incurring the wrath of the powerful in Chiapas. Those men of the world eventually

[8] Starr, *Continental Ambitions*, 34.
[9] Ibid., 35.

succeeded in forcing him out. In 1550, he resigned from his diocese and returned to Spain, where he spent the rest of his life (sixteen years) training young Dominican missionaries for work in New Spain.

Francisco Orozco was inspired by this sixteenth-century missionary, and during his time in Chiapas emulated his love for the indigenous peoples of the state. Like Las Casas, Orozco educated himself in their culture and dialect and, to give employment to them, he established a factory for making tubular organs, many of which adorned the churches in the diocese. In his memoir, he writes with particular pride about the Indians of Chamula, a tribe with a long history of fighting white people in Chiapas. This tribe had never fully accepted the Christian religion and when they did practice it, it was their own version of the faith. At one point, they crucified a member of the tribe so that they could have a "Christ of their own race". With patience and perseverance, Orozco won the confidence of these Indians, weaning them away from their previous customs and in the process becoming a hero among them. Whenever he went back to visit San Cristóbal, they came out to meet him "with such delirious demonstrations of joy that my coming constituted a holiday of rejoicing for all the town".[10] Ironically, it was this popularity with Indians that dragged Orozco into an unusual controversy— one that would haunt him for the rest of his life.

The controversy began fifteen years earlier when the governor of Chiapas decided that the city of Tuxtla would be the capital of the state, not San Cristóbal, which had had that title for four hundred years. Not surprisingly, San Cristóbal resented the change, and during the chaos of the

---

[10] Francisco Orozco y Jiménez, *Memoir of the Most Reverend Francisco Orozco y Jiménez* (Chicago: Extension Print, 1918), 23.

revolution that brought President Francisco Madero to power, that city launched a military-style attack on Tuxtla, thus moving the government back to San Cristóbal by force. To ensure the security of the newly moved municipal government, the San Cristóbal authorities recruited an army of Indians, using the bishop's popularity to do the recruiting. It didn't work because the capital eventually moved back to Tuxtla anyway. However, in the fingerpointing that followed, the Tuxtla politicians blamed Bishop Orozco for masterminding the attack on their city and using the Indians to carry it out.

It was a report in the Mexico City newspaper, *El Imparcial*, that brought the controversy to a boiling point. In a lengthy article about this "Tale of Two Cities", the newspaper flatly accused the bishop of Chiapas of inciting the Indians there to rebel against the government of the state, a charge that was picked up by four other major newspapers. The people of San Cristóbal were appalled. While they were sympathetic to the idea of moving the government back to their city, they knew that Bishop Orozco had nothing to do with it, and they expressed their anger in a letter (signed by hundreds) that didn't mince words. "The yellow daily *El Imparcial*, vomited with the shamelessness which characterizes it," their letter stated, adding that the publication "has beaten the record for lies, fiction and effrontery."[11] The priests of the diocese also came to

---

[11] Orozco, *Memoir*, 17. The letter from the people of San Cristóbal, dated July 10, 1911, has a heading that says "Infamous Falsehood—El Imparcial Basely Calumniates the Worthy Bishop of Chiapas—Energetic Protest by the Whole Town". It is signed by Lindoro Castellanas, José Castellanas, Antonio Herrera, and two pages of names. The letter from the clergy, dated July 26, 1911, and addressed to President Francisco de la Barra in Mexico City, is signed by eighteen prominent priests, including the archdean, three canons of the cathedral, and the rector of the seminary.

the bishop's defense, although with more restrained language. To the bishop's great relief, the governor of the state eventually investigated the issue and concluded that Orozco was not an actor in the attack on Tuxtla. But unfortunately, he was an actor in a related issue: the question of where to locate the seat of the diocese (the cathedral and administrative offices). For four hundred years it had been in San Cristóbal, and when the capital moved to Tuxtla fifteen years before, the bishop of that time refused to move with it. The leaders of Tuxtla were not happy. They disliked the Catholic Church, but they wanted the diocesan seat in Tuxtla because of the prestige it would bring the city and the defeat it would deliver to San Cristóbal. But when they asked the new bishop (Orozco) to move, he flatly refused just like his predecessor. A campaign of anti-Catholic vitriol ensued, with the perpetrators using language that was unworthy of any self-respecting civic leader. Inevitably, the fight aggravated the already tense relationship between the two cities, one of which was mostly indigenous and Catholic (San Cristóbal) and the other mostly white and anti-Catholic (Tuxtla).

What made the civic leaders of Tuxtla so anti-Catholic was their membership in a powerful fraternity that controlled the politics of Mexico in those days. They were Masons. Freemasonry is one of the world's oldest and largest fraternities, and its membership has been a Who's Who of famous leaders in many parts of the world. A considerable number of the Founding Fathers of the United States were Masons. Because of its hostility to the doctrines of the Catholic Church, however, membership in the movement has been forbidden to Catholics, especially in Mexico, where the movement's hostility of Catholicism has been particularly intense, going back to the struggle for independence from Spain and the War of the Reform in the nineteenth century. Beginning at that time, the Masons in Mexico saw themselves as the standard-bearers of civilization, called upon to save the fatherland from the destructive influence of the Catholic Church. "The Apostolic Roman Catholic clergy, converted into a rapacious, obstructive, conservative, and retrogressive political party, has been the sole cause of the misfortunes which have affected Mexico from the days of the Spanish Conquest until our own time," said Minister of War Joaquín Amaro, who was a Mason, in a speech in 1929.[12] By that time, the Masons had become such a force in politics that it was impossible to get any position of importance in the government or the military without being active in the movement. "In Mexico, the State and Freemasonry have been one and the same thing in recent years," Emilio Portes Gil admitted when he was president.[13]

But if the Masons of Tuxtla were confrontational in their approach to the Catholic bishop, the Catholic bishop did nothing to lower the tension. Like his hero, Bartolomé de Las Casas, Orozco was never afraid of a political fight, especially when it concerned blatant injustice. At one point, he put the city of Tuxtla under interdict, thus forbidding the celebration of any sacraments there for a time and forcing people to seek the sacraments elsewhere. (Interdicts are rare censures imposed by Church authorities on jurisdictions that plot to destroy the Church and her mission.) At another point, he had to go into hiding because of threats to his life.

Critics of Orozco point to this as an example of an autocratic, proud personality who was not well suited to the

[12] Jean Meyer, *The Cristero Rebellion* (London: Cambridge University Press, 1976), 29.
[13] Ibid., 27.

anti-Catholic state of Chiapas. Orozco had grown up in Zamora, where Catholicism was in the air they breathed, and the bishop's word was taken as law. Chiapas was very different. The Catholics there were fewer and more independent (because of the shortage of priests), and the Masons were more fanatically anticlerical. A patient and more diplomatic approach would have been less polarizing.

Ironically, it was at the height of this crisis that Pope Pius X appointed Francisco Orozco to the Archdiocese of Guadalajara, one of the oldest and most prestigious dioceses in the nation. In the eyes of the anticlerical elements in both Chiapas and Guadalajara, the message was unmistakable. The man who stirred up a revolt in Chiapas was now being promoted to Jalisco to do the same thing there. With the help of the press, they conducted a campaign to have his appointment blocked, which didn't work of course. If anything, it enhanced his image as a hero in the eyes of Catholics everywhere. Guadalajaran Catholics were overjoyed at the news of his appointment, and Church officials there were full of hope for the future. With a new president (Francisco Madero) installed in Mexico City, and a more tolerant era in church-state relations already under way, the dynamic Orozco looked like the right man in the right place. Several days of festivities and receptions were organized, with the streets decorated in streamers and eye-catching triumphal arches: "Viva el Mártir de Chiapas" (Long live the martyr of Chiapas), people cheered with understandable exaggeration, as they strained to get a glimpse of their new archbishop.

Orozco was installed in the majestic three-hundred-year-old cathedral in a solemn ceremony that included hundreds of bishops and priests and thousands of the faithful. One witness remembered the crowd flowing out onto the streets nearby and onlookers filling the balconies and roofs of the nearby houses. The date was February 9, 1913, a date that should have gone down as a milestone in the history of Guadalajara. Unfortunately, the date would be remembered for another reason. On that day four hundred miles away, a military coup broke out in Mexico City against President Francisco Madero, a development that would turn out to be a turning point in Mexican history. One can only speculate about how the new archbishop heard the ominous news. Did somebody tell him during the celebrations that day, or did he hear it later? In any case, he probably didn't give the news much attention, because there had been five failed coups against the hapless Madero in the previous two years. Orozco had no way of knowing that this sixth coup would succeed, with disastrous consequences for the country and for the Catholic Church. The War of the Generals was about to begin in Mexico, a period of unthinkable chaos and destruction that would engulf the city in which Orozco had just been installed. In less than eighteen months, the majestic cathedral in Guadalajara would be desecrated, and acts of wanton destruction would be perpetrated by out-of-control troops in an orgy of exuberant sacrilege.

War of the Generals

The crisis began when a couple of generals marched on the National Palace in Mexico City, and after being repulsed by troops loyal to President Madero, withdrew and established themselves in a well-fortified army arsenal in the other side of the city. What followed was ten days of brutal fighting, known in the history books as the Decena Trágica or Tragic Ten, with neither side getting the upper hand. Downtown streets were strewn with burning cars, runaway horses, and bloated bodies, as the civilian casualties mounted into the thousands. The one who finally emerged as president from this destruction was Victoriano Huerta, an ambitious general who used deception and betrayal to grab power. Madero had foolishly put him in charge of suppressing the coup, but when the time was ripe he switched sides and put Madero under arrest.[14] Three nights later, the president of Mexico and the vice president were "mysteriously" shot in a prison yard in Mexico City while the outdoor flood lights were "mysteriously" turned off. From there, things went from bad to worse. It was Mexico's darkest hour, a period of political assassination, civil war, and anarchy known in the history books as the War of the Generals. The players in this tragedy are well known to this day: Pancho Villa, Emilio Zapata, Venustiano Carranza, Álvaro Obregón, and Plutarco Elías Calles.

The nightmare went on for almost three years, and the loss of life to violence and starvation was enormous. For Catholics there was the added trauma of anticlericalism, as revolutionary generals vented their anger against priests, Church property, religious symbols—anything to do with the faith of the people. The city of Guadalajara was one of the hardest hit by this rampage. Archbishop Orozco was a little over a year in his archdiocese when, in July of 1914, the armies of General Álvaro Obregón marched into Guadalajara and unleashed a torrent of wanton destruction

[14] The American ambassador to Mexico, Henry Lane Wilson, helped broker the agreement under which Huerta joined the rebels. A diplomat of the dollar diplomacy era, Henry Wilson is remembered for his brash interference in Mexico's internal affairs. However, the U.S. president (Woodrow Wilson) never did recognize Huerta. In fact he brought about Huerta's downfall when he ordered the naval occupation of Veracruz in April 1914.

that brought back memories of the War of the Reform in the previous century. Undisciplined soldiers roamed the streets, desecrating church sanctuaries, smashing altars, and selling sacred books for ten cents a volume. They drank beer from chalices, burned religious art in the streets, and danced around the fires wearing vestments they found in the sacristy. In some places, they lined up statues on the sidewalks and conducted mock trials of the saints for the entertainment of anyone who cared to watch. One of their more famous acts of barbarism was perpetrated in the Guadalajara cathedral. Soldiers broke into the tombs in the crypt and desecrated the remains of the former bishops, some of which had been resting there for nearly three hundred years. The cathedral became a barracks for the troops, and the altar railing was so damaged that it had to be replaced later.

At the same time, the governor of the state, Manuel Diéguez, ordered all priests in Guadalajara imprisoned, and all churches taken over on the pretext that they were hiding arms. Soldiers rounded up priests and church workers wherever they could find them, robbed them of anything they had, and threw them into filthy dungeons. The seminary became a barracks for the troops, as did the Jesuit University of Guadalajara. About eighty priests in all were imprisoned, and a hundred foreign-born priests and nuns were banished from the country. Most of the Mexican priests were released after ten days (no arms were found of course), but the governor then levied a penalty of one hundred thousand dollars on the archdiocese for no reason. A couple of days later, he demanded more money. When the vicar general protested that raising that kind of money was quite impossible, he had to go into hiding for fear of his life. The governor retaliated by stealing all the chalices and other sacred vessels from the cathedral, "valued at one million dollars".[15] Nine of the churches were never given back, nor was any of the nonworship property, such as convents, residences, hospitals, orphanages, the seminary, or the Jesuit university.[16]

By this time, Archbishop Orozco was in exile. He had been forced to leave Guadalajara because of threats to his life and well-founded rumors that the government planned to arrest "the troublemaker from Chiapas". He fled to Mexico City, and from there to Europe, eventually ending up in New York. But he continued to direct his archdiocese from exile through the vicar general, who was picking up the pieces and trying to return to some semblance of normal life. Their first challenge was to find housing for the two hundred seminarians whom Obregón threw out on the street, and it was the generosity of the people that led them to a solution. They divided the forty theology students into four groups and hid them in four ranches where they continued their classes; two professors were assigned to each group. After two years, they sent them to Spain to complete their studies. The remaining 160 were given hospitality by generous parishioners who lived near an abandoned sculpture workshop, where the students gathered each day for class and Mass. The sleeping conditions were primitive and the food was scarce, and they lived in constant fear of being discovered. The local

---

[15] Orozco, *Memoir*, 9.

[16] The Archdiocese of Guadalajara has had to survive the loss of several seminary buildings over the years. The first one, beside the cathedral, was closed in 1696 because it was too small; a revolutionary monument stands there today. The second one, also next to the cathedral, was confiscated in the anti-Catholic turmoil of the nineteenth century and is now a museum. The third one, a few blocks from the cathedral, was confiscated in 1914 and is still in government hands today; until recent years it served as an army barracks. Today, the archdiocese has two separate seminaries out in the suburbs, one for philosophy and the other for theology.

pastor, who arranged the hiding places, told them to cover themselves in dust and to pretend to be sculpture apprentices if they saw danger coming. By November 1916, Orozco was back in the archdiocese and ready to go to work—in disguise. He avoided the big city, where the military was concentrated, and began clandestine pastoral visits to the remote regions of Zacatecas and Nayarit to administer the sacraments and comfort the people. By now, the authorities had issued orders for his immediate arrest, but he ignored them and continued moving from town to town, always exhorting the people not to divulge his whereabouts. Somehow it worked. Several times the authorities caught up with him, and several times he got away. God was protecting him, the people said. At one point, in El Tule, Zacatecas, the official sent to capture him, got typhoid and died before he could complete his mission. (On his deathbed the official was reconciled to the Church, much to the chagrin of fellow soldiers who tried to talk him out of it.) Exasperated, the authorities then sent a company of one hundred soldiers to bring him in, but instead of capturing Orozco, they found another bishop they were looking for: Bishop Miguel de la Mora of Zacatecas. On another occasion, several army units chased him around a remote region of Nayarit, armed with information they got from a priest who was tricked into talking. Finally, a detachment of fifteen soldiers found him in the village of Huajimic, but incredibly, they decided not to arrest him after all because "they were afraid to do so."[17]

The military police in Jalisco were equally helpless and frustrated. "It is known," a supervising officer wrote, "that in one of the villages of the district under your operating

[17] Orozco, *Memoir*, 6.

zone is the archbishop of the Catholic faith, Francisco
Orozco Jimenez, an arch-traitor to his country.... I hereby
command you to immediately proceed to the arrest of said
Orozco Jimenez with all the necessary precaution, and this
before complying with any other orders you may have
received."[18] Several days later, the supervising officer's
orders became more threatening: "From your communication No. 24, dated 15th of this month, I note that you did
not arrest Archbishop Orozco Jimenez," he wrote.

> I beg to state that the general commanding this division
> and I think very badly of this—your fault—because we
> know that you even accompanied and guarded him on the
> trip that said archbishop made from Saint Martin to Chi-
> maltitán. I make this statement so that it may be known
> to you that said general and I know perfectly well what is
> happening in that region under your orders.[19]

So the elusive archbishop continued his pastoral visits, celebrating Masses and Baptisms, hearing confessions,
even ordaining young men to the priesthood on the hidden ranches of people willing to host him. During 1917
and 1918, while on the run, he ordained sixteen young
priests and seventeen deacons and conferred minor orders
on another fifty-four young men—remarkable numbers
by any standards.[20] He even celebrated a Pontifical Mass
(in San Juan de los Lagos) to mark the publication of the
new Code of Canon Law and ordered all churches in
the diocese to do likewise.[21]

---

[18] Ibid.
[19] Ibid., 7.
[20] Ibid., 12, 26.
[21] The Code of Canon Law, promulgated by Pope Benedict XV in May
1917, brought all the rules and regulations developed over the centuries into
one single volume of organized legislation. An updated version was promulgated by Pope John Paul II in 1983.

A Country in Ruins

The human suffering the archbishop was seeing firsthand at this time was appalling. Historians have calculated that for every famous revolutionary who died between 1910 and 1920, a hundred thousand nameless Mexicans also died. In a country of about 15 million, between 1.5 and 2 million lost their lives to violence or starvation as troops wreaked havoc on the countryside. Two months spent clearing a field and planting under the burning sun could be wiped out in minutes as an army of five thousand horsemen galloped through the carefully tilled rows of corn and beans. And before moving on, they might even stop at the owner's one-room hut and confiscate the one milking cow and couple of turkeys the family was counting on for food.[22]

The year 1917 was the worst, going down in history as the "Year of Hunger". Venustiano Carranza had finally emerged from the civil war as the victorious strongman, and Mexico had a president again, but the country was in ruins.[23] Mines and industries had closed, railroads had been destroyed, and crops lay rotting in the fields. Banks failed, the government was buried in debt, and what money there was available went to the crushing military budget. Starvation was rampant, and those at the bottom of the economic ladder ate bran mixed with sawdust. In some places, people had to overcome their innate revulsion against killing and eating horses.[24] In the face of this suffering, the archbishop continued his visits, over "ravines

[22] Michael Meyer, William Sherman, and Susan Deeds, *The Course of Mexican History* (New York: Oxford University Press, 2007), 484.

[23] In April 1915, Álvaro Obregón, an ally of Venustiano Carranza, finally defeated Pancho Villa in the Battle of Celaya.

[24] Enrique Krauze, *Mexico: Biography of Power* (New York: HarperCollins, 1998), 367.

and perilous pathways, through villages decimated by emigration, typhus fever and famine. From all these villages I received marks of love and sympathy," he wrote in his memoir, "and they were greatly consoled by my presence among them."[25]

But 1917 was also notorious for something else. That was the year the anticlerical constitution (detailed in chapter 1) was written in the city of Querétaro. Orozco, who stayed out of politics and ordered his priests to do likewise, nonetheless published a carefully worded pastoral letter protesting the crass anticlericalism of this new constitution, which only made authorities more determined than ever to catch him. It didn't matter that other Mexican bishops had put out similar statements of protest, as had hierarchies in other parts of Latin America and the United States. They accused Orozco of inciting the people to rebellion, and they ordered the closing of seven churches where the letter was read during Sunday Mass. (After some months, they were reopened.) A short time after this, his luck finally ran out. He was in Lagos de Moreno and had just celebrated Mass in a church packed with parishioners when military officers arrived at the rectory without warning and arrested him in the middle of dinner. They had no warrant, and the officers declined to state any reasons.

News of his detention spread quickly, and by one o'clock in the morning, a large crowd had gathered outside the military headquarters in Lagos de Moreno. When the telegraph office opened in the morning, the rest of the world learned that the archbishop of Guadalajara had been finally caught, and messages of support began to pour in from clergy and laity all over the world. Meanwhile, a

[25] Orozco, *Memoir*, 5, 6.

Catholic lawyer succeeded in getting a writ of habeas corpus from a local judge, which was hand-delivered to the barracks, as people waited to see if it would do any good. It didn't. The officer in charge received blunt orders from his superiors: "Put judge, habeas corpus and laws into the mouth of a cannon!"²⁶ Within hours, the archbishop was on a military train heading for the border and exile in the United States, a trip that would take fourteen days and five stops, including a bout in prison. The train had one comfortable car, which was used by the general and his officers, and a flatbed for transporting the general's automobile. Everybody else had to use cattle cars that had no seats. One of the priests traveling with the archbishop got an old suitcase for the prelate, which he used as a seat during the day and a pillow at night.

At every train stop—Aguascalientes, San Luis Potosí, Monterrey, Ciudad Victoria, Tampico, Nuevo Laredo—people gathered and tried to see the archbishop but were not allowed. Lawyers and priests, including diocesan officials from Guadalajara, pleaded with the military to respect the writ of habeas corpus, also to no avail. The consuls from several nations, including the United States, Great Britain, and Japan, also tried to intervene, as did the apostolic delegate to the United States, again without success. The response of the general in charge was to the point. "Señor Archbishop," he said, "we know you have committed no crime, but we have a supreme order to override the habeas corpus, supreme court and everything else."²⁷ As if to add insult to injury, the general

---

²⁶José Garibi y Rivera, "Capture and Expulsion of the Most Reverend Francisco Orozco y Jiménez" in Orozco, *Memoir*, 30. Rivera was the archbishop's secretary and later succeeded him as archbishop of Guadalajara.
²⁷Ibid., 33.

then demanded that he sign a document renouncing his legal right to a writ of habeas corpus. Orozco refused, but when the general said that "a stray bullet will end this trouble",[28] his friends put pressure on him not to risk his life over this issue. (What his friends did not know was that the Mexican authorities had decided not to kill him; they had been advised by some interested Americans that the execution of Orozco would be counterproductive.) Orozco finally did sign, and shortly afterward found himself over the border in Laredo, Texas. He went immediately to join his fellow bishops in San Antonio, and from there to Chicago and then Rome.

The irrepressible Orozco was back in Guadalajara by the end of that year (1918), this time bearing gifts—papal honors for two prominent Guadalajara laymen. At his request, Pope Benedict XV conferred the Knighthood of St. Gregory on Miguel Palomar y Vizcarra and Pedro Vázquez Cisneros. Palomar y Vizcarra had been a prominent member of the National Catholic Party during its brief success and was an outspoken advocate of Pope Leo XIII's 1891 *Rerum Novarum*. Cisneros was a leader in the ACJM (Asociación Católica de la Juventud Mexicana) and (with Anacleto Gonzáles Flores) was instrumental in organizing the boycott that forced the Jalisco legislature to rescind its implementation of the 1917 Constitution. Orozco had been a strong supporter of that boycott.

The Calm before the Storm

With the accession to power of General Álvaro Obregón (1920–1924), there was some let-up in the persecution of the Church. Despite his anticlerical record during the War

[28] Ibid., 33.

of the Generals, Obregón was not interested in implementing the 1917 Constitution too literally, and as president he pursued a policy of live and let live. Not that harassment and threats against the Church stopped completely. In 1921, a small bomb went off outside Orozco's residence, and the same happened to the archbishop's residence in Mexico City. But these attacks were coming from extremists rather than the president himself, and the bishops saw them as such. They wanted to work with the new president where possible.

Archbishop Orozco took advantage of this calm to rebuild his archdiocese. He reopened Catholic schools and colleges, and he moved the seminarians to a retreat house that could accommodate two hundred people. He also threw his weight behind the implementation of Pope Leo XIII's encyclical *Rerum Novarum* and made Guadalajara the center of Catholic social action for the nation. Orozco was an unapologetic proponent of social justice, something that drew more than a little criticism from Conservatives, including his fellow bishops. The bishops of his time, he wrote later, fell into two groups: those like himself who "attempted to orientate the people towards carrying out their obligations", and those who "felt disinclined to sponsor any form of resistance or opposition, confining themselves exclusively to their ecclesiastical ministrations". Quite naturally, he wrote, "the activities of the first group were scrutinized and opposed with hostility by their episcopal counterparts in the second group."[29] That criticism didn't stop the energetic Orozco, however. He was especially interested in the Catholic union movement, and one of his proudest moments was the opportunity to host the

[29] Francisco Orozco y Jiménez, *Memorandum: An Apologia Pro Vita Sua*, 8. The memorandum, which was written in 1929, was edited by Monsignor Francis J. Webber and printed privately by the Archdiocese of Los Angeles in 1968.

meeting of the National Workers Congress in Guadalajara in 1922. That congress brought together twelve hundred Catholic worker-delegates representing some eighty thousand Catholic union members from all over the country, and several bishops also attended. As usual, there were violent threats from the anticlerical diehards, but President Obregón himself had no objections to the congress.

"I notified the President of the Republic, General Obregón, of the event well in advance," he wrote. "He sent a polite reply approving the event. As a matter of fact," he added with amusement, "the government placed a cavalry guard at the door of the congress hall, and the military saluted me respectfully whenever I passed."[30]

Salutes of respect from the military! That would be nice if it lasted. By 1924, Plutarco Elías Calles had come to power and had ushered in an era of persecution against the Catholic Church that made previous eras look tame. Within weeks, he enacted the new penal code (the Calles Law), mandating that all priests would have to register with the state in order to minister in a parish. The Catholics of Guadalajara had seen it all before (the 1918 law passed by the Jalisco state legislators was similar), but this was more ominous. It was coming from the federal government and applied to the entire nation.

As youthful leaders of the powerful ACJM geared up for an all-out fight, the worried bishops met at the capital, and not surprisingly Orozco played a prominent role in the debate. He spoke against the bishops who wanted to wait and see how the new law played out before acting, reminding them that under the Calles Law they would no longer have any say in choosing the priests who ran their parishes. But he was ambivalent when it came to deciding

[30] Ibid., 11.

exactly what to do. The most radical idea under consideration (what one would call the "nuclear option" in today's politics) was to suspend worship in the entire nation as a protest, but that idea scared Orozco, despite the fact that he himself had done something similar in Guadalajara in 1918. Would people fall away from the Church if the sacraments were not available, he wondered. In the end, the bishops apparently made a decision to take this radical step, although it is unclear in retrospect how unified the decision was. Up until recent years, it was assumed that the bishops' decision was nearly unanimous, but studies of the Vatican secret files (opened up in 2006) have shown that a radical minority of bishops deceived the pope into thinking that their fellow bishops were of one mind when in fact they were seriously divided.[31] In any event, the fateful decision to suspend worship on August 1, 1926 (the day the Calles Law was scheduled to go into effect), got the pope's approval, and the rest is history.

Two weeks later, the members of the episcopal committee on church-state relations tried a last-ditch effort to find common ground with the government. They sent a letter to Calles expressing a desire for a reasonable solution, pointing out that worship could be restored immediately if the draconian provisions in the law were reformed. Calles' response was cold and to the point. The Church as an institution did not have any legal existence, he said, but individual Catholics were free to seek changes to the new constitution through the proper channels. The bishops immediately took him up on the challenge, turning to their network of parishes and Catholic action groups

[31] Irene Savio, "Cuando los obispos mexicanos engañaron al Papa" (When the Mexican Bishops Deceived the Pope), *Proceso*, November 26, 2017, https://translate.google.com/translate?hl=en&sl=es&u=https://www.proceso.com.mx/512521/cuando-los-obispos-mexicanos-enganaron-al-papa&prev=search.

across the nation for help in launching a campaign. A month later they submitted a petition to Congress, backed up by two million signatures, requesting changes to five particularly offensive articles of the 1917 Constitution. As it turned out they were wasting their time. The Chamber of Deputies voted overwhelmingly (171 to 1) to reject the petition on the grounds that the bishops had lost their right to citizenship because they had conspired with a foreign power (the Vatican) to disobey the constitution of the Mexican Republic.[32]

By the time Archbishop Orozco received this bad news, however, he was in hiding—again! He had received an order to appear at the office of the interior minister in Mexico City and had decided not to show up because a confidential source had warned him that they were planning to execute him. It was his third exile. For the next twenty months, he ran the archdiocese as a fugitive, hiding first in the region northeast of Guadalajara known as Los Altos, and later in the canyons near Tequila. He mostly avoided the residences of the wealthy hacendados, staying instead in the dwellings of poor Indians where it was less likely that the authorities would find him. He endured "a thousand hardships", he wrote later. One night while reading by candlelight in an Indian hut, he noticed a poisonous snake crawling over his bare feet, and he had to force himself to remain calm until the unwelcome visitor moved

[32] David Bailey, ¡Viva Cristo Rey!: The Cristero Rebellion and the Church-State Conflict in Mexico (Austin: University of Texas Press, 1974), 94. At this time Mexico did not have a democracy as we know it. Male landowners voted for municipal authorities. The municipal authorities in turn voted for members of Congress, who in turn voted for the president. (Indians and women could not vote.) Consequently, President Calles was the undisputed dictator of Mexico. Here is how U.S. Ambassador Dwight Morrow described it: The government is Calles, the constitution is a farce, and Congress and the judiciary are simply agents of Calles (John Sheerin, Never Look Back: The Career and Concerns of John J. Burke [New York: Paulist Press, 1975], 120).

on.[33] Twice he was struck down by malaria; apparently a priest cured him by injecting him with quinine. Despite these conditions, he remained faithful to his daily regimen of prayer and study (he read a history of the Church and commentaries on Scripture, among other things), and he kept a diary, which he penned in Latin and sent to Pope Pius XI.[34] More important, he continued to stay on top of administration issues in his archdiocese.

Jesuit Father Wilfrid Parsons, who interviewed him many times, describes how he stayed in touch with Church officials in Guadalajara during this time.[35] A young Indian man traveled to the city once a week, carrying the diocesan mail on foot. He usually left the hiding place (sixty miles from Guadalajara) at five in the evening, and when he got close to the city he lay down for a couple of hours sleep. By eight o'clock in the morning he was in the city to make his rounds, delivering the archbishop's mail to five different people, none of them knowing who the other recipients were, and picking up the return mail for his boss. At nightfall he set out on the journey back and was at the archbishop's hiding place by morning. Eventually, a wealthy friend of the archbishop gave the young man a car, which he immediately learned to drive. On a number of occasions, he persuaded the archbishop to come with him on those visits to Guadalajara. The young driver once invited some of his friends to come along, and all enjoyed their ride through the big city, with the archbishop hidden in the middle of a group of boisterous young people.

Meanwhile, the authorities continually let him slip through their fingers, despite their best efforts. Orozco

---

[33] Wilfrid Parsons, *Mexican Martyrdom* (Rockford, Illinois: Tan Books and Publishers, 1987), 58.
[34] Ibid.
[35] Ibid., 56. Wilfrid Parsons, S.J., was the editor of *America Magazine* from 1925 to 1936 and was an outspoken critic of the Calles government.

was back in the cat-and-mouse game he played in 1917
and 1918, relying on the loyalty of the people to protect
him, which they did. "The simple truth of the matter is,"
he wrote, "that I was protected by the reverend silence of
some fifteen thousand of my people, all of them aware
of my movements, who were scattered through a poor
mountainous region—a people whom I shall continue to
bless forever."[36] Neither did Anacleto González Flores
divulge a word despite the brutal torture he suffered at
this time in the *Cuarto Colorado* in Guadalajara. So the
archbishop continued to celebrate Masses and other sacraments, including the ordination of young priests. On
one occasion, a group of seminarians came close to getting
caught by soldiers while walking back to Guadalajara after
visiting him, and only escaped because they were able to
run faster than the soldiers.

But if the frustrated authorities failed to catch him, they
wasted no time in defaming his name, putting out stories
that Orozco was personally leading the Cristero troops in
battle. Outlandish as the story was, some believed it, and
the *Daily Express* even sent a reporter from London to
check it out. The reporter decided the charge was ground-
less, but Orozco was surprisingly defensive about the issue
when he described it in his memoir. Clearly, the Chiapas
controversy of earlier years made him overly sensitive, and
he went to extra lengths to protest his innocence, insisting
that the government could never produce a single piece of
evidence to back up their accusations.

"It could not have been otherwise, for I never had any
contact with the rebel forces nor did any of them know
where my place of hiding had been," he wrote later.[37]

[36] Orozco, *Memorandum*, p. 14.
[37] Ibid., 13.

Some priests in his archdiocese did have contact with the Cristeros, however, albeit in nonviolent ways. They were acting as chaplains, administering the sacraments to the soldiers and tending to the dying. For that they paid the ultimate price: torture and death at the hands of the government. When news reached the archbishop that the number of murdered priests in his archdiocese had reached six (it would eventually be many more than that), he wrote a pastoral letter to the people that is remarkable for its tone. Despite his personal policy of avoiding contact with the Cristero soldiers, he was filled with admiration at the self-sacrifice of the priests who did have contact. He expressed frustration about knowing so few details of their deaths (he was in hiding), but he wanted to speak out anyway. "Levanto hoy mi voz," he said, "que quisiera resonar por todas partes pregonando la gran gloria y la incomparable aureola con que mi amada esposa, la Iglesia de Guadalajara, ciñe su frente" (Today I lift up my voice, which I would like to resonate throughout the whole world, proclaiming the glory and saintly radiance that my loving spouse, the Archdiocese of Guadalajara, bestows on them). Orozco then called attention to a larger group: "los no menos gloriosus nombres de tantos que en el campo de batalla han sucumbido heroicamente por su religion" (the no-less-glorious names of so many who have heroically died for their faith on the battlefield).[38] He ended the pastoral letter by stating his intention of submitting the stories of these priests and laity to the judgment of the Holy See, words that turned out to be prophetic. Of the twenty-five priests and laymen canonized by Pope John Paul II in

[38] Javier Navarro Rodríguez, *Tierra de Mártires* (Diocese of San Juan de los Lagos, 2002), my translation. The booklet is a brief history of the martyrs and is quoting from a pastoral letter written by Archbishop Orozco y Jiménez to the people of the Archdiocese of Guadalajara.

2000, fifteen were from the Archdiocese of Guadalajara. Additional people are in the process of canonization.

Victim of a Peace Agreement

When the Mexican bishops and the government of President Emilio Portes Gil finally reached an agreement in 1929 to end the Cristero War, Archbishop Orozco requested a meeting with the president in the hope of getting permission to return to Mexico. The meeting, which lasted an hour and a half, did not go well, even though the apostolic delegate and the archbishop of Mexico City came with him for support. It began with some lighthearted bantering between Orozco and Portes Gil about how the police had failed to catch him during all those months in hiding, but the conversation soon changed and the tone became ominous. "I was listened to with excessive serenity, or rather coolness, on the part of the president," he wrote, "and at the conclusion of my remarks, his only comment was that it had been decided that I should return to exile, this time in a place outside the country."[39] The archbishop of Guadalajara was singled out by Gil despite his long record of nonviolence, and his fellow bishops were unable to correct the false rumors about him. He left his homeland and went into exile for the fourth time.

A year later, however, there were changes in the Mexican government that looked hopeful. Emilio Portes Gil was pushed out of office, and another Calles puppet, Pascual Ortiz Rubio, was made president in his place. Orozco decided to take his chances, and so he returned to Guadalajara for the ordination of José Garibi Rivera,

[39] Orozco, *Memorandum*, p. 14.

who had been appointed an auxiliary bishop of the archdiocese. Rivera had been his secretary and constant companion during his years in exile. After that ordination, he
stayed on in Guadalajara, keeping a low profile and hoping
that the government would leave him in peace. It did for
a while, but after some eighteen months the authorities
arrested him again without warning and kicked him out
of the country. It was his fifth exile. He spent the following years on the road, a sacrificial lamb in the agreement that was negotiated to end the Cristero War. At one
time he was in Europe, at another in the United States,
celebrating Masses, visiting friends and saying his prayers.
On December 12, 1933, he found himself in St. Peter's
Basilica in Rome, invited by Pope Pius XI, as the main
celebrant in a Solemn High Mass to proclaim Our Lady
of Guadalupe the patroness of all Latin America and the
Philippines. When he returned to the United States, he
brought another papal honor with him—the *Pro Pontifice et
Ecclesia* medal—this time to honor American Marie Walsh
Harrington, a lady in whose Los Angeles home he stayed
many times while in exile.[40]

But he missed his native land, and he missed the people in whose service he had been ordained a priest and a
bishop. In 1935, he told Father Wilfred Parsons in New
York that he was determined to go back to Mexico, with
or without the permission of the government.

"But you can't go back," Father Parsons protested.
"This time they will kill you."

[40] However, the local archbishop, John Joseph Cantwell, was irritated at
Orozco's gesture and forbade the lady from ever wearing the medal in public, an order she conscientiously obeyed. But Monsignor Francis Webber, the
archivist for the Archdiocese of Los Angeles, had the last word. He told this
writer that he had the privilege of pinning the medal on Marie Walsh Harrington's mortal remains during her funeral Mass.

"I do not care," he replied. "I cannot die in this country."[41] He did go back (Lázaro Cárdenas was president), and this time they did leave him alone, probably because he was no longer a threat to anyone. His auxiliary, José Garibi Rivera, had been appointed coadjutor archbishop and was in effect running the archdiocese. Six years had passed since the agreement with the government that ended the Cristero War, and Orozco could see that nothing had changed. The government continued to restrict the number of priests who could serve in parishes, blatantly ignoring the provisions of the peace agreement. In many states, practically all the churches had been closed, and priests were nowhere to be found.

But Francisco Orozco y Jiménez was done fighting and concerned himself instead with preparation for death. The following year (1936), he died peacefully at the age of seventy-one, and he is buried in the cathedral in Guadalajara where a wounded lion, sculptured in white marble, marks his tomb. It is a fitting symbol for the man who was so lionized by the people of his own day and is so venerated by the people of Guadalajara to this day.

The Vatican has opened the cause of canonization for Francisco Orozco y Jiménez. If he is canonized, he will join the long list of priests from the Guadalajara archdiocese who are already canonized, priests of whom Orozco was so proud. One of those was Toribio Romo, who was ordained by Orozco in 1922 and was martyred in 1927. His story is next.

---

[41] Parsons, *Mexican Martyrdom*, 59.

Chapter 7

Saint Toribio Romo
and the Catacombs

Argentine artist Judi Werthein some years ago designed
an unusual walking shoe for immigrants. Called a Brinco
sneaker, it was made for those trying to cross the U.S.-
Mexican border on foot, and it has several practical aids
to avoid getting lost in the desert: a flashlight and compass
attached to the shoelaces, a map on a removable insole
showing the most popular illegal routes from Tijuana to
San Diego, and a small pocket in the tongue for carrying money and pain relievers. The sneaker has one more
important detail. On the back ankle is a small portrait of
a figure all immigrants turn to for protection when they
attempt that dangerous crossing from Mexico into the
United States. His name is Saint Toribio Romo González.[1]

Saint Toribio is one of twenty-five martyrs canonized
by Pope John Paul II in the year 2000, but he is the best
known of the twenty-five on the U.S. side of the border
and one of the best known on the Mexican side. Several churches across the United States have relics of the

[1] The artist produced a thousand of these sneakers. She gave some to immigrants at the border for free. The rest she made available as art in a boutique in
San Diego for $215 per pair. They are featured in the booth for the nonprofit
organization Printed Matter at Art Basel, an international art fair.

saint, including the Cathedral of the Blessed Sacrament in Sacramento, California, where the main altar enshrines a bone fragment of the saint. In 2014, the Archdiocese of Los Angeles hosted a four-foot-high statue of the saint that came from Mexico and was carried to churches across three counties in Southern California, as thousands of the faithful gathered to celebrate Mass and pray to the martyr who was shot in his bed one morning in February 1928.

In Mexico itself he is popular also. Mothers put small pictures of the saint in their sons' backpacks before they leave home to immigrate to the United States, and many take a side trip to his famous shrine in Santa Ana, Jalisco, before heading north to attempt the border crossing. Newspapers on both sides of the border in recent years have carried stories of the saint's miraculous appearances to immigrants who get lost in that unforgiving desert on the American side.[2] As the lore goes, a mysterious person in dark clothing appears out of nowhere just in time to save them from death and leads them to safety or to a place where they can find work. His only request is that they come to visit him some day in his hometown of Santa Ana, and those who do make it to Santa Ana are stunned to discover that Toribio Romo, the person in the giant photo there, is the same person who had come to save their lives in the desert.

The Catholic Church has not authenticated these stories, but as their number has increased, so have the crowds of people visiting that tiny community of Santa Ana. In Toribio's day, it was too small even to have its own resident priest, but today it a lively pilgrim destination with a

---

[2] Ginger Thompson, "Santa Ana de Guadalupe Journal; Saint Who Guides Migrants to a Promised Land", *New York Times*, August 14, 2002, https://www.nytimes.com/2002/08/14/world/santa-ana-de-guadalupe-journal-a-saint-who-guides-migrants-to-a-promised-land.html.

new thousand-seat church, a twenty-four-bedroom retreat center, a Toribio Romo museum, and a booming souvenir business selling key chains, comic books, and T-shirts with the image of the saint on them. The person who is believed to have appeared in the desert is no longer the stranger he used to be, at least not among immigrants.

Simple Country Boy

Toribio Romo was born on a small plot of land in Santa Ana on April 16, 1900. His parents, Patricio and Juana Romo, were descendants of Spanish families that had moved to the area some two hundred years earlier, and they eked out a living from the soil, raising seven children (Toribio was the fifth) on a diet of corn, beans, chili, onions, and once in a while meat. The food was adequate but boring, as was the way they dressed. Everyone (children and adults) wore the same thing: a shirt and pants made from cheap, off-white cotton material called manta and a hat made from cactus fiber. Like all children, Toribio went barefoot during the week, wearing his sandals (called huaraches) only for special occasions like attending Mass on Sundays.[3]

Because Santa Ana did not have a resident priest, the people belonged to the parish of Jalostotitlán (known as Jalos), some two hours' journey on foot—longer if you had to drag children along. Every Sunday, people walked that long journey for Mass without complaint, and many of them went back on first Fridays to honor the Sacred Heart. The comforting devotions of the Church brought

[3] James Murphy, *The Martyrdom of Saint Toribio Romo* (Liguori, Mo.: Liguori Publications, 2007), 14.

both structure and meaning to their lives: devotions to Our Lady of Refuge in June and July, prayers to Our Lady of the Rosary in October, outdoor processions to honor Saint Ann during the rainy season. Most families prayed the Rosary every night, and during Lent they religiously followed the Church regulations about fasting and abstinence. Like so many rural communities in Mexico, the people of Santa Ana loved the Church, and they were thankful to be living in a time when it was possible to practice their faith without interference from the state. Older folk could remember times when things were different, in particular the War of the Reform in the previous century, when radicals took pickaxes to destroy churches and attack priests. But that was in the past. Don Porfirio was now president, and he had no interest in fighting with the Catholic Church. Priests could go about their business freely, without constantly worrying about harassment from civil authorities.[4]

The priests from Jalos came to Santa Ana every few weeks to celebrate Mass, hear confessions, and visit the sick, and when they stayed overnight, it was from the Romo family that they received hospitality. That is what sowed the seeds of Toribio's vocation. Up to that point, nobody from Santa Ana had ever even thought of entering the priesthood, but from a young age Toribio showed signs that he might be the first. He couldn't take his eyes off the visiting priest, who sat and engaged the adults in conversation; when he observed his sisters making a new alb (the long white vestment worn at Mass) for the priest, it made his young mind wonder.

"Do you think I will ever wear a garment like that?" he asked.

[4] Ibid.

"No," his sister Hipólita answered dismissively. "Honey is not made for the mouth of an ass." (A Spanish expression similar to "casting pearls before swine".)

"True, honey is not made for the mouth of an ass," another sister, Quica, interjected, "but someday you will wear a garment like this, Toribio."[5]

There is another story told about a conversation Quica had with Toribio while he was still very young. One night while both were admiring the starlit sky and pondering the grandeur of God, Toribio pointed to a table-shaped hill nearby and said, "Quica, I think heaven is right there on that *mesita*." Years later, that story took on added significance when people in the area were looking for a suitable place to build a church. They chose the top of that same hill, and Toribio Romo eventually celebrated his first Mass in that new church.[6]

But that was a long way off. For now, Toribio needed to go to school, and because Santa Ana had no school (most people there were illiterate), he had to move to Jalos for his elementary education. It was at this point that Quica made a surprising announcement to the family. She intended to break off her engagement to be married, she told them, and would move to Jalos to help her brother get through school. It was a remarkable sacrifice and the beginning of a relationship that would last throughout Toribio's life as a priest.

When brother and sister finally got to Jalos, however, they found the school to be less than stellar. It was owned by a single lady who ran the operation in her backyard, a ramshackle patio with caged canaries along the wall and baskets full of tobacco and paper on the desk; she was

[5] Ibid., 15.
[6] Ibid., 16.

earning extra money rolling cigarettes for the local stores. But Quica and Toribio made the best of their situation, and Toribio continued to attend the school. They earned a living the hard way. She washed clothes and made tortillas for the neighbors, and he pitched in after school delivering the packages to customers. They also found time for prayer: Mass every morning, a visit to the Blessed Sacrament during the day, and the Rosary together at night. Eventually the whole family moved to Jalos, and things became a little easier for everyone. Toribio became an altar boy in the local church, and Quica became more confident that her brother would enter the seminary someday.[7]

Sure enough, he did. At age twelve, to Quica's great joy, Toribio entered the minor seminary in San Juan de los Lagos, a city that was famous for its shrine of our Lady. The new surroundings must have been a culture shock for the country boy from Santa Ana, but by all accounts these were happy days for him. He loved the daily rhythm of study and prayer, and he basked in the care of his superiors as much as the friendship of his classmates. His Spanish appearance made him stand out (he was tall and light skinned with blue eyes), but he had little interest in being tidy and well groomed; his disheveled appearance just added to his charm among the students.

Academically, Toribio was at the top of his class. He had a special love of Latin and used to take over the class when the professor could not make it. Not surprisingly, he was elected class president. But the most noteworthy thing about these early years was his interest in *Rerum Novarum*, the encyclical of Pope Leo XIII on the rights of workers to unionize. Toribio was chairman of a student group

---

[7] Ibid., 17.

that met to study that encyclical, and these seminarians did more than just study the pages of the text. They organized classes for workers in the local parishes, opening their minds to the social teaching of the Church and the prophetic message of the Scriptures. Years later, as a priest, he would organize similar study groups for his parishioners.[8]

In 1920, Toribio entered the major seminary in Guadalajara to complete his theology studies. At first the students there joked about the *rancherito* (country boy), but his friendly personality and simplicity soon won the students over. To the faculty members, it was apparent that he could roll with the punches, and he didn't take himself too seriously—an important quality in a priest. He also showed a special interest in the problems facing Mexican immigrants in the United States, and he even wrote a one-act comedy about it. Called *Let's Go North*, it portrays a cultural clash between a Mexican immigrant who returns to his home village to show off his command of English and liberal American views, and a local campesino who is not impressed by the visitor's newfound sophistication. As the play unfolds, the well-dressed visitor lets it be known that he does not believe in God anymore, and he denounces the village priests as "money-grubbing retrograde obscurantists".[9] Before long, however, the simple campesino has exposed the shallowness and poverty of this immigrant's soul, and has underlined the temptation facing so many immigrants who forget their spiritual roots when they move north of the border. The play is a remarkably mature work coming from a twenty-year-old seminarian.

[8] Ibid., 20.
[9] David Romo, "My Tío, the Saint", *Texas Monthly* magazine, November 2010, https://www.texasmonthly.com/articles/my-tio-the-saint/.

Ordained in Troubled Times

Finally, on December 22, 1922, Toribio reached the goal for which he had been preparing for so many years: ordination to the priesthood. It was a proud occasion, not just for Toribio but also for his parents and siblings who traveled all the way from Jalos to Guadalajara to be part of the ceremony, and to be in the presence of Francisco Orozco y Jiménez, the most famous archbishop of his day. As the chief shepherd of Guadalajara, he was the ordaining prelate, and now he would be Toribio's superior as the newly ordained priest began his ministry in some corner of this huge archdiocese. A few years earlier, Toribio had been the student representative chosen to welcome the archbishop to the seminary for a visit with the seminarians.

"Do you promise obedience to me and my successors?" the archbishop asked him in the cathedral ceremony that day. "Yes, I do," Toribio responded, knowing full well that he was entering the priesthood in troubled times.[10]

As Providence would have it, Toribio's adult life coincided with the most chaotic period in Mexican history, in particular the most brutal persecution of the Catholic Church in Mexico. Toribio was thirteen years old when the War of the Generals started. During the turmoil of the following ten years he was in the tranquil surroundings of the seminary, but the never-ending stream of bad news from the outside world must have been the subject of many a discussion in class: the sack of Guadalajara and desecration of the cathedral by Obregón's soldiers in 1914; the passing of the notoriously anti-Catholic constitution in 1917; the bomb (hidden in a bouquet of flowers) that went off in front of the image of Our Lady of Guadalupe

[10] *Rites of Ordination of a Bishop, of Priests, and of Deacons* (Washington, D.C.: United States Conference of Catholic Bishops, 2003), 78.

in Mexico City in 1922 (one month before his ordination), to mention a few.[11] It would be difficult to imagine a more unsettling time for a young man to begin his ministry as a priest, but there was worse to come. The month following his ordination, the apostolic delegate to Mexico was expelled from the country after participating in a ceremony dedicating a statue honoring Christ the King on a mountain in central Guanajuato.[12] The following year, all foreign clergy were expelled from the country. And then the worst of all: the infamous Calles Law in 1926, which stipulated that the government rather than the archbishop would decide if he could minister as a priest. Like many priests, Toribio ignored the order to register with the government, which made him liable for prosecution and prison time, but that did not bother him unduly.[13] By this time he was already in trouble with the law anyway, because of something he did in his parish the previous year. In October of 1925 in Cuquio, he and his pastor organized an outdoor Mass to celebrate the Feast of Christ the King. Fifteen thousand people came to the emotionally charged celebration on a hill outside the town that day, in deliberate defiance of the government's policy forbidding outdoor Masses. During exposition of the Blessed Sacrament

[11] The explosion did not damage the image of our Lady, but the high altar was badly damaged. A heavy bronze crucifix that was bent by the blast is on display today in the basilica in Mexico City.

[12] The statue was later bombed by Obregón's successor, Plutarco Calles, who also expelled two succeeding apostolic delegates. The present-day statue was built in the late 1940s. The seventy-five-foot-tall statue is part of one of Mexico's most famous shrines, the Cerro del Cubilete, standing on top of a mountain that is almost nine thousand feet high.

[13] At first, the bishops as a group forbade the priests to register with the government. However, by 1929 some bishops had decided to abide by the law. In February of that year, twenty-six hundred priests and five bishops registered with the authorities (Jean Meyer, *The Cristero Rebellion* [London: Cambridge University Press, 1976], 71).

after Mass, the people took an oath to defend their faith in the face of mounting government atrocities—even if it meant doing so with their lives—and Father Toribio and his pastor joined in that public oath. It was a "heavenly experience", Toribio's brother Román said later as "the mountains vibrated with the cries of *Viva Cristo Rey*".[14] The following year, the tension escalated when three hundred Cristero soldiers took over the city hall in Cuquio and held it for several months with the support of the people. Neither Father Toribio nor his pastor was involved in that Cristero operation, but in the eyes of the authorities they were the masterminds, and the two priests ended up on a watch list. Toribio must have gone into hiding at this time, because by the time he was assigned to Tequila ten months later, he did not move into the rectory. Instead, he hid in a canyon outside the town where the authorities would have difficulty finding him.

Life for Catholics at this time in Mexico was like living in the catacombs of Rome. Priests like Father Toribio who continued to minister had to live like fugitives from the law, and the parishioners who sheltered them did so at the risk of becoming fugitives also. (The two men who were shot with Anacleto González Flores were members of the family that gave him refuge.) The Catholics who got caught harboring a priest or hosting a secret Mass in their homes would have to pay off the police, and if that did not work they could see their land confiscated and given to an upstart army officer or to some turncoat who had been a paid hand on the ranch a few weeks earlier. For the priest, the risk was equally high. Some were shot

---

[14] Román Romo González, *Santo Toribio Romo* (Jalisco, Mexico: Diocese of San Juan de los Lagos, 2001), 42. This booklet consists of personal memories of Toribio Romo that had been recorded earlier by his brother Fr. Román Romo.

on the spot, with their vestments still on, for not revealing what they heard in confessions. In one rural parish, government agents posed as priests and used the information gained in the confessional to arrest the parishioners. Nothing like this had ever been known in history, not even in the first centuries of the Church.

But persecution always brings out the best in people. When the suspension of worship became effective (August 1, 1926), Catholics immediately organized themselves to keep parish life going without the presence of a priest. Volunteers (both men and women) stepped forward to lead services in the churches every morning and evening, using familiar prayers such as the Rosary, or devotions to particular saints, or some other assortment of prayers from an old prayer book. In some places, this eventually developed into what came to be called "White Masses": liturgies consisting of the opening prayers of the Mass (the Confiteor, Gloria, and Creed), followed by a Gospel and a commentary on the Gospel that was provided by the bishop's office.[15] People were also encouraged to practice "spiritual communion", a traditional devotion among Catholics who have a desire to receive Communion but cannot get to Mass at a particular time.

Planning to have a real Mass required more work, of course. The local leader had to find a priest and then schedule the ceremony for a safe place, at a safe time of day, inviting only people that were known to be real Catholics. In Jiquilpan, Michoacán, for example, Masses were celebrated at three o'clock in the morning in a remote canyon, or somebody's orchard, and participants had to

[15] Matthew Butler, "Revolution and the Ritual Year: Religious Conflict and Innovation in Cristero Mexico", *Journal of Latin American Studies* 38, no. 3 (August 1, 2006): 476.

know the password to get in. Volunteers took turns as sentries watching out for trouble, and when it became too dangerous, the location was changed to neighboring Sahuayo. People were more than willing to travel the extra distance to Mass despite these dangers, and it was not uncommon to see people cry with joy at the prospect of receiving the *Santissimo*. A visitor from England who happened to find out about one such Mass describes her experience as follows: "Just before leaving Veracruz after my illness, the Sisters of Charity who nursed me let me into the secret that a priest would be saying Mass very early one April morning, and if I could be there at 5.30 A.M. I could go to Confession, Holy Communion and hear Mass—if I never mentioned it to a soul. Of course I got there . . . The priest was in lay dress with several day's beard, but it was a great privilege."[16]

The frequency of those secret Masses varied from state to state, depending on how the local governor felt about implementing the religious provisions of the constitution. The state of Chihuahua, for example, eventually allowed only 10 priests for some 440,000 people scattered over a vast territory. (It is the largest state in Mexico.) The next governor was even worse; he banned all priests. So the people began to flock to the border town of Juárez on Sundays, and from there, they slipped across the bridge into El Paso, Texas, for Mass. At one point, the governor offered special low railroad fares on Sundays to encourage people from the countryside to patronize the bull fights in Juárez, but he cancelled the offer when he realized that hundreds were taking advantage of the cheap train ride to

[16] Mrs. George Norman, *The Life and Martyrdom of Father Michael Pro, S.J.* (London: Catholic Book Club, 1938), 124. Mrs. Norman adds this comment: "These dear nuns, since we left, have been disbanded and who knows what happened to them" (ibid.).

get to Mass in the United States.[17] The bishop in El Paso at this time, Bishop Anthony Schuler, was host to more than a few refugees who were able to flee the ferocity of the persecution. Bishop Arthur Drossaerts of San Antonio and Archbishop John Cantwell of Los Angeles–San Diego were also known for their generosity.

As the church-state crisis dragged on, and the priests were harder to find in rural areas, Church leaders were forced to find creative ways to keep the faith alive. Out of necessity, three new forms of lay ministry gradually developed:

1. *Self-administered Communion*: With the approval of Rome, the bishops allowed people to keep consecrated Hosts in certain homes and to administer Communion to themselves, provided they followed strict guidelines that would ensure respect for the sacrament. An altar should be set up with white linens, candles, and a glass of water, the guidelines stated. Communicants should meditate for thirty minutes, recite the Confiteor, then reverently come forward with recently washed hands to take Communion. On approaching the altar, they should genuflect one by one, then take the host between thumb and forefinger and place it on the tongue, making sure no particles fell from the Host. Before retiring to their places, they should purify their fingers in the glass of water, and someone should consume that water at the end of the service.[18] Preserving that sense of respect was not easy, however, when it came to finding a suitable place to store the consecrated Hosts. Diocesan officials apparently were envisioning some kind

[17] Wilfrid Parsons, *Mexican Martyrdom* (Rockford, Ill.: Tan Books and Publishers, 1987), 172.
[18] Butler, "Revolution and the Ritual Year", 483.

of homemade tabernacle with a lit candle, and they were horrified when they heard about people sticking the Hosts in clothes closets, or under beds, or in the dark corner of some basement. They soon found out the reason. People had to hide the consecrated Hosts from the sacrilegious raids of the police.

Interestingly, the bishops insisted that people must self-administer Communion rather than receive it from somebody else, a stipulation that (presumably) was meant to avoid blurring the distinction between the lay priesthood and Holy Orders. But there was one exception to this. Designated lay leaders were allowed to bring Communion to the dying. Some pastoral letters appealed to the practice of the early Church to justify this, in particular a third-century layman called Tarcisius who was martyred while bringing Communion to Christians in a Roman prison. According to the Mexican guidelines, the patient was asked to say the Act of Contrition before receiving the Host, and some of the dying even made a nonsacramental confession, sharing his sins with a trusted friend or family member. One priest in Querétaro actively encouraged this practice of nonsacramental confession, pointing out that God's forgiveness is not limited by the vicissitudes of human affairs.[19]

2. *Holy Hours*: This practice seems to have developed spontaneously. People began to schedule Holy Hours in the presence of the Blessed Sacrament, something that became all the more precious as Mass became less available. For some communities, the Holy Hour became a substitute celebration on major feasts if a priest could not be found. The people of one border town in Baja California had

[19] Ibid., 475.

planned on a day of adoration before the Blessed Sacrament to celebrate Holy Thursday, but there was a problem. They had consumed all the consecrated Hosts. So they dressed up a ten-year-old boy in white (white shoes, stockings, pants, and coat), and a group of armed men drove him by automobile into the United States to get a Host from the nearest Catholic Church. When the men got back to their town, they enthroned the Host in a monstrance in the church, surrounded by candles and flowers, as the crowded congregation prayed and sang hymns for several hours. At the end of the day, the boy in white was driven back so that he could return the Host to the American pastor. (Presumably, the pastor had insisted that the sacred Host and lunette be returned.)[20]

3. *Marriages without a priest*: This development caught many Catholics by surprise. As the Cristero War dragged on with no end in sight, the bishops in some places were forced to give lay leaders authorization to witness marriages.[21] Information about how this worked in practice is scant, but one case in Guanajuato is worth quoting. Cecilio Valtierra was a twenty-nine-year-old member of the Unión Popular (founded by Anacleto González Flores) who became a leader in Jalpa after the priest was exiled for allegedly supporting the Cristeros. Like many lay volunteers, he had been leading morning and evening prayer, and had arranged for a priest (if he could find one) to celebrate the sacraments occasionally. Those were standard duties at the time and they didn't surprise him, but he was surprised when his priest-contact at the diocese told him in a letter that he had

[20] Parsons, *Mexican Martyrdom*, 172.
[21] According to the Catholic understanding of marriage, the bride and groom are the ministers of the sacrament. The priest is a witness, which is why members of the laity can take the place of the priest with ecclesiastical permission.

permission to witness Catholic marriages. The letter went on to assure him that those marriages would be valid, and included instructions on how to do the ceremony. However, the priest's assurances did not ease Cecilio's doubts about this upgrade in his ministerial powers. "I read the letter and the formula again and again, and I couldn't believe that it was all real," he said.[22] Despite his misgivings, Cecilo began celebrating marriages, following the instructions of his superior and hoping that people would eventually get used to the idea. Here is his own description of how those marriage ceremonies were conducted:

> In a few words I explained to the *novios* and the witnesses the aim of that ceremony, and all that they had to do. I asked the *novios* if it was their wish to join themselves together in matrimony, each with the other, in accordance with the Law of God and the Holy Mother Church, and on answering that it was, I ordered all those present to kneel down, and with devotion and honest intention to recite the Creed three times. That was all that had to be done according to the printed formula.[23]

But that printed formula wasn't enough. Many people continued to question the validity of the marriage ceremonies Cecilio was performing. "Some said I had been a busybody, others that I was an imposter, others that I was a usurper of faculties," he said.[24] Eventually he resigned.

Exactly what level of lay involvement was allowed in Father Toribio's corner of the Lord's Vineyard is difficult to know because he has left no record, but it is safe to assume that it did not include performing marriages. The

[22] Butler, "Revolution and the Ritual Year", 478.
[23] Ibid.
[24] Ibid., 479.

Archdiocese of Guadalajara was relatively rich in priests and probably would not have needed a ministry like Cecilio Valtierra's, but the other forms of lay ministry were probably necessary in the Guadalajara archdiocese like everywhere else. Like so many fellow priests, Father Toribio ministered underground, which meant he could only function with the help of lay leaders who ministered above ground, conducting morning and evening prayers and keeping the churches open. And every time he celebrated a secret Mass or Baptism, he knew that this could be his last.

Death in Tequila

Tequila, in the state of Jalisco, has given its name to the famous drink made from the agave plant, and thousands of tourists visit there every year to tour distilleries with famous brand names like Sauza and Jose Cuervo. But an abandoned distillery in a remote canyon outside the town has become equally famous in recent years—as a destination for pilgrims. It was in that old building, surrounded by a quiet landscape of exceptional beauty, that Father Toribio Romo spent his last five months and met his death. Situated fifty miles from Guadalajara, in the central-western highlands of Mexico, it is surrounded by craggy volcanic hills that are covered in rich fauna and lush vegetation. During the day a gentle breeze wafts through the canyon, carrying the singing of birds that belie the place's connection to the violence and sorrow of the past. Archbishop Francisco Orozco hid in this area for a while when he was on the run from the Calles government, and Toribio Romo died here on February 25, 1928.

Unlike Santa Ana, Jalisco (the place of Toribio's birth), the canyon near Tequila is still relatively unchanged since

Toribio's time, probably because it is so inaccessible from the road. It takes about twenty minutes to climb down there on foot, much less in a car if the steep pathway doesn't scare off the driver. The abandoned tequila building has mostly fallen down, but the location of Toribio's murder is clearly marked, and there is a recently built chapel there where groups of pilgrims can celebrate Mass. As in so many pilgrimage destinations in Mexico, pieces of paper adorn one of the chapel walls with scribbled notes about the favors that Toribio has granted to grateful pilgrims. "Thank you for all you did; I pray that my son will turn his life around," one pilgrim wrote. Another prayed for the health of a baby called Varisma and attached the note to some baby clothes. Another scribbled the words "Thank you" on a dollar bill and pinned it to the wall. Yet another left a government document on which he wrote: "Thank you for your help." The document was a form letter from the U.S. Immigration and Naturalization Service, informing him that he had been approved for citizenship.

Toribio Romo moved into this remote canyon in September 1927, with the authorization of Archbishop Orozco, presumably because he had volunteered to take on this dangerous assignment. By this time, the Cristero War had already gone on for two years, and bishops had given priests the choice of either going to the cities to wait out the crisis or continuing their ministry at the risk of their lives. Two of Toribio's siblings volunteered to come with him: his brother Román, who was newly ordained and wanted to be his assistant, and his sister Quica, who offered to be their housekeeper.

And so it was that a run-down tequila facility in a remote canyon outside Tequila became a clandestine parish center of sorts, run by three members of the same family, one of whom would sanctify the place with his martyrdom. The siblings used two small storage rooms as bedrooms and converted the warehouse into a makeshift chapel for Mass and a classroom for catechism. The courageous people who owned the warehouse provided the Romo siblings with food and even took care of their laundry—at the risk of being caught, of course.

Father Toribio immediately set about doing what he loved best: setting up centers for catechism instruction in homes on nearby ranches, in addition to classes in the warehouse. Many nights he went into town to visit the sick and celebrate Mass in the homes of those brave enough to host a Mass for people in their neighborhoods. The two brothers worked quietly in a stealth ministry, hoping nobody would say or do anything to attract the attention of the authorities. That went on for five months without any problems, but then one night something happened that made everyone nervous. Word passed around that soldiers would be searching the area for Catholics conducting illegal services, so Father Toribio and his siblings decided to hide outdoors under bushes until the danger passed. Early the following morning the three siblings, who had been up all night, returned to the warehouse where they found people waiting for Mass; it was Ash Wednesday. After they celebrated the Eucharist, people began to relax, believing that the danger had passed, at least for now. It hadn't.

Looking back now, it is clear that Father Toribio sensed something sinister at this point, but didn't talk to his siblings about it. In fact, his brother and sister thought he was acting strangely, and they were even more puzzled when he suddenly told Román to get to bed early because he would have to go to Guadalajara early the next day. When Román asked why, Father Toribio refused to explain, simply saying: "Brother, I am ordering you because I am your superior here."[25] After Mass the following morning, a saddled horse was waiting to take Román to the city. Before his brother could depart, Toribio asked him to hear his confession, and then he gave him a sealed letter, instructing him not to open it until he was told to. Father Toribio then returned to the makeshift chapel, and Román disappeared up the trail out of the canyon as his bewildered sister looked on, not knowing what to think.

All through that day and the following one, Father Toribio was pensive, saying little and obviously preoccupied with his own thoughts. One has to wonder what he thought about during those final hours in that remote canyon. Certainly, the previous twelve months did nothing to brighten his mood. They had been like a year out of Hell: the closing of the churches, the persecution of the archbishop, the order for all priests to register with the state, the murder of so many priests, including many he knew personally. Those priests were martyrs for the faith, the people kept saying to him, and now he himself would probably be numbered among them. He must have asked God to give him the strength to go on.[26]

He kept himself occupied throughout Friday, recording Baptisms and weddings in the parish books, and writing out certificates for families who had celebrated the sacraments in recent days. He continued working into the night, occasionally taking naps or brief breaks but never going to bed. On Saturday at 4:00 A.M. he woke Quica, who had fallen asleep on the floor near him and asked her to prepare the altar for Mass. The Eucharist—the celebration of Christ's death and Resurrection—had always been the central pillar of his spirituality, and it would be especially comforting in a

[25] Murphy, *Martyrdom*, 43.
[26] Ibid.

time of crisis such as this. "Lord, do not leave me, nor permit a day of my life to pass without my saying the Mass," he had often prayed, "without my receiving your embrace in Communion."[27] But when he got to the chapel that morning, he told Quica he was too tired even to celebrate Mass. He returned to his room, took off his alb, threw himself on the bed, and finally fell asleep.

About an hour later, federal troops found him there in a peaceful slumber, with one arm covering his face. A soldier moved the arm to get a close look at him, and then yelled, "This is the priest! Kill him!" Father Toribio woke up, sat up in the bed, and said, "I am the priest, but do not kill me."[28] Before he could say more, a shot rang out along with more shouts of "Kill the priest!" He got up and staggered a dozen steps out of the building before a second shot rang out, and he fell into the arms of his horrified sister who had followed him. Quica looked into his anguished eyes one last time, and he died. She had supported her brother's vocation in both childhood and adulthood, and now God had given her the privilege of holding him in her arms during his last agony.

What happened next could be considered a small gesture of mercy. The officer in charge of the troops allowed the people to put Father Toribio's body on an improvised stretcher, so they could carry it in procession up the trail out of the canyon and into Tequila. The gesture was soon diminished, however, when unruly soldiers began to whistle and sing vulgar songs along the way, which Quica ignored as she walked barefoot behind the body while praying the Rosary. In Tequila the time for kind gestures was over. Soldiers dumped the body in front of

[27] Ibid., 44.
[28] Ibid.

city hall and forced the weak and pale Quica to walk bare-foot to the barracks, where they subjected her to hunger and ridicule for three days before releasing her. But when she joined her family in Guadalajara, she was the one on whom they leaned for words that would make sense of it all. "We should not cry," she told her shocked siblings. "Padre Toribio is in heaven."[29] When Román finally opened the sealed letter his brother had given him, he found a final testament requesting that he "please take care of our dear and aging parents" and similar expressions of concerns for his siblings.

The body of the twenty-seven-year-old Father Toribio was buried in the cemetery in Tequila, where it remained for twenty years. Eventually the family moved the remains to Santa Ana, to the chapel on the *mesita*, where it lies today. Quica lived to an old age, spending the rest of her life supporting seminarians in Guadalajara, where she founded a house of residence for them. She died in 1959 at the age of seventy-three. Román became a priest and survived the Calles regime, eventually becoming a pastor of Santa Teresita Church in Guadalajara, where he served for almost fifty years. He died in 1981 at the age of seventy-six.

There were twenty-four other martyrs canonized with Toribio Romo in the year 2000 by Pope John Paul II, twenty-three of them priests. Surprisingly, Father Miguel Pro was not on that list of martyrs, although his death was even more famous than that of Toribio Romo and is better documented. He was killed just three months before Toribio, but in very different circumstances—circumstances that have made his case more complicated and the process of canonization much slower. The next chapter will tell his story.

[29] Ibid., 45.

Chapter 8

Miguel Pro and Photographs
That Shocked the World

According to historian Jean Meyer, some ninety Catholic priests were shot during the Calles presidency, but none of those killings was as famous as that of Miguel Pro. Father Pro worked under the noses of government officials in Mexico City in 1926 and 1927, and not only spoke out fearlessly against the policies of Calles and his henchmen, but also ran an information center that coached others to do the same. He celebrated Mass openly all over the city, despite being on the capital's most wanted list for over six months, and each time the authorities caught up with him he slipped through their fingers, using his acting skills and quick thinking. He was known as God's Jester. Ironically, Pro was also a Jesuit, a member of that order that was hated by the Liberals ever since the Bourbon king Charles III expelled the Society of Jesus from Mexico in 1767. Their reputation for brilliance in education and courage in speaking for the most vulnerable was no less a legend in Calles' time, especially in the area of Catholic Action. The Jesuits were the masterminds behind two of the most effective Catholic lay organizations challenging the Calles regime: the ACJM (Asociación Católica de la Juventud Mexicana) and the Damas Católicas.

When Calles finally caught up with Pro at the end of 1927, he decided to turn his execution into a public event that would serve as a warning to other priests. He invited a crowd of public officials, military brass, and journalists to attend the spectacle, and press photographers were allowed to record the event for the whole world to see. The result was that the death of Father Miguel Pro, S.J., by firing squad on November 23, 1927, became the best-documented killing of the time, with photographs of the gruesome scene appearing in newspapers around the world. Reaction from the international public, however, was not what Calles expected. Rather than feeling sympathy for the Mexican government's problem with "clerical subversives", there was surprise and revulsion that a Catholic priest would be summarily shot in a civilized country without formal charges or a trial.[1] An estimated twenty thousand people (some said thirty thousand) attended his funeral, and five hundred cars followed the hearse to the cemetery.

A Born Actor

Miguel Agustín Pro Juárez was born on January 13, 1891, in Zacatecas, one of the chief silver mining states in Mexico. He was the third child and first son of Don Miguel Pro and Josefa Juárez, a comfortable middle-class couple who were able to raise their children in the relative security of Mexico during the Porfirio Díaz presidency. As a mining engineer (like his father before him), the senior Miguel supervised

---

[1] Marisol López-Menéndez, *Miguel Pro: Martyrdom, Politics, and Society in Twentieth-Century Mexico* (Lanham, Md.: Lexington Books, 2016), 123. See also Jean Meyer, *La Cristiado* (Garden City Park, N.Y.: SquareOne Publishers, 2013), 88.

large numbers of workers in the booming mining industry, eventually becoming a representative for the government in the Division of Mining. The junior Miguel showed signs of talent from an early age, especially as an actor. At the age of five, his father bought him a tiny theatre with puppets, which the child immediately put to good use entertaining his brothers and sisters with a skill one would expect in a much older boy. He was also a mimic and a practical joker. One day while out walking with his sister Concepcion, he embarrassed her by suddenly knocking on the door of a house they were passing and telling the owner that his sister had noticed a beautiful statue of the Blessed Mother in the window and wanted to buy it. Much to the relief of Concepción, the man refused to part with it, and the two left to continue their walk. It was the ugliest statue she had even seen, she said later as her siblings laughed about the antics of their comic brother. Miguel's musical talent was also apparent from a young age. He quickly learned the guitar and mandolin, and eventually the five oldest Pro children formed a homespun string quintet that was kept busy performing for visitors to the Pro home. Miguel's guitar and mandolin would be a support to him in future years as a priest on the run.

Miguel's education (and that of his siblings) was interrupted quite a bit because his father's job caused the family to move a lot: from Zacatecas to Monterrey and then back to Zacatecas. At one point, the parents homeschooled the children. Then they put Miguel into a boarding school, which did not go well; he wasn't happy there. At another time, they hired an instructor who came to the home to teach the Pro children. But if Miguel lacked stability in his formal education, he gained valuable experience working in his father's office, where he organized the files and helped with payroll. This work also gave him an opportunity to see the mine workers close-up and to observe their appalling working conditions—an experience that would remain with him for the rest of his life.

Mining had been a critical part of the Mexican economy for five hundred years, with huge quantities of gold, silver, copper, and other metals going overseas to satisfy the insatiable appetite of the Spanish Crown. From the late sixteenth century to the late nineteenth century, precious metals (especially silver) accounted for more than 70 percent of Mexico's exports, coming from thousands of mines in the central and northern regions of the country. The state of Zacatecas alone had some five thousand mines. The profits from this boom brought relative affluence to many people; large cities like Zacatecas (at one point the third largest city in the country) grew up around the industry, and haciendas teaming with cattle and sheep soon blanketed the countryside. But not much of that profit reached the thousands of laborers who worked underground. These workers (mostly Indians) had to climb down slender shafts and feel their way along damp tunnels that carried the risk of flooding or some other accident. They hauled the ore out of the mines by climbing up notched logs that served as crude sets of stairs, carrying their heavy loads in the same blankets they used to sleep in at night.[2] Many of them died of exhaustion or malnutrition or poison from the bad air. Conditions improved a bit with the new mining methods introduced during the Porfiriato, but mine workers continued to be the most miserable group in a Mexican work force full of misery. They worked long hours seven days a week with no benefits, receiving pay that was far below what U.S. workers earned, even though the mines were mostly owned by American and European companies.

[2] Michael Meyer, William Sherman, and Susan Deeds, *The Course of Mexican History* (New York: Oxford University Press, 2007), 150.

The young Miguel Pro probably climbed down those shafts with his father more than once, where he saw those working conditions firsthand. At any rate, we know from his writing that he developed a deep affection for mine workers, an affection that was only reinforced by his father's compassion as a boss and his mother's frequent visits to miner families in need. His mother even organized a clinic where workers could avail of free services, but it was closed by the local mayor who objected to the administration of the sacraments among other things. The young Miguel never forgot what he saw during those days.

Neither did he forget another painful image from that time. In 1907, a riot broke out when a crowd of mine workers surrounded his father's government office (despite his record of compassion as a boss), shouting, "Exploiters," and demanding to see the mine-property titles so they could destroy them. Luckily, the senior Miguel had already taken the files from his office to his living quarters upstairs as a precaution. When he saw the noisy crowd outside his house, his first instinct was to face the protesters and reason with them, but he thought better of it when his family pleaded with him not to go outside. Instead, he pushed the dining room table against the door and prayed that his family would not be physically attacked. Eventually, help came in the form of the Rurales, the much-feared elite guards that the Porfirio regime used to bludgeon people into submission when they disturbed the peace. True to their reputation, they galloped over the demonstrators and put a quick end to the protest, while young Miguel peered through the shutters horrified at the sight of innocent workers being "killed like dogs".[3] Years later, while studying Pope Leo's encyclical *Rerum*

[3] Ann Ball, *Blessed Miguel Pro* (Rockford, Ill.: Tan Books and Publishers, 1996), 16.

Novarum in the seminary, the memories from this time flooded his mind and became for him a personal example of the injustice the pope was talking about. Throughout his life, he frequently signed his letters with his favorite nickname, El Barretero (the Miner).

Joins the Jesuits

Curiously, Pro's vocation to the Jesuits began with a crisis of sorts. One of his older sisters, María de la Luz, had entered the convent, and the family had come to attend her formal "reception of the habit" in Aguascalientes, when there was a surprising announcement. Before they left the convent that day, his other older sister, Concepción, announced that she also wished to enter the convent. The news threw the nineteen-year-old Miguel into a mild depression that dampened his sunny personality and made him reserved and pensive for several weeks. Why would she want to leave her loved ones, he tearfully asked her, and when she said it was the will of God he gave her a bewildered look.[4] He did not like her answer, but nonetheless asked her for prayers that he would learn the will of God for his own life.

Miguel grew up in a very Catholic family, but he wasn't particularly pious as a youth. In fact, on the night his father pushed the dining room table against the door for protection, he made a promise to God that he would not have a special girlfriend for a year, and then changed his mind. "Pardon me, Lord, I didn't know what I was doing," he told God.[5] However, a Jesuit retreat he attended at this

[4] Ibid., 19.
[5] Ibid.

time in a neighboring parish showed a different side of him. During the retreat, he borrowed a cassock without permission and went on a "pastoral visit" to the neighboring ranches, posing as a young priest. The simple ranch folk, who did not know any better, took him seriously and loaded the young "Padre" with eggs and cheese and other foods.[6] Was this just one more Pro prank or was he saying something more serious about his plans for life? Soon after, Miguel Pro did decide to choose the path of his two older sisters. On August 10, 1911, at the age of twenty, he entered the Jesuits and began the rigorous training required to become a member of the Society of Jesus.

"Are you willing to renounce the world, all possessions, and all hope of temporal goods," he was asked in the ceremony to become a postulant.

"Are you ready if necessary to beg your bread from door to door for the love of Jesus Christ?

"Are you ready to reside in any country and to embrace any employment where your superior may think you to be most useful to the glory of God and the good of souls?

"Do you consent to put on the livery of humiliation worn by Jesus Christ, to suffer as he did and for love of Him, contempt, calumnies and insults?"[7]

The formation house for the new Jesuit recruits was in El Llano, a small town not far from Zamora, which was known for the beauty of its landscape. Everywhere there was the "Mexican profusion of color", Mrs. George Norman writes about the place, with great red and yellow flowers cascading from tubs and swarming up pillars.[8] Miguel Pro was happy there. His comic personality made him one

<hr>

[6] Ibid., 14.
[7] One of the rites used by the Society of Jesus along the path to Ordination.
[8] Mrs. George Norman, *The Life and Martyrdom of Father Michael Pro, S.J.* (London: Catholic Book Club, 1938), 18.

of the most popular members of the class, but there was a serious side to him also. Classmates later recalled observing the "two Pros in one: the one who played and the one who prayed",[9] and there was little doubt in their minds that Miguel had a religious calling. Two years after entering, on August 15, 1913 (the Feast of the Assumption), he and his classmates made their first vows as Jesuits.

Meanwhile, outside the peaceful walls of the novitiate, things were falling apart in Mexico. President Victoriano Huerta, who had overthrown President Francisco Madero (February 1913), was himself overthrown the following year when President Woodrow Wilson intervened directly in the Mexican turmoil by sending the U.S. Marines into Veracruz. The result—in addition to strong anti-American protests—was even more chaos, with four warring generals fighting each other for control of the country, while innocent bystanders suffered.[10] The casualties in this multisided civil war included the Pro family members, all of whom had to flee their home in Saltillo when General Pancho Villa overran the state early in 1914. (The senior Miguel had worked for the hated Porfirio administration.) It was inevitable that this chaos and destruction would catch up with the junior Miguel Pro also, and it finally did one night in early August 1914, when twenty-two followers of General Venustiano Carranza broke their way into the El Llano novitiate, brandishing guns and ordering the terrified Jesuits to produce the account books. While one of the priests went to find the accounts, the others went

        [9] Ball, *Blessed Miguel Pro*, 21.
        [10] President Woodrow Wilson's naval occupation of Veracruz in April 1914 brought about the downfall of Victoriano Huerta. This intervention in Mexico's internal affairs caused widespread anti-American protests in that country. In Mexico City, an American flag was tied to the tail of a donkey and used to sweep the streets of Cathedral Plaza.

to the chapel to consume the consecrated Hosts and get ready to defend the chapel from desecration.[11] Ironically, the date was August 4, 1914, and the community was in the midst of preparations for an important celebration: the Centenary of the Restoration of the Society of Jesus.[12] The house had already been decorated with colorful festoons and flags, the work of Miguel Pro who had been put in charge of that chore.

As it turned out, nothing more happened that night; apparently, the soldiers found nothing of interest in the account books and left without harming anybody. Two days later, the community went ahead with the celebration of the centenary, thanking God for Pope Pius VII's decision to restore the Jesuit order after forty years of nonexistence. But as those novices contemplated the agony and ecstasy of their Jesuit past, their superiors could not have missed the irony of the Mexican present. Difficult times were back for the Church in their country, and the superiors were deeply worried about the safety of the novices under their care. In fact, by the time the Carranza attack took place, they had already begun preparations to flee El Llano, although they had not told the novices yet. They had acquired the necessary lay clothes (disguises) to be worn while on the run, and they were taking an inventory of the library treasures and other valuables to be hidden

[11] Norman, *Life and Martyrdom*, 38.

[12] John Henry Cardinal Newman has called the suppression of the Jesuits one of the great mysteries of the Catholic Church. It is a complicated and controversial subject for historians. In 1773 Pope Clement XIV, under fierce pressure from the Bourbon courts and other European powers, suppressed the order worldwide. Somehow it survived quietly for forty-one years with the help of powers like Catherine the Great of Russia (who was not even Catholic); she refused to promulgate the papal bull to her dominions, Pope Pius VII finally restored the order in 1814. The Jesuits who were still alive reorganized themselves and succeeded in reviving the Society.

in the basement or sent to friends in Zamora. They set August 15 as the day that evacuation of the house would begin, and the students were finally informed of the decision at a special meeting in the chapel the evening before. We don't have a record of how Miguel Pro felt about this sudden evacuation, but a classmate's diary gives us some details. That last morning, the novices visited every room and corner of the house to say goodbye, while the superior ordered the nameplates removed from the doors of the rooms used by the priests. A large statue of our Lady was also removed. In effect, any signs or symbols that would indicate the house was a religious one were hidden or destroyed.[13] During the midday meal, the novices pledged to pray for each other, as each one checked which small group he was assigned to and at what time that group was scheduled to leave. All were instructed to bring as little baggage as possible—no books that would betray their identity. The plan was to hide in neighboring haciendas or in homes in nearby Zamora until a safe place could be found where they could resume their religious formation.

Miguel Pro's group of four left in the late afternoon, on foot (some were provided with horses), and headed for Zamora where they found shelter in the home of a fellow novice. They stayed there two weeks, and in that short time they saw close-up the full extent of the religious persecution being visited on the Catholic Church in their country. The scene was surprisingly quiet for the first couple of days—the novices were even able to attend morning Mass—but then the Carranzistas (followers of General Carranza) put out an order for all churches in the town to be closed. The general in charge had set up headquarters in the residence of the bishop of Zamora, and from there he

---

[13] Norman, *Life and Martyrdom*, 42.

issued an order for all priests to report to him. Those who did were immediately thrown in jail, some subsequently tortured. Those who didn't had to flee to the hills. One day Miguel's group brought food to some priests who were hiding in a remote area outside the town, but on their way they had to hide themselves in a field of corn when armed revolutionaries rode by. Some hours later, still hiding in the corn, they saw the same revolutionaries return with about fifty horses they had stolen from the ranches in the area. Another day they saw the commanding general violently beat an old priest just to prove to his troops that the blood of a priest would not wither his hand.[14] By now, it was obvious that Zamora was not a safe place for any Catholic, let alone seminarians, and the superiors put out an order for all novices to make their way to Guadalajara immediately. The persecution was in full swing there also, but at least the bigger city offered more places to hide.

It was in Guadalajara that Miguel finally connected with his family again. His mother and younger siblings had fled to that city also, and by a happy coincidence they were living close to where he and his fellow novices were housed. However, the young Miguel was not prepared for what he saw when he finally made his way to where his mother and siblings were staying. They had settled into a boarding house in a poor part of the city, living in one room with two beds, a couple of chairs, and a picture of the Sacred Heart on the wall. (That picture was one of the few things they succeeded in grabbing before they fled from Saltillo.) To eke out a living, his mother was taking in laundry and doing other humble work wherever she could find it. She did not know where her husband was, she told her son, but she had heard that he was living in a safe place somewhere.

14 Ibid., 48.

It was a far cry from the comfortable circumstances the family had known when Miguel was growing up, and it broke his heart even as the family put on a brave face and didn't complain.

Miguel spent two months in Guadalajara, attending Mass when he could and following a flexible prayer schedule, as he and his fellow novices waited for word about their future. True to himself, he continued to be the class jester and joy-maker, playing tricks on people and pulling out his guitar or mandolin at a moment's notice. Finally, word came that he and thirteen others would be going to Los Gatos, in Northern California, to continue their studies in the Jesuit novitiate there. When the departure day arrived, his mother and younger siblings came to the train station to see him off, embracing him with tears and wondering what the future held in store for all of them. It would be the last time Miguel Pro would see his mother in this world.

Seminary Training

Los Gatos was a small California town, near San Francisco, that had its own unique hint of past danger; it got the name "Gatos" from the cougars and bobcats that used to come down from the Santa Cruz Mountains back in the days when there were fewer people around. The territory was originally part of Mexico (as was all of California, Texas, and New Mexico), and Miguel and his companions saw signs of that Mexican heritage everywhere: the Spanish architecture, the Spanish city names, the Spanish missions built by the Franciscans up and down the California coast.[15]

---

[15] Mexico ceded California, Texas, and New Mexico (half of its territory) to the United States in the Treaty of Guadalupe Hidalgo in 1848.

This was clearly a Catholic part of the United States, and the Jesuit refugees received a warm welcome from their American counterparts who must have been eager to learn more about what was happening south of the border. Nevertheless, conditions in the Los Gatos community were not easy for the fourteen new arrivals. Because all the rooms were occupied by American seminarians, the visitors had to make do with cramped quarters that were improvised on the top floor of the building. Moreover, the library was not equipped with Spanish books, and they knew little English; when the group arrived, all they had was one Spanish grammar. But they eventually found more Spanish texts and returned to their studies while their superiors waited for things to improve back in Mexico. They didn't. In fact the first half of 1915 was even worse than the previous years, with civilian casualties and atrocities mounting in the civil war; Miguel's superiors decided that he and his companions would have to go to Spain to continue their studies.

In June 1915, they boarded a train for Florida and from there took a ship across the Atlantic to the port of Cadiz in southwestern Spain. Their final destination was Granada, a Moorish-style city with a pleasant climate at the foot of the Sierra Nevada mountains, about an hour by car from the Mediterranean coast. Nearby is the famous Alhambra, the Islamic fortress and palace that originally served as the headquarters of the Moors, and later as a royal court for Ferdinand and Isabella. It was here that Christopher Columbus received the royal nod to go forward with his plan to discover the New World. Seeing it for the first time must have been an exciting experience for the recently arrived novices from the New World, but they soon found themselves confined to the large Jesuit novitiate outside the town, which included an observatory and professional-grade telescope. Miguel and his companions spent five years here, taking the required philosophy courses and continuing their formation in the Spiritual Exercises of Saint Ignatius.[16] Outside class, Miguel was his usual funny self, making people laugh and always willing to help when he could be useful. When an epidemic of influenza broke out in the community, he insisted on helping the overworked caregivers, despite the fact that his own health was not perfect. At this time, he began to feel an internal pain that the doctors could not diagnose, but he rarely talked about it and always tried to see the bright side in everything.

At the end of the fifth year (1920), Miguel went to Nicaragua for the standard two years of pastoral experience, teaching in a boarding high school where the climate was humid and the mosquitos were ubiquitous. When the two years were up, he returned to Spain (this time Barcelona), probably happy to be back in the more pleasant climate of the Mediterranean. It was here that he experienced one of the high points of his life as a Jesuit novice.

During Holy Week of 1924, he was allowed to do a retreat in nearby Manresa, the place where Saint Ignatius of Loyola spent a year of prayer and extreme mortification in 1522, begging for his keep and doing menial chores in exchange for food and lodging. At that time, Ignatius was going through the intensely personal trials that would make him not only the founder of the Society of Jesus but one of the spiritual giants of the Catholic Church. In a cave outside this town, he wrote down the fundamentals of what would eventually become the famous Spiritual Exercises, the rigorous regimen of prayer that has since been practiced by millions of people, clerical and lay alike. It must have been an awe-filled experience for the

---

[16] The Spiritual Exercises of Saint Ignatius are explained below.

thirty-three-year-old Miguel Pro to kneel and pray in that sacred place—the cradle of the Society of Jesus.

At the end of two years, he was on the move again, this time to Enghien in Belgium, a large Jesuit institution with so many nationalities that they had to communicate in Latin. It was here that he finished his study requirements and was finally ordained on August 31, 1925, at the age of thirty-four. Eighteen French Jesuits were ordained with him for the missions in China and Madagascar; also ordained were a Dutchman, an American, and a Brazilian.[17] It is unlikely that the ordaining bishop that day even noticed the slim, bronze-skinned Mexican in the group, let alone suspect that he was ordaining a future martyr. In little more than three years, photographs of this young man—his arms outstretched before a firing squad—would appear in newspapers in Europe and around the world. Did Miguel Pro himself sense any of the impending doom? We will never know, but we do know that his ordination day was tinged with sadness, despite the joy of Holy Orders. While the newly ordained priests were giving their first blessings to parents and family, he disappeared to his room to look at some family photographs, which he blessed as he wept. All through his studies in Europe, he had worried about his family back home, and the image of his mother living in that boarding house room must have haunted him the most. "I grow older day by day and I fear you will scarcely find me here on your return," she wrote to him at this time. "I think God asks the sacrifice from me of never seeing you at the altar." She died a few days after writing those words, on February 8, 1926.[18]

[17] Norman, *Life and Martyrdom*, 83.
[18] Ibid., 93.

Pro's health at this time was another cross. The internal pain that he quietly suffered through most of his seminary training came to a climax right after his ordination and could no longer be ignored. He had scarcely finished his month-long vacation when he was sent to Brussels for an evaluation, which resulted in an operation. But the procedure seems not to have worked, because the doctors immediately ordered a second operation (this one without an anesthetic, for some reason), and then a third one. A period of recuperation in a house run by nuns in the South of France followed, where as usual he showed more concern for others than for himself. He insisted on celebrating the earliest daily Mass saying, "I do not sleep anyhow; it will not be a sacrifice,"[19] which was true. All his life, long before he got sick, he had been troubled by insomnia. He visited the other sick priests regularly and at one point would have stayed up all night with a dying priest, if the superior had not forbade him. He also found time to talk to the gardener who was a lapsed Catholic and brought him back to the Church.

Miguel was never shy about talking religion to complete strangers, and if they were poor so much the better. His conversation with a group of mine workers on a train in Belgium was a striking example. After his ordination, he volunteered to spend his vacation visiting the Belgian Black Country, a coal mining area south of Brussels that was famous for huge factory chimneys and troublesome labor strikes. As soon as he arrived there, he put on the dark blue overalls of the miners and went down into the bowels of the mine, to scenes that were all too familiar to the young man from Zacatecas. When he got back to the surface, he joined a group of young miners on their

[19] Ibid., 99

train ride home, still dressed like them in dirty overalls. However, it soon became clear that he was not welcome in their company.

"We are socialists," one of them said to him with a hostile look.

"Excellent," the young priest said; "I am a socialist also."

"There are Communists here too," the miner said a minute later.

"Better still," the priest said, "for I am even a Communist. For instance, it is one o'clock. You have some food and I too am hungry. Won't you share your food with me."[20]

The miners were disarmed. When they asked him why he was not scared of them, he told them he was armed— with a crucifix. At the next train stop, one of them picked up some chocolates at the vending machine and shared them with everyone in the train carriage, including the young priest.

Back to Mexico

Why Pro's provincial called him home to Mexico is not clear, but it may be because of his ability to communicate with manual laborers. With *Rerum Novarum* becoming increasingly important in Mexico, there was a need for a priest with his personality and deep convictions about social justice for the workingman.[21] Besides, he missed his homeland and worried as much about the fate of the Church there as he did about his own family. Despite the stepped-up persecution of the Church by Plutarco

[20] Ibid., 87.
[21] López-Menéndez, *Miguel Pro*, 102.

Calles—rather because of it—he wanted to go home and work as a priest among his own people. In the eyes of the world it was sheer folly, but it was what many Jesuits before him had done going back to the foundation of the order. That is what Edmund Campion had done when he returned to England in the sixteenth century, only to be hanged, drawn, and quartered by the order of Queen Elizabeth I. That is what Isaac Jogues had done when he returned to the Indian tribes near Quebec in the seventeenth century, only to be brutally tortured and tomahawked at the hands of the Mohawks. What Miguel Pro was doing was no different.

"Three more days and I shall be in Mexico," he wrote while on the high seas. "Will it be difficult for me to get back, priest and religious that I am? I do not know." And he did not care. During the voyage, he made no effort to conceal his identity—he celebrated Mass every day on the ship—and when they arrived in Veracruz on July 7, he just walked up to the immigration and customs stand without a care and took his chances. Incredibly, he got through without any problem. "It was a special dispensation of God," he wrote, "that I re-entered my country.... I do not know how I did it."[22] He left the port at six in the evening and reported to his superiors in Mexico City the following morning.

He could not have returned to Mexico at a worse time—or at a better time. This was July 1926, and President Calles had just issued his ominous order that all priests must register with the government, a development that was immediately followed by the equally ominous decision of the Mexican bishops to suspend all worship in the country, beginning July 31. There was chaos and panic everywhere,

[22] Norman, *Life and Martyrdom*, 116.

as people crowded into churches and besieged priests with urgent requests to administer needed sacraments before the July 31 deadline: requests to get married, to get babies baptized, to go to Confession. The provincial immediately put Father Pro to work at Holy Family Church, the large newly built Jesuit church in the city (where his remains lie today). There he heard daily Confessions from 5:30 A.M. to 11:00 A.M. and again from 3:00 P.M. to 8:00 P.M.—a heavy schedule for a man in good health, let alone one who was still fragile after three surgeries. Twice he collapsed in the confessional and had to be carried out for fresh air. When the suspension of worship became effective July 31, he continued this frenzy of activity underground, celebrating Masses and distributing Communion in secret locations called "Communion Stations" to countless numbers of people. One day he administered Communion to twelve hundred people, he told his provincial. It was at one such Communion service (which met at 6 A.M.), that he had one of his first run-ins with the police. In the middle of the service, a maid ran in and shouted, "The police are coming."[23] Reminding the people to keep calm (which they did not do), Father Pro told them to hide all religious emblems and quietly disperse to the various rooms in the house. He then put the Blessed Sacrament into an inside pocket (he was wearing a shabby old gray suit), pulled out a cigarette that he put into a long holder, and calmly opened the door.

Police: "There is public worship going on here."

Pro: "There is not."

Police: "Yes, yes, there is public worship here."

Pro: "Well, this time you are going to be forced to admit that somebody was pulling your leg."

[23] Ibid., 127.

Police: "How? We saw the priest come in here. Anyhow we have orders to search the premises. Follow us."

Pro: "I like that. This is the last straw. Follow you? And by what right can you make me? Show me your warrants. Anyway, if you are bent on it, go all over the house and if you find public worship going on, come and tell me so I can attend Mass."[24]

When the frustrated police found no priest, they decided to put a guard at the house entrance for the rest of the day. To mock them further, Father Pro apologized that he could not help them with their search because he had to go to work. He departed to distribute Communion at other stations, and when he was finished, he returned to check on the police who were still waiting to catch the priest!

Another morning, he arrived at a house at dawn to celebrate a secret Mass, only to find two policemen at the door waiting to arrest the priest. Here is his own description of what happened next: "I pulled myself together and went straight up to the policemen. With an important air, I took down in a notebook the number of the house. Then I opened my coat as if showing them my secret police badge, and said with an air of conviction: something fishy going on here. . . . ? They gave me a military salute and let me pass, convinced that I was a police agent and that I had really shown them the badge they wear."[25] Obviously, he did not celebrate Mass for the nervous people upstairs that morning. After assuring them there was nothing to worry about, he left and got another military salute on the way out the door. These Pro exploits were made possible by his array of disguises, as well as his way with words. Sometimes he dressed like a government official (he had

24 Ibid.
25 Ibid., 164.

a "magnificent police dog" somebody gave him), other times like an old man with a cane, other times like a student riding his brother's bicycle, "which has already given me a fine bruise on my arm and a huge lump on my head," he said to his brother.[26]

He did in fact get arrested several times, but it was always in sweeps that involved a group of people, and each time the police let him go not realizing who they had within their grasp. So his secret ministry continued at an astonishing pace, and included activities you would not associate with a priest who had to work in the underground church:

- With the help of the ACJM, he trained a team of speakers that numbered 150, and he kept in contact with them to answer questions about the teaching of the Church. He had four mailing addresses.

- He gave retreats to a wide variety of groups: ninety elderly ladies who had to meet in a different place each day; fifty chauffeurs who arrived to find their priest-director dressed as a mechanic; eighty state workers who smiled at the idea of saying the Rosary in a government office, surrounded by desks and typewriters.

- He helped poor families, especially the families of Cristero soldiers. "My purse is as dry as Calles soul," he wrote to his provincial about the shortage of money. He helped about one hundred families, "taking advantage" of his rich friends. On one occasion, he was seen carrying six chickens and a turkey through the streets—all of them alive.

- He found foster families for babies who were left at his doorstep. "I need not tell you how damp my clothes were," he said about one baby he carried on his lap

---

[26] Wilfred Parsons, *Mexican Martyrdom* (Rockford, Ill.: Tan Books and Publishers, 1987), 45.

while driving the car. His family ended up adopting one of those babies, which led to no small amount of scandalous talk about who was the father of the child!

- He continued to study for his final theology exams, which had not been completed in Spain. Finally, on September 16, 1927, the busy young Jesuit met that obligation.[27]

Martyrdom

Miguel Pro was ready for martyrdom when it finally came; he even desired it. That is clear from comments he made on several occasions. "News of abuse and retaliation come from everywhere," he wrote after arriving back in Mexico. "The victims are plenty; there are more martyrs every day.... Oh, if only (I got) the lucky number."[28] A few weeks later, he was promising to be an advocate for his friends when he got to Heaven, telling them to "get ready with your petitions."[29] What eventually caused him to draw the "lucky number" was an assassination attempt against Álvaro Obregón, Calles' predecessor, who had just been reelected president. On Sunday afternoon, November 13, 1927, Obregón and some friends were driving through Chapultepec Park in Mexico City on their way to a bullfight when four men in a Hudson Essex sedan pulled up alongside their

[27] See Ball, *Blessed Miguel Pro*, 68.

[28] López-Menéndez, *Miguel Pro*, 30. A copy of this important letter is in the Jesuit archives in Mexico City. It was transcribed by Father Antonio Dragon, S.J., a friend of Pro who was ordained the year before him. Dragon wrote two biographies of Pro, which have been an essential source of information for all the books written later.

[29] Norman, *Life and Martyrdom*, 137.

Cadillac and threw a couple of homemade bombs at the car. Nobody in the Cadillac was seriously injured, and after a brief return home to treat some minor scratches, Obregón went to the bullfight as originally planned. Meanwhile, Obregón's friends, who had been following the Cadillac in a second car, pursued the Essex and after a shootout succeeded in grabbing two of the four attackers: Juan Tirado, who was immediately incarcerated, and Nahum Lamberto Ruiz, who died shortly afterward from his injuries. The other two fled on foot.

The mastermind of the plot was one of the two who fled on foot. His name was Luis Segura Vilchis, a young engineer and friend of Father Miguel Pro (he helped Pro organize the team of speakers) who had been working on the assassination plot for a year. The previous April he had cancelled a plan to blow up the train that Obregón was traveling on when he discovered that his target was using a passenger train instead of a private one. Not phased by this second failure, Vilchis brazenly decided to go to the bullfight that Obregón was attending and even got close enough to the president-elect to congratulate him on his narrow escape in the park. Some days later, when the police arrested him and questioned him about the assassination attempt, he denied any involvement and produced the ticket to the bullfight as proof. Obregón himself, who remembered meeting him at the bullfight, confirmed the alibi, and he was let go. But things changed quickly when Vilchis learned that Father Pro and his two brothers had been arrested at the home of a friend where they were hiding, and that they also were being questioned about the assassination attempt. Vilchis immediately went back to the police and confessed his role in the plot, adding that the Pro brothers were innocent and should be released. However, after doing further investigation, the authorities decided to detain all four men—Miguel Pro, Humberto Pro, Roberto Pro, and Luis Segura Vilchis—and charge all of them with complicity in the crime.

The Pro brothers in fact had nothing to do with the assassination attempt, but unfortunately a superficial glance at the facts could lead one to suspect that they were involved somehow (which may be why Miguel's canonization process is slower than that of other Calles victims).[30] Father Pro's outspoken criticism of the government and his work helping the families of Cristero soldiers were enough to put him on the suspect list. His brother Humberto was also suspect because of his propaganda activities for the League and ACJM; he had been arrested for those activities the previous year. More important, the Essex used in the plot had been registered in his name (although he had sold it to a friend three days before the crime), and his identification and driver's license were still in the car on the afternoon of the crime.[31] Police Chief Roberto Cruz, who had been giving Calles daily briefings on the investigation, put those facts together in a report to the president, recommending that all five (Juan Tirado was the fifth) be put on trial. Calles accepted his report but not his recommendation, instead ordering that all five be shot immediately without trial. "So there is proof of the guilt of these individuals, and of the priest who was the mastermind behind it," he said to the police chief. "Here it was General Obregón, tomorrow it will be me, and then you."[32]

[30] Pope John Paul II beatified Miguel Pro in 1988, stating that hatred toward his faith was the reason for his death.

[31] López-Menéndez, *Miguel Pro*, 23.

[32] David Bailey, *¡Viva Cristo Rey!* (Austin: University of Texas Press, 1974), 169. Ironically, Obregón at first wanted a trial because he suspected that political enemies (other than Catholic activists) might be behind the plot. So did many others. It was a tense time in the nation.

Miguel Pro had finally drawn the "lucky number", but he didn't know it yet. This could not be it, he said, because the charge against him was so ludicrous that even the Calles regime would need a better excuse than this to kill them. As soon as he and his brothers appeared before a competent authority, he said, they would be released and he would continue his underground ministry until God was ready to call him. Consequently, he and his brothers settled into a relaxed routine in prison, praying the Rosary and singing joyful hymns. When their sister brought food to the prison each day, they shared it with everyone, even the prison guards. One guard had a lengthy conversation that brought him back to the Church. Photographers and reporters were allowed into the prison on the fifth day, and Miguel and his companions talked freely with them, confidently predicting that they would soon be set free. However, when guards appeared unexpectedly in his cell early the following morning, Miguel apparently had a premonition because he suddenly changed his mind. "This morning all three of us are going to be shot," he told his shocked brothers. "Don't worry," he added, "rather let us thank God that we have been chosen; let us renew our offering and let us pardon our enemies."[33] On their way out of his cell, one of the guards asked him for forgiveness, which Pro gladly gave him, putting his arm around the guard's shoulders as he did so.

Moments later, Pro stepped outside into the daylight and found himself in a walled enclosure the size of a large oval-shaped garden, where a number of army chiefs, public

[33] Parsons, *Mexican Martyrdom*, 50. Parsons is quoting from an account of those final hours by Roberto Pro, who was in jail for the same crime, but was released at the last minute. By "all three of us" Miguel meant himself and his two brothers, Humberto and Roberto.

officials, and photographers were standing to the side, waiting to get their first look at the condemned priest.[34] Pro was dressed in the clothes he brought with him to the police station six days earlier: a shabby dark suit, woolen cardigan (brown with wavy stripes), white shirt, and dark tie.[35] At the far end of the enclosure was a bullet-marked barrier or stockade made of tall rough-hewn wooden stakes, and in front of that structure were three cutouts of a human form that the soldiers used for target practice. (All this can be seen clearly in the black-and-white photographs that appeared in the press.) "Miguel Agustín Pro," an officer called out, and Pro was immediately led to that end of the garden space, to a spot in front of the stockade between two of the human cutouts. "Any last request," an officer asked him, to which he answered: "That I may be allowed to pray."[36] Meanwhile, the photographers were busy recording everything the priest did.

An Irish journalist, Francis McCullagh who was present that day, describes what he saw next: "The young priest knelt bolt upright, his eyes closed, his arms folded on his breast. Even in that place of squalor and death, he was a picture of saintly dignity and recollection."[37] After

[34] The police headquarters, where Pro and his companions were executed, was originally a luxurious private home, built near the Plaza de la Reforma in the center of the city. Executions took place in what was originally the oval-shaped garden at the back. Today the National Lottery Building occupies that space.

[35] The prisoners did not wear uniforms, and family members were allowed to bring in food.

[36] Norman, *Life and Martyrdom*, 198.

[37] Captain Francis McCullagh, *Red Mexico: A Reign of Terror in America* (New York: Louis Carrier, 1928), quoted in Norman, *Life and Martyrdom*, 198. McCullagh was a war correspondent for the *New York Herald* and the English language *Japan Times*. He was one of the journalists invited to witness the execution of Father Pro. Some of his articles were published in *America* magazine.

two minutes of prayer, he stood up and facing the crowd stretched out his arms in the form of a cross. In one hand he held the crucifix he was given on the morning he made his first vows as a Jesuit and in the other his rosary beads. "Dios tenga compasión de vosotros," he said. "Que Dios los bendiga. Señor, Tu sabes que soy inocente! Perdono de todo corazón a mis enemigos" (May God have mercy on you. May God bless you. Lord, you know that I am innocent. With all my heart, I forgive my enemies).[38] By this time, the guards had stepped back, out of the range of fire, leaving Miguel alone and without a blindfold, facing a firing squad at the other end of the enclosure. "Prepare," a senior officer shouted to the five members of the firing squad. They immediately discharged their rifles into the chest of the young priest, as he collapsed between the cut-outs. "Viva Cristo Rey" were his last words before falling to the ground. When the soldiers saw that he was still alive, one of them came forward and finished him off with a shot into the side of his head at close range. "There was no sense of loneliness and abandonment in the last look he gave to the world," McCullagh said. "On the contrary, a strange exultation shone in his face as if he already felt himself shaded by the mighty wings of his patron, San Miguel, the Archangel."[39] The scene made one feel pity rather than hate for Roberto Cruz and his henchmen, McCullagh said.

The execution of the others followed immediately: Humberto Pro, who was as innocent as his ordained brother; Luis Segura Vilchis, who had confessed to the crime; and Juan Tirado, who had been captured at the scene of the crime. Roberto Pro was released at the last minute through

[38] Norman, *Life and Martyrdom*, 199.
[39] Ibid.

the intervention of the Argentine ambassador to Mexico. The body of each victim was left on the ground where it fell until all four were shot. They were all then taken to the military hospital morgue in a waiting ambulance, which was forced to push slowly through the large crowd of people that had gathered outside the police headquarters, some crying, "Viva Cristo Rey," others kneeling in reverent silence as the vehicle passed. Soon after, the heartbroken senior Miguel Pro arrived at the morgue to claim the bodies of his sons. The old mining engineer, who had been reduced to penury by the turmoil of the times and had lost his wife the previous year, was now losing two of his sons. It must have been small consolation that a third son, Roberto, could also have been in the morgue that day were it not for the last-minute action of the Argentine ambassador. That son ended up in exile in Cuba.

Later that evening and the following day, the crowds that gathered at the Pro residence were enormous, as thousands of people filed through the house to kiss the caskets and touch them with their rosaries and other pious objects. Jesuit priests recited the Office of the Dead, as the Blessed Sacrament reposed on top of the two caskets alternately. Later, the priests discussed the details of the funeral and decided which priests would be pallbearers. Don Miguel, Sr., simply knelt before the bodies, at times touching the caskets, at times just peacefully praying in the presence of this mystery.

A U.S. English language news service that was used by American diocesan newspapers describes what the scene was like the following day, November 24:

"At least 20,000, probably the greatest crowd that ever gathered for the funerals of private persons in Mexico, must have assembled along the line of march and at the cemetery." Every class of society was represented, the article said, "from the wealthy and fashionably dressed persons, who came in fine automobiles, to entire families of bare-footed Indians who had walked miles to the funeral."

"All carried floral offerings of some kind, even if only wild flowers picked along the roadside and rained these flowers upon the coffins as they passed, while they prayed and chanted for the dead 'martyrs' and to 'Christ the King'."[40] The streets and avenues along the way (3.5 miles) were carpeted with flowers, and the graves in Dolores Cemetery became veritable mountains of flowers.

By coincidence, President Calles had a get-acquainted lunch that day with Dwight Morrow, the new American ambassador to Mexico.[41] Was the lunch delayed by the traffic jams in the city? Did the Miguel Pro affair come up in discussion? Very probably! This much we know for sure: the following day, the new ambassador received a carefully worded document protesting the execution of Father Pro and his companions that was signed by the directors of the National League for the Defense of Religious Liberty. They were hoping that the new ambassador would do more than his predecessor to stop the brutal attacks on the Catholic Church in Mexico. Ambassador Morrow simply sent the document to the U.S. State Department without comment. He had nothing to say about the problem at this time, but before long that would change. Morrow would become a key player in bringing the war to an end, as we will see in the next chapter.

---

[40] "Ruthless Tyranny Fails to Daunt Mexican Masses", *Catholic Herald*, December 3, 1927, front page; the *Catholic Herald* is the newspaper of the Dio-cese of Sacramento, California.

[41] López-Menéndez, *Miguel Pro*, 66.

Chapter 9

Father John Burke and the Tireless Ambassador

The two Americans who worked together to negotiate an end to the Cristero War in Mexico were an unlikely team. One was a Catholic priest and well-connected Church bureaucrat—not the kind of person who would normally endear himself to the anticlerical Plutarco Calles. The other was a businessman who was once a partner with the powerful commercial and investment bank J. P. Morgan—again not a particularly nice person in the mind of Calles, who distrusted the "dollar diplomacy" of U.S. foreign policy. But what both Americans had in common was an uncanny ability to win the confidence of people who distrusted them and a genuine desire to solve Mexico's religious problem.

The Catholic priest was John Burke, an Irish American from New York City (his parents came from the "ould sod") who entered the Missionary Society of St. Paul the Apostle (known as the Paulists) and studied at the Catholic University of America in Washington, D.C. There he came under the influence of the encyclical *Rerum Novarum*. After some years in parish work, his superiors appointed him editor of *Catholic World*, the respected liberal magazine of the Paulists, where he spent eighteen years preaching social justice and advocating for the millions of immigrants arriving on U.S. shores, most of whom were Irish Catholics. This was still the era of anti-Irish prejudice, when many native Americans were deeply threatened by the stereotype of the spalpeen—the illiterate Irishman who spent his life living in squalor and drinking cheap whiskey. If these immigrants would only get a fair chance, Burke kept saying, they would revitalize America, and the Catholic Church would play a central role in that revitalization. His own family was a good example. His older brother, Thomas, had entered the Paulist Fathers before him and eventually became a well-known preacher and superior general of the order. His brother James became a vice president in a large trust company.

When the United States entered World War I in 1917, Father Burke used the magazine to throw his support behind President Woodrow Wilson, for more reasons than one. He sincerely believed in the war cause, but he also knew that American Catholics were on trial. He wanted to prove that they could be loyal citizens of the United States like everyone else. There were other Catholic leaders who shared that same conviction, of course, in particular, James Cardinal Gibbons of Baltimore, who publicly pledged the support of the Catholic Church for the war effort, and James Flaherty of the Knights of Columbus, who launched a million-dollar drive to support Catholics in the armed services. But Father Burke soon became frustrated with the lack of coordination in these efforts to support the war. The Catholic Church in America, he said, was too splintered and unorganized to run an efficient national campaign, which was true. In those days, the U.S. bishops never met or talked to each other in formal meetings (except for the fourteen archbishops who met once a year), and the fifteen thousand Catholic societies around the country had practically no communication or coordination either. The nearest thing to a national Catholic voice was the four-hundred-thousand-member Knights of Columbus, but their relative efficiency only served to underline the lack of efficiency in the rest of the Church. It was this situation that eventually made Father John Burke famous, demonstrating his genius as an organizer.

It began with a meeting he had with Cardinal Gibbons in the summer of 1917 in which he discussed the lack of communication in the Church and the confusion this was causing in supporting the war effort. To address the problem, he proposed a national gathering of all Catholic leaders to discuss setting up an agency that would centralize the war campaign and coordinate the activities of so many well-meaning Catholic organizations. Burke left that meeting with the cardinal's full support and wasted no time in following up. A few weeks later (August 11–12, 1917), his alma mater, Catholic University, was the setting for a meeting that drew 115 clerical and lay representatives from sixty-eight dioceses, and a host of national Catholic organizations—the first meeting of its kind in the history of the Catholic Church in America. Several times at that meeting, the discussion got sidetracked by petty self-interest and misconceptions about why they were there; but somehow Father Burke pulled them together, and by the end of the second day they had agreed to establish a national Catholic organization called the National Catholic War Council. That organization would turn out to be the key factor in the Catholic war effort of 1917–1918, an effort that many at the time called "the greatest promotion and public relations program the American Catholic Church had ever known".[1]

[1] John B. Sheerin, Never Look Back: The Career and Concerns of John J. Burke (New York: Paulist Press, 1975), 57.

But what would happen when the war ended and the National Catholic War Council was not needed anymore? Would the bishops return to the isolation of their dioceses and be content with the splintered Church of the past? John Burke did not want that to happen, and at this time Divine Providence handed him a blessed opportunity to do something more. On February 20, 1919, seventy-seven bishops gathered (again at Catholic University) for the golden jubilee of Cardinal Gibbons' episcopal ordination, a grand celebration that included a Roman cardinal who came as the personal representative of Pope Benedict XV. During those activities, Father Burke's idea of having regular meetings of bishops came up a lot, so much so that Gibbons appointed a committee to investigate it further. A few months later, the bishops were back at the Catholic University campus with a plan in mind and the approval of the Holy See. This time they voted to establish a permanent organization called the National Catholic Welfare Council (NCWC, the predecessor of the National Conference of Catholic Bishops and the United States Catholic Conference, which later combined to form today's United States Conference of Catholic Bishops); they established an administrative committee of seven bishops, under the chairmanship of Archbishop Edward Hanna of San Francisco, to handle affairs between the annual meetings. Participation in the new organization was to be voluntary, which meant it would have no legislative authority or coercive power, an important provision in winning the support of some bishops who were skeptical about a new level of bureaucracy in their lives. Not surprisingly, Father John Burke was appointed general secretary by the administrative committee a few weeks later, which meant he had to move from New York to Washington, D.C., where he would spend the rest of his life overseeing the new NCWC headquarters and staff. During those years, he consulted with some fifty Catholic hierarchies in other countries, assisting them in establishing episcopal conferences based on the American model. The twenty million Catholics in the United States now had a high-profile voice in Washington, D.C., who could command attention at the top levels of the U.S. government. During his tenure as general secretary, Burke won the respect of five U.S. presidents and many career officials at the top of the U.S. State Department, contacts that would be vitally important when he eventually got directly involved in the Mexican religious issue. His first official communication with Mexico came in November 1925, when the aging Archbishop Mora of Mexico City telegrammed his office to inform him about the new law in the state of Tabasco mandating that Catholic priests had to be married and over forty years of age to minister in that state. That telegram initiated a contact between the American bishops and the Mexican bishops that would become more significant as time passed, and it also initiated an official dialogue between Father John Burke and the U.S. government because the first thing Burke did was forward the telegram to the U.S. State Department.

The Ambassador Enters the Discussion

On October 13, 1927, a two-hour meeting took place at the Mayflower Hotel in Washington, D.C., between Father John Burke and Dwight Morrow, the newly

---

[2] Ibid., 117.

appointed American ambassador to Mexico.[2] Morrow had
not even taken up his new job yet, but Burke was asked
to brief him on the persecution of the Catholic Church in
Mexico before he headed south. (Patrick Cardinal Hayes
of New York and the New York judge Morgan O'Brien,
a prominent Catholic layman, had suggested that the
new ambassador talk to Father Burke.) In fact, Morrow
was already well aware of the problem. Studying the role
of religion in society was a favorite pastime of his, and
although not a Catholic himself, one of his favorite authors
was Lord Acton, the English Catholic politician and historian. Like many fair-minded Americans, he was appalled
by the prospect of Mexican bishops having to live in exile
in San Antonio, Texas, because of persecution in their
own country—a scandal that had continued on and off
for fifteen years.[3] Moreover, as a partner in J. P. Morgan
and chairman of the International Committee of Bank-
ers in Mexico, he had been involved in Mexican financial issues for several years and was a personal friend of
Agustín Legorreta, head of the Bank of Mexico. In a letter

[3] The Mexican refugee crisis began to impact the Catholic Church in
America as far back as 1914, when hundreds of priests and sisters were exiled
from Mexico by the anticlerical strongmen who fought in the War of the
Generals. The Knights of Columbus immediately began to provide generous
financial support to the new arrivals. When the Mexican bishops were exiled
also, most of them found refuge in San Antonio, Texas, through the generosity of Bishop John Shaw and later Bishop Arthur Drossaerts. Shortly after
the Mexican bishops' arrival, Father Francis Kelley (later bishop of Oklahoma
City) helped found a seminary in Texas for the exiled Mexican seminarians; Kelley got money from the Catholic Extension Society to purchase the
building from a group of nuns in Castroville, not far from San Antonio. That
seminary had 108 seminarians at its peak, and eventually graduated 59 priests.
From that point on, the American Catholic press followed the Mexican religious crisis closely, and some Catholic leaders wrote books about it: Bishop
Francis Kelley wrote a book called *Blood-Drenched Altars* (Rockford, Ill.: Tan
Books and Publishers, 1935).

to Legorreta just months before being appointed ambassador, he brought up the religious issue, stating bluntly that it was an obstacle to good relations between their two countries. He was referring to the twenty million Catholics in the United States who, he said, were watching the persecution of their coreligionists with increasing horror. There must be a way to resolve this issue, he told his Mexican banker friend.

Morrow was also a personal friend of President Calvin Coolidge, going back to their days as classmates at Amherst College, and it was natural that the president would turn to him to fill this particular post at this particular time. Coolidge needed an ambassador in Mexico City with a more delicate approach. The previous ambassador, James Sheffield, had a visceral dislike for Plutarco Calles and was even accused of making racist comments about Mexican government officials on occasion. Not surprisingly, relations between the United States and Mexico steadily declined during his four years as ambassador, and President Coolidge wanted a change in Washington's way of dealing with his neighbor south of the border.

At the meeting in the Mayflower Hotel, Ambassador Morrow was immediately impressed with Father Burke and found himself in full agreement with the priest on the urgency of the Mexican religious question. "What do you think I should do," he asked Burke at the end of the meeting. Burke did not have a specific answer, but said he would stay in contact with Undersecretary of State Robert E. Olds, who was also at the meeting that day. In a subsequent letter to Olds from Mexico City, Morrow was already more optimistic about dealing with President Calles, saying that he felt "a *modus vivendi* could be worked out without loss of dignity to either side if there were any method by which a liberal Catholic of the type of Father

Burke, who talked to us in Washington, were dealing directly with President Calles."[4]

The wheels were also beginning to turn on the ecclesiastical side. Around this time, the NCWC's administrative committee gave Father Burke permission to meet with President Coolidge (who already heard about Burke from his friend Morrow) to discuss the Mexican problem. At that meeting, Burke stressed the need to give Calles a frank report on how American Catholics felt about the persecution of their Mexican coreligionists, but Coolidge expressed extreme caution saying that this was an internal issue and to intervene could lead to armed conflict. But Burke had made his point, and at a follow-up meeting with Secretary of State Frank Kellogg, he brought along a chronological list of the hostile acts committed by the Calles regime in the twenty-one-month period from February 1926 to November 1927. It was forty-three pages long.

Meanwhile, the suggestion that Father Burke meet face-to-face with President Calles came up again, this time at a meeting between Burke and Olds in the undersecretary's office in the State Department (the two were becoming close friends), an idea that Burke did not dismiss out of hand. Such a meeting, he said, would require permission from his superiors, the NCWC's administrative committee and the U.S. apostolic delegate, Archbishop Pietro Fumasoni Biondi, who was now responsible for Mexico as well as the United States. Fumasoni Biondi was at first skeptical that any good would come from such a meeting, dismissing Morrow as just another arrogant banker in the "dollar diplomacy" tradition, but then changed his mind and gave Burke permission. The meeting would take careful planning, however, and Morrow suggested that he and

[4]John Sheerin, *Never Look Back: The Career and Concerns of John J. Burke* (New York: Paulist Press, 1975), 118.

Burke begin with a preparatory meeting, which they did in Havana during the sixth Pan-American Congress in January 1928. By this time, Morrow was having weekly breakfast meetings with Calles on the president's ranch outside Mexico City, which the American press began calling "ham and eggs diplomacy",[5] and relations between the two countries were already warming up significantly. Nonetheless, the private meeting between Morrow and Burke (held in Morrow's hotel room in Havana) was difficult. Morrow readily admitted to Burke that Calles was a fanatic and that the Mexican constitution was a farce, but he said that the Catholic Church in Mexico was leading a rebellion against the state—at least that was how President Calles saw it. In response, Burke denied the accusation of rebellion and insisted that no peace could be reached until Calles allowed the exiled Mexican bishops to return to their dioceses, and an apostolic delegate must be allowed to function in Mexico. It was a tough first day. "Spent four hours with him (Morrow) and came home disappointed and depressed," Burke wrote in his diary that night.[6] The following day the argument continued, with Burke urging the skeptical ambassador to at least try convincing Calles to allow an apostolic delegate to return to Mexico. Morrow was reluctant, saying that pushing Calles too far could cost him his ambassadorship, but in the end he said he would try. Before departing, Morrow again brought up the idea of a face-to-face meeting. "If Calles shows himself willing to receive you and discuss this matter with you," he asked, "will you come to Mexico to talk to him?" Burke said yes, on condition that he got permission from his superiors.[7]

[5] David Bailey, ¡Viva Cristo Rey! (Austin: University of Texas Press, 1974), 176.
[6] Sheerin, Never Look Back, 121.
[7] Ibid.

Morrow returned to Mexico City, met with Calles again, and was pleasantly surprised. After reciting his usual list of complaints about the Catholic Church, the president did agree to talk to the American priest. A meeting was immediately arranged, but it never happened. Somebody talked, and on February 9, 1928, word reached the *New York Herald Tribune*, which angered Calles, but he remained open and discussions went ahead to get a new date.

At this point another admirer of John Burke entered the picture. Walter Lippmann, the American writer and political commentator who had been covering the Mexican religious problem in his newspaper columns, had two lengthy interviews with Calles in Mexico City and was surprised by the president's flexibility. Lippmann (on the urging of contacts in the U.S. State Department) immediately wrote to Father John Burke, explaining that two of the most contentious laws—the one concerning registration of priests and the one limiting the number of priests in each state—could be interpreted in a way that could be acceptable to the bishops of Mexico. Shortly after that, the two men met in Burke's home in Washington for a discussion that lasted three hours, followed by more meetings over the following two days in Lippmann's room at the Carton Hotel. Like Morrow, Lippmann was deeply impressed with Burke, and before long the two men were busy sketching a peace plan—a modus vivendi—that might bring an end to the Cristero War.

However, it was Ambassador Morrow rather than Lippmann who worked out the details. With both sides now willing to meet, Morrow drafted a letter that Burke could send to Calles, expressing his hopes for peace in Mexico. The carefully worded draft made a number of diplomatic concessions to the Mexican Revolution: that Burke believed the Mexican president was not seeking "to destroy the identity of the Church nor to interfere with its spiritual function"; that the purpose of the Mexican constitution and its enforcement "has been and will be to keep churchmen from being implicated in political struggles while at the same time leaving them free to dedicate themselves to the welfare of souls"; that the hierarchy wanted to resume public worship if it could be assured of "a tolerance within the law", permitting the Church freedom to live and exercise its spiritual function.[8] The draft did not demand a change in the Mexican constitution because Morrow believed that such a demand would immediately kill the chances of success. (No one but a madman would endeavor to settle the question of principle between the Church and Mexico, he had written earlier to Olds.) However, the text did suggest a discussion about the constitution at some future date—"in an atmosphere of good will". The last paragraph stated that if the president saw merit in his ideas, he (Burke) would be willing to travel to Mexico City to discuss the issues in more detail. After Burke and the apostolic delegate gave their approval to the letter, Morrow drafted a second letter—the response that President Calles would give to Father Burke—and immediately showed both drafts to Calles himself. It worked. To Morrow's relief, Calles expressed his satisfaction with both drafts, which meant he was open to Burke's offer to meet face-to-face. Hours later, on March 29, Father Burke set the process in motion by signing the letter on his side— what would become known as "Father Burke's March 29 Letter"—and gave it to Undersecretary of State Robert Olds, who immediately dispatched it to Mexico City by diplomatic pouch. Burke then left Washington for Mexico City by train, accompanied by William Montavon, the

---

[8] Bailey, *¡Viva Cristo Rey!*, 193.

head of the NCWC's legal department, who would be his personal assistant and interpreter throughout the entire process. He was dressed in civilian clothing because he did not want to be recognized by anyone, but also because by now it was against Mexican law to wear religious garb in public. Near the border, at Laredo, the two Americans were met by officials of the Calles government who assisted them with immigration and put them on a train for Mexico City. Ambassador Morrow met them in the capital, and the group immediately headed east by car to a secret meeting place on the Gulf of Mexico.

The Secret Meeting Place

San Juan de Ulúa is a complex of fortresses on an island overlooking the port of Veracruz that has a long and varied Mexican history. Built by the Spaniards in the sixteenth century, it was a giant storage facility for the precious metals that left New Spain for Madrid during the colonial period—a kind of Mexican Fort Knox—and the massive strong rooms there give a hint at just how much wealth the Spanish Crown plundered from New Spain during those centuries. With walls that are twenty-five feet thick in some places, and surrounded by shark-infested waters, it was a formidable place to store the bullion that would eventually be sent across the Atlantic. It was also a formidable place to hold prisoners, similar to the Alcatraz federal penitentiary in the San Francisco Bay, except that the Mexican one had a much more notorious reputation for brutality; some compared the conditions suffered by the inmates there to the horrors of Dante's *Inferno*.

Intimidating as its profile was, however, people sometimes tried to break in—not to free the prisoners but to steal the treasure. Pirates, who were operating in the Caribbean, often raided the island, and for those who were successful the reward could be considerable. Legend has it that one sixteenth-century Dutch pirate (his name was Piet Heyn) made off with some ninety tons of pure gold and silver. Other unwanted foreigners also broke in on occasion, with more grandiose plans in mind. The armed forces of France landed there twice in the nineteenth century for the purpose of taking over Mexico, and President Woodrow Wilson sent in the marines in 1914 to get rid of a dictator, Victoriano Huerta. San Juan de Ulúa had become a symbol of foreign interference in Mexican affairs on top of its other bitter memories.

President Calles may have had this history in mind when he chose San Juan de Ulúa as a meeting place for the Americans, but he was also preoccupied with the pressing problems of his own day. The Mexican army was losing close to a thousand men a month by some estimates, and agricultural production had fallen by 34 percent because of the war. For Calles the meeting with the American priest was a gamble, but given the improvement in Mexican-American relations it was worth a try. It was also a gamble for Father Burke. He had signed a letter that made concessions to Calles and the revolution, without knowing how the Holy See would react, even if Calles accepted the terms. The apostolic delegate, Pietro Fumasoni Biondi, had given his approval, but the delegate could not speak for the Holy See. Nor could he speak for the Mexican bishops who did not even know the meeting was taking place. It was common knowledge that most of them were adamantly opposed to any negotiations with Calles, and when they found out about the first meeting (the one that got cancelled because of leaks), they were not pleased.

The meeting, which lasted five hours, took place in the presidential castle that was part of the San Juan de Ulúa fortress, and sitting at the table that day were Plutarco Calles, Father Burke, Ambassador Morrow, and two Calles representatives, one of whom was the interpreter. The meeting was tense at first. Burke began the conversation by explaining that he represented the U.S. apostolic delegate, Fumasoni Biondi, and that his boss wanted to find out if the offending laws in Mexico could be interpreted in a way that would allow the bishops to return to their spiritual duties. Burke added that the Mexican government should not judge the policy and views of the Holy See by the actions of individual Mexican bishops. Calles' response was immediate and blunt. "Father Burke, you are all wrong with regard to the facts," he said.[9] He condemned the Mexican bishops for stirring up trouble among uneducated people who blindly obeyed them and accused them of trying to weaken (if not destroy) the Mexican government. He cited the boycott and suspension of worship as examples, saying that what the bishops wanted was political control, with no interest in improving the standard of living of the poor. He had never tried to destroy the Catholic Church, he said, but was simply demanding "fidelity to the institutions and laws of Mexico".[10] In his response, Burke resisted the temptation to answer him back point by point, but simply stated that the pope fully supported efforts to help the poor and would never support any move to weaken the government. As the hours rolled on, the mood slowly changed, and both sides turned their attention to Father Burke's March 29 letter as the basis for a modus vivendi. Incredibly, by the

[9] Sheerin, *Never Look Back*, 127.
[10] Bailey, *¡Viva Cristo Rey!*, 196.

end of the day, Calles had signed the response Morrow
had drafted for him, with only minor changes. In that
statement Calles said that "it is not the purpose of the
constitution nor of the laws, nor my own purpose, to
destroy the identity of any church, nor to interfere in any
way with its spiritual function." He called attention to
his oath of office, saying that it was his duty to enforce
the constitution, but also "to see that the laws be applied
in a spirit of reasonableness and without prejudice". He
even agreed to allow an apostolic delegate into the country, with the stipulation that he would not be given official diplomatic recognition. Calles was clearly in a better
mood, and before leaving he asked Burke what the next
step would be. Burke explained that he would have to
report back to the apostolic delegate, who in turn would
send a report to Rome. Calles thanked Burke for coming to meet him, and added (to "my utter amazement",
Burke said): "I hope your visit means a new era for the life
and people of Mexico."[11]

The encounter that both sides feared so much was
already lowering tensions between church and state in
Mexico, and Calles was beginning to see the Catholic
Church in a different light. Burke and Morrow were also
thankful for another reason. There were no leaks. The
Mexico City press carried a routine report that the American ambassador met the Mexican president in Veracruz,
where the president happened to be that day.[12]

Days later, the Mexican government brought the initiative into the public forum, using an event that had already
been planned in Celaya. With both President Calles and
President-elect Obregón present, the education minister

[11] Ibid.
[12] Ibid., 197.

(J. M. Puig Casauranc was his name) spoke about the government's policy of tolerance for all Mexicans, "whether in their hearts is lodged a Masonic belief or whether they have an altar of the Lady of Guadalupe, the blessed virgin who signifies comfort and a feeling of love for the Mexican people".[13] The surprising speech, which became known as the "Mea Culpa de Celaya", made immediate news because of its conciliatory tone, and one newspaper (*El Universal*) reported that the minister's words were giving rise to rumors in the United States about a possible settlement to the religious question.[14]

Back in Washington, the focus now shifted to the Mexican bishops who so far had been kept in the dark about Burke's secret meeting, except for one prelate: Leopoldo Ruiz. He was the seasoned archbishop of Morelia (who coincidentally was staying with Father Burke), a pragmatist with a history of adapting to different political conditions over the years, from the dictatorship of Porfirio Díaz, to the idealism of Francisco Madero, to the chaos caused by the War of the Generals. With the death in San Antonio of Archbishop Mora, he became the de facto leader of the Mexican hierarchy, and the apostolic delegate now looked to him to take on a difficult task. His assignment was to convince his fellow bishops in San Antonio (some of whom were outspoken supporters of the Cristeros), to sign on to a statement containing concessions similar to those in Father Burke's March 29 letter, but without telling them about the existence of the letter or the secret meeting.

Ruiz's approach, when he met with his fellow bishops, was to couch the discussion in Vatican terms. The

[13] Ibid.
[14] *El Universal*, April 29, 1928, cited in Bailey, *¡Viva Cristo Rey!*, 198.

Holy See, he said, was aware that the Cristero War had reached a stalemate, and the pope wanted the Mexican bishops to come to consensus about settlement terms, just in case an opportunity for peace should present itself. However, the discussion that ensued soon uncovered the hardline attitude shared by the majority of Mexican bishops, and the resolution they eventually passed reflected that uncompromising stand. They invoked the memory of the martyrs who had died for the faith, and they paid tribute to the sacrifices made by the League, adding that the League directors should be consulted before a settlement would be reached. Moreover, a settlement would have to include a change in the constitution that was the cause of the brutal persecution in the first place, and also the return of church buildings that had been confiscated by the state. And they brought up amnesty: a guarantee that Catholics who fought in the war would be allowed to return to normal life peacefully without facing revenge. It was the kind of uncompromising consensus that Ruiz had feared, but there was one bright spot—a loophole—in their resolution. It stated that in the final analysis the bishops would obey any decision that the Holy Father would make about Mexico.

Father Burke tried to make the best of it. In order to bridge this gap between the Mexican bishops and Calles, he volunteered to write a diplomatic letter to Calles appealing for more concessions from the Mexican government, but Morrow vetoed the idea saying a letter would be a waste of time. Burke would have to come to Mexico again and talk to the president face-to-face, he said. Burke agreed and Morrow succeeded in getting a date from the president, but then another obstacle reared its head. The president vigorously objected to including Archbishop Ruiz in any meeting, and Morrow had to use all of his diplomatic skills to convince Calles that an agreement without the Mexican bishops' participation would be meaningless. In the end Calles gave in but he was not happy, and when they finally met on May 18 at Chapultepec Castle in Mexico City, Calles was noticeably cold to Ruiz. His handshake was stiff, and his face had no hint of the pleasantness he showed to the others as they entered.[15] Ignoring the bad omen, Burke began the discussion by reporting on the San Antonio bishops' meeting, giving it as positive a spin as he could. The bishops sincerely wanted to return to their dioceses in peace, he said, and they also wanted to know if it was true that the laws on registration and the allocation of priests could be interpreted in an acceptable way. In addition, they wanted clarification on the religious instruction of children in Catholic schools (which was forbidden by the constitution), and also the return of church buildings that had been confiscated by the state. Calles responded that he would consider requests for the return of the buildings but some had been sold; on religious instruction, he said that religion could not be taught in any schools, Catholic or otherwise.

Ironically, it was the unwelcome guest who turned the tide. When his turn came, Archbishop Ruiz struck a conciliatory note, assuring the Mexican president of the bishops' sincere desire to return to the spiritual care of their people. He volunteered to write a formal letter to him (Calles) that would contain the concessions in Father Burke's March 29 letter, with an additional paragraph quoting the conciliatory words in the "Mea Culpa de Celaya" speech. The offer satisfied Calles, and a step-by-step plan of action soon emerged. First, the text of Ruiz's letter would be submitted to the Holy See for approval,

[15] Sheerin, *Never Look Back*, 129.

after which it would be sent as a formal letter to Calles, who would then reciprocate with a formal letter to Ruiz endorsing the points in the first letter and also the sentiments expressed in the "Mea Culpa de Celaya" speech. At that point, the two letters would be published with the following announcement: "In the light of the attached two letters, the Holy See has authorized the resumption of religious worship in Mexico."[16]

Morrow and Burke were elated and immediately got to work putting together a long telegram to Archbishop Fumasoni Biondi in Washington. In the telegram, they described the settlement plan in detail, but also urged him to get the word to Rome as soon as possible so that the churches of Mexico could be reopened by Pentecost, which was only ten days away (May 27, 1928). Excited staff members at the U.S. State Department stayed up all night to transmit the telegram to the apostolic delegate, and they volunteered to handle the follow-up communications between Rome, Washington, and Mexico City.[17] As it turned out, those U.S. State Department services would not be needed. Morrow and Burke were about to get a big surprise.

Slow Down!

The "Americans are crazy", Archbishop Fumasoni Biondi muttered to a staff member when he saw the telegram from Mexico City. Rome does not act on "mere telegraphic advices", he said. "They want to rush things.

---

[16] Ibid.

[17] Ibid., 130. The apostolic delegates of those days did not make much use of telegrams because they were expensive, especially when the documents were lengthy. There was also a concern about confidentiality.

It can't be done. Rome does not act in that way. She is eternal."[18] The telegram was never forwarded to the officials in Rome (they would get a summary). Instead the delegate sent a frigid reply to Ruiz and Burke saying that someone would have to go to Rome personally to handle this matter. The ship "Leviathan" was sailing for Europe on May 26, he told them. It was crushing news for the two Americans, and there was worse to come. Vatican officials were unimpressed when they got news of the settlement, saying that any realistic agreement with the Calles government would have to include guarantees that the anticlerical parts of the Mexican constitution would be changed. To make things worse, Ruiz on his way to Rome leaked the negotiations, which got Calles upset and motivated the militant Mexican Catholics to redouble their efforts to oppose any negotiations. Then the Vatican newspaper *L'Osservatore Romano* ran a series of articles on Mexico that caught Burke and Morrow badly off guard.[19] The articles not only delivered a blistering attack on Calles at a sensitive time, but also attacked Ambassador Morrow, whom they described as a tool of U.S. financial interests. For both Ambassador Morrow and Father Burke, this was a low point in their careers, a period that was marked by confusion and self-doubt.

Ambassador Morrow (a non-Catholic) was disheartened and bewildered by the contradictory messages he was getting from the Catholic Church. If Mexican Catholics were serious about reopening the churches in Mexico, he wondered why the bishops were so adamantly opposed to negotiations with Calles. And if the Vatican was really opposed to the use of violence, as Father Burke had

[18] Ibid.
[19] See ibid., 133.

assured him, how could the directors of the League claim that they had the full support of the pope? Not one to give up, however, Morrow decided to put these questions to Bishop Pascual Díaz, the secretary of the episcopal committee on church-state relations. What was the official policy of the Catholic Church regarding Mexico, he asked him, and exactly who had authority to speak on behalf of the Church? As it turned out, he was asking the right person. Díaz, a Jesuit who had been appointed bishop of Tabasco in 1922, was by this time in close contact with the Holy See and was instrumental in clarifying the Holy See's policy on exactly these questions.

Up to this time, a commission of three bishops, representing the Mexican hierarchy, had been living in Rome to advise the Holy See on the religious issue, and all of them were strongly opposed to negotiations with the Calles government.[20] The truth is they were counting on a Cristero victory in Mexico. What this meant was that the Cristeros had a direct pipeline to Pope Pius XI and were in effect dictating Vatican policy—a situation that Bishop Díaz was determined to change. In November

---

[20] Bailey, ¡Viva Cristo Rey!, 131. In fall 1926, the episcopal committee on church-state relations sent three Mexican bishops to Rome to represent them at the Vatican. All three of them were strong supporters of the League and the Cristero War: Archbishop José Maria González y Valencia of Durango, Bishop Emeterio Valverde y Téllez of León, and Bishop Jenaro Méndez del Rio of Tehuantepec. Their effectiveness in influencing Vatican policy was seen in the words used by Pope Pius XI when he praised a group of young Mexicans who were in Rome for the commemoration of the birth of Saint Luis Gonzaga in January 1927. The pope told the visitors that they were the "sons of a people who are offering their blood for the faith". He then sent greetings to all Mexicans, especially the young, saying: "Tell them that We know all they are doing, that We know they are fighting, and how they are fighting in that great war that can be called the battle for Christ" (ibid., 132). The November 1927 visit of Bishop Pascual Díaz to Rome changed the pope's view of that "battle for Christ".

1927, he went to Rome and bluntly told Vatican officials that a Cristero victory was not possible without U.S. aid, and that U.S. aid was out of the question in the current political climate. With the churches closed in Mexico and the sacramental life of the people at a virtual standstill, the Church could suffer irreparable damage, he said, if the war dragged on much longer. His intervention was successful, so successful that Pietro Cardinal Gasparri, secretary of state, called in the three Mexican bishops and told them that their services were no longer needed in Rome.[21] (From that day forward, Bishop Díaz was seen as an implacable enemy by the Cristeros.)

By the time Bishop Díaz got Ambassador Morrow's list of questions, he was able to give the ambassador up-to-date answers that were clear and definitive: the official spokesman for the Catholic Church in Mexico, he said, was Archbishop Fumasoni Biondi, since he was the apostolic delegate for Mexico as well as for the United States. He stated that Father John Burke was the delegate's representative and he (Díaz) was the official liaison between the apostolic delegate and the Mexican hierarchy. On the question of the League's status, he indicated that the Holy Father had given his full support to that organization the previous year on condition that it stayed out of politics and remained nonviolent. Obviously that condition was no longer being fulfilled, he said, and the pope no longer recognized it as a lay Catholic organization.[22]

(It should be noted that the pope was not actually condemning the Cristero Rebellion and never did. He was simply distancing the Church from the rebellion by stating that Catholics who participated in it were doing so

[21] Ibid., 181.
[22] Ibid., 23.

as individual Catholics in good standing, not as members of an official Catholic organization. The subtlety may not have satisfied Morrow, but at least he knew now which voices to listen to.)

For his part, Father John Burke was also having a difficult time. He was not surprised by the contradictory messages coming from the different levels of authority in the Church; he was too familiar with how the Church works to be bothered by that. But he was frustrated with the Vatican's hard line. He agreed with the U.S. ambassador that to demand immediate changes to the Mexican constitution was unrealistic, given the mindset of Calles. He believed worship in Mexico would never be restored if the Catholic Church insisted on that demand, and restoring worship for the people of Mexico was his main priority. That was also a Vatican priority, of course, but only as part of a bigger picture. Vatican officials feared that the anticlerical articles in the constitution would come back to haunt the bishops if they rushed into an agreement that did not clearly address those articles. (As it turned out, the Vatican's fears were well founded, as we will see in the epilogue.)

Burke was also frustrated with the militancy of the Mexican bishops.[23] With the exception of Ruiz and Díaz, the Mexican bishops wanted the overthrow of Calles rather than a peace agreement, and they believed that outcome was not unrealistic given the success being enjoyed by

---

[23] Archbishop Fumasoni Biondi was also frustrated with the militancy of the Mexican bishops and felt that, except for Ruiz and Díaz, they never accepted him as their apostolic delegate. He also felt that the Vatican had lost confidence in him and was listening to everybody except him. In fact, Vatican officials were listening to many different voices, but they had to pay special attention to the views of the Mexican bishops because, after all, they were the ones with the most personal experience of the religious persecution.

the Cristeros on the battlefield. Some of them even put out pastoral letters calling on American Catholics to send money and arms to the Cristeros. Burke was deeply critical of this policy, though he was careful not to say it in public. He wrote it in his diary. The Mexican bishops had never— not even once—expressed regret for all the atrocities perpetrated against Mexican government officials, he wrote; they would rather "let souls starve and go un-shepherded" than talk peace. As for American intervention of any kind, he said that such foreign intervention would be a betrayal of Mexico's sovereignty. "We have no more right to go in (to Mexico) than England had to go into and dominate Ireland," he wrote.[24]

Then something else happened to add to Burke's frustrations. Father Edmund Walsh, S.J., vice president of Georgetown University, appeared on the scene to the surprise of Burke, Fumasoni Biondi, and Morrow. As head of Georgetown's School of Foreign Service, Walsh was already well known in Rome, and he was asked by Pope Pius XI to do an independent evaluation of the Mexican religious problem.[25] He would eventually be instrumental in convincing the more militant elements of the Mexican Church (lay and clerical) to accept a peace settlement, but what hurt Burke's feelings was the secret nature of his assignment. He

[24] Sheerin, *Never Look Back*, 144.

[25] Father Edmund Walsh, S.J., was an author and professor of geopolitics, and a respected diplomat in his own right. He directed the Papal Famine Mission in Russia during the Bolshevik Revolution, and later he was asked by President Coolidge to use his influence with Archbishop Michael Curley of Baltimore; Curley was a firebrand who was conducting a blistering campaign of criticism against Coolidge's do-nothing policy toward Mexico. More important, Walsh was the founder of Georgetown University's School of Foreign Service, which predated the U.S. Foreign Service by several years. Graduates of Georgetown's School of Foreign Service include President Bill Clinton and President Barak Obama.

was instructed not to inform Burke of his involvement in the issue. Moreover, Burke had the impression that Walsh was now authorized to conduct official negotiations with President Calles. In fact he wasn't.[26]

Burke was now suffering from self-doubt, wondering if he had been pushed aside by the Vatican, and the fact that he remained so unflappable through this period is a tribute to his spirituality. During his life, he had occasionally confided to coworkers that it was his prayer that sustained him in times of trial. After one difficult day of meetings in the apostolic delegate's office, in which they discussed the militancy of some Mexican bishops, he wrote in his diary: "Thus ended the evening at the delegation: I to my house where I composed a so-called poem to Our Lady of the Cenacle."[27] Burke loved to write short verses to the Blessed Mother, which he would send to his friends as Easter greetings or to mark important occasions in their lives.

As it turned out, Burke need not have worried about his role in the Mexican peace negotiations. The key to his importance was his unlikely relationship with Plutarco Calles, and the Mexican president's uncharacteristic trust in him despite the fact that he was a Catholic priest. "Calles' admiration for Father Burke was one of the curious features of the negotiations," says Father John Sheerin, Burke's biographer. "He hated the Church yet showed almost filial reverence for Burke."[28] An example of this reverence was the response of Calles when Morrow asked him not to make their secret meetings public. Morrow secured a promise from Calles to keep the meetings confidential, but

[26] Sheerin, *Never Look Back*, 147.
[27] Ibid., 140.
[28] Ibid., 138.

it was his respect for Burke that caused Calles to make that promise. If Father Burke thought the negotiations should be kept confidential, they would be kept confidential, Calles said. He even went further, saying that "any official the Church might wish to appoint might come and live in freedom in Mexico" as long as that name was suggested by Father Burke.[29] Coming from a president whose policies had murdered some ninety priests, that was unusual.

On February 13, 1929, the importance of the Calles-Burke relationship became apparent again. During a meeting that day between Emilio Portes Gil (the new president of Mexico) and Ambassador Morrow, Portes Gil surprised the ambassador by asking if Father Burke would come down to Mexico at once to see him. Doubtless, Calles had suggested the meeting from behind the scenes. As it turned out, Burke had to decline graciously because he was scheduled to go to Rome with Fumasoni Biondi to discuss the Mexican issue, but the proposal to meet again (the third in a little over a year) was noted with interest by Vatican officials. Two months later, Burke wired his assistant from Rome to say that the Vatican was open to negotiations with the new president of Mexico, based on his March 29 letter of the previous year. Peace negotiations were back on track.

Church-state relations in Mexico had come a long way since the Burke-Morrow meeting in the Mayflower Hotel some twenty months earlier. Both sides were now looking for common ground rather than for excuses to condemn each other. The president of Mexico was no longer accusing the Catholic bishops of directing the Cristero War or other rebellions against the state; he was making a distinction between the official Catholic Church and the

[29] Ibid., 137.

militants. On the other hand, Archbishop Ruiz was reassuring that president of the spiritual, not political, nature of a bishop's mission in the Catholic Church, and he was not demanding that constitutional changes be a precondition to negotiations. In effect, the two sides were accepting the basics of the agreement that Burke and Calles had crafted the previous year.[30] And there was also another important development. To give the discussions more weight, Archbishop Ruiz was now the ad hoc apostolic delegate to Mexico ("ad referendum" was the technical term used by the Vatican). All that was needed now was a meeting date.

Final Settlement

Ambassador Dwight Morrow left Washington by train for St. Louis on June 4, 1929, on the first stage of his trip back to Mexico City. At the request of President Portes Gil, he had cut his vacation short in order to be in the Mexican capital for the upcoming meeting between the president and Archbishop Leopoldo Ruiz, which had been scheduled for June 12. Archbishop Ruiz, accompanied by Bishop Díaz, left Washington on a different train the same day, and because Morrow knew that Ruiz's train was arriving in St. Louis around the same time as his, he arranged to have his private carriage switched to Ruiz's train for the next leg of the trip, to San Antonio. Then he sent his secretary to invite the two churchmen to join him in his carriage so they could talk more about the upcoming meeting. He was still nervous about the details.[31]

[30] Bailey, ¡Viva Cristo Rey!, 254.
[31] Ibid., 270.

For several months, Morrow had continued his role as the behind-the-scenes cheerleader and architect, reminding both sides of the common ground already achieved in the Burke-Calles meetings and drafting new letters that were really not new. It was not smooth sailing, however, especially on the Church side. When it seemed like all the details of the agreement had been nailed down, the archbishop dropped a bombshell that almost derailed the entire peace plan. The Vatican officials, he announced, had changed their minds. They wanted a change in the constitution as a precondition to negotiations after all. Morrow was stunned, and it took all of the skill and patience he could muster to convince Ruiz that such a demand would doom all changes for peace. Ruiz (and the Vatican) backtracked.

It was to make sure there were no more such surprises that Morrow requested a last-minute meeting on the train to San Antonio, and to his relief there were none. The Holy See had reluctantly agreed not to insist on changes to the Mexican constitution at this meeting, the archbishop assured him, on condition that the issue would be addressed as soon as possible. Morrow was satisfied, and when the train arrived in San Antonio, he disconnected his carriage and stayed behind in San Antonio (presumably for some business), while the two bishops continued their journey to Nuevo Laredo, where Mexican officials welcomed them and expedited their passage through immigration. For the remainder of the journey south, Ruiz requested that the doors and windows of their Pullman be kept closed, a request that the employees respected. He did not want word of their return to Mexico, after years of exile, leaking out. The precaution didn't work. In Querétaro a message was delivered to them that they would not be picked up in the Tacuba station as planned, but at a station further into the city. However, even there reporters were waiting with a flurry of questions, which the churchmen carefully evaded. Ruiz simply said that he was happy to be back in Mexico, and that the government had been hospitable to them at the border crossing.

The meeting took place over two days in a large formal room called the Salon de Acuerdos in Chapultepec Castle, but neither Ambassador Morrow nor Father Burke were at the table. Portes Gil wanted to meet with the two Mexican churchmen only. Morrow was active behind the scenes, however, as usual, drafting the amended statement for both sides and making sure that those drafts got the approval of the Jefe Máximo before being submitted to the formal meeting. It worked. Two statements were eventually agreed to, one by Gil and another by Ruiz. Portes Gil's statement assured the Catholics of Mexico that it was not the aim of the Mexican constitution "to destroy the identity of the Catholic Church or of any other (religious organization), nor to interfere in any way with its spiritual functions". Referring to the registration of priests (which "had been misunderstood"), he said that the government could not register any priest who had not been named by proper ecclesiastical authority. He also gave a clarification about religious education, stating that teaching the faith was legal so long as it was carried out within the bounds of the Church. The companion statement by Ruiz was briefer, simply stating that because of the assurances given by President Portes Gil, "the Mexican clergy will resume religious services pursuant to the laws in force".[32]

All that remained was getting approval from the Holy See. To assist with this, Father Walsh (who came to Mexico City even though he was not allowed into the

[32] Ibid., 280.

meetings) used contacts he had at the Chilean Embassy in Mexico City to ensure rapid communication with the Vatican. It was the Chilean cable and code facilities that transmitted the final documents to Rome for approval and received the reply from Vatican Secretary of State Pietro Gasparri. The embassy also made staff available to translate the reply from Italian into Spanish—something that turned out to be a bad idea. The person who did the translating unwittingly mistranslated a critical sentence in Gasparri's reply that touched on the important problem of the Mexican constitution and in so doing gave the false impression that the pope was not demanding (eventual) changes to the Mexican constitution after all. The surprised bishops immediately asked the Vatican for a clarification, but unfortunately Gasparri's response did not clarify the issue because he had no way of knowing that they were working from an erroneous translation. The result was that Ruiz and Díaz went into the final negotiation with Portes Gil on June 21 seriously misinformed about the one issue that worried Vatican officials most—the Mexican constitution—and as a result they were more willing to compromise than they would otherwise have been.[33]

At that final meeting (on June 21), Ruiz did bring up two other issues that had been flagged by Garparri: amnesty for the Cristero soldiers and the return of church buildings. As it turned out, Portes Gil was surprisingly flexible and made generous promises on both counts, but then he brought up a concern of his own. He wanted two "troublesome

[33] Irene Savio, "Cuando los obispos mexicanos engañaron al Papa" (When the Mexican Bishops Deceived the Pope), *Procesco*, November 26, 2017, https://translate.google.com/translate?hl=en&sl=es&u=https://www.proceso.com.mx/512521/cuando-los-obispos-mexicanos-enganaron-al-papa&prev=search. Whether or not this mishap made any difference in the final outcome is a matter for historians to debate.

churchmen"—Archbishop Orozco of Guadalajara and Bishop Manríquez of Huejutla—exiled from the country until more calm conditions would prevail among the people.[34] In response, the surprised Ruiz spoke up in Orozco's defense, but he didn't dwell on the point and Gil got his way. Orozco would have to be a sacrificial lamb. (He did not even try to defend the militant Bishop Manríquez.) The two statements were finally signed in duplicate and exchanged.

Archbishop Ruiz and Bishop Díaz left Chapultepec Castle feeling satisfied with the result, and they drove directly to the Basilica of Our Lady of Guadalupe for a prayer of thanksgiving before the main altar. On their way out of the basilica, Ruiz turned to his companion and gave him some unexpected news. Pope Pius XI had just appointed a new archbishop to Mexico City, he said, and his name was Díaz.

There is a charming follow-up story told about Ambassador Dwight Morrow. On the Sunday that churches finally reopened in Mexico City, he and his wife were in Cuernavaca (where they had a weekend house), and while they were having breakfast on the veranda, the bells at the cathedral nearby began to ring. "Do you hear those bells," he said to his wife. "I had a small role in bringing back those bells." His priest friend wasn't present to enjoy the moment, but the ambassador had not forgotten him. In a personal message to Burke, he congratulated him on "the happy outcome of the work you started more than a year and a half ago", and he praised his "courage, patience, and faith".[35] Undersecretary Robert Olds wrote to Burke also,

----

[34] Bishop José de Jesús Manríquez y Zárate was one of the more outspoken supporters of the Cristeros. Archbishop Orozco never supported them.

[35] Bailey, ¡Viva Cristo Rey!, 284.

saying this: "Perhaps nobody can appreciate as I do that the result would have been quite impossible without your understanding personality and tireless effort. Your superiors owe you more than they will ever realize or ever can repay."[36]

[36] Sheerin, *Never Look Back*, 154.

EPILOGUE

The year was 1934—five years after the settlement that ended the Cristero War—and Lázaro Cárdenas had just been elected president of Mexico. Like his three predecessors, he got the position only because he had the approval of Plutarco Calles, the power behind the scenes in Mexico, and he immediately went about filling his cabinet with names that also had the approval of the Jefe Máximo. They were all anticlerical, but the most famous was the one who got the post of minister of agriculture. His name was Tomás Garrido Canabal, a farmer-turned-lawyer from Tabasco, one of the most fertile regions of Mexico, where the soil was rich and the rainfall plentiful. His father owned large estates there, and as a child Tomás had everything that money could buy except refinement and good manners. "He grew up a rough, uncouth, uncultured, most ill-mannered cattle rancher, and all of his life he never learned to sit properly on a chair," says one historian. "But he had an insatiable and bestial lust for power."[1]

As governor of Tabasco for fifteen years, Garrido became known for his policy toward religion more than his knowledge of agriculture, making Tabasco a laboratory of anti-Catholicism for the rest of the nation. The "most frenzied anti-Catholic ever born in Mexico", historian Enrique Krauze calls him, a man who made Plutarco Calles

---

[1] Joseph Schlarman, *Mexico: A Land of Volcanoes* (Milwaukee: Bruce Publishing, 1950), 535.

look like "a model of Catholic piety".[2] Some examples of his idiosyncrasies and buffoonery: he named his sons Lenin and Lucifer, and it was said that on one of his ranches he had a bull called "God", a hog called "Pope", and a donkey called "Christ". It was this Garrido who issued the famous ruling in 1925 that all priests in his state would have to be married and over forty in order to function, a ruling that caused Archbishop Mora of Mexico City to contact Father John Burke and the U.S. Catholic bishops. Ten years had passed since that communication, and things had not changed very much in Mexico. If anything, the persecution had escalated.

One of Garrido's most famous initiatives was the creation of the Red Shirts (*Rojinegros*), a paramilitary force of young people, dressed in red shirts with black pants or black skirts, whose sole purpose was to terrorize the Catholics of Tabasco with assassination and torture. Graham Greene, whose novel *The Power and the Glory* is set in this part of Mexico, describes what he saw when he visited Villahermosa, the capital of Tabasco. The police there were the "lowest of the population", he says, and even the casual visitor was overwhelmed by their brutality. "These were the men who a few weeks later were to fire into a crowd of unarmed peasants attempting to pray in the ruins of a church," he says. "Garrido did his job well: he knew that the stones cry, and he did not leave any stones."[3] The evil lieutenant in Green's novel is based on Garrido.

When he took up his cabinet post in the Cárdenas administration, Garrido made sure to bring this youth militia with him, much to the horror of Catholics in Mexico City. People had heard about the Red Shirts of

---

[2] Enrique Krauze, *Mexico: Biography of Power* (New York: HarperCollins, 1998), 495.

[3] Schlarman, *Mexico*, 542.

Tabasco, but to see them elevated to the federal level was a shocking reminder of how bad things had become in their country. "Hay Dios?" (Is there a God?), Garrido would yell when he saluted a group of them. "Nunca lo hubo" (There never was), the youths would yell back as they went on another destructive rampage in the city.[4] One of their high-profile activities was what they called "Red Saturdays", a weekly celebration in the courtyard of the Department of Agriculture when religious articles and prayer books were burned to the accompaniment of dancing and song. Churches and private homes were constantly raided to keep up the supply of religious articles for these "Red Saturdays", but the article they wanted most was the image of Our Lady of Guadalupe in the national basilica of that name. They never could get their hand on it because Catholic volunteers organized a round-the-clock guard at the basilica.

An American Protestant minister, Dr. Charles Macfarland, went to Mexico at this time because he wanted to find out for himself if it was really true that the Mexican government was persecuting the Roman Catholic Church. "Is not that question answered sufficiently when I pass the beautiful Cathedral," he wrote in his report,

> and find flaming posters of the State plastered on its walls attacking it in violent terms as an institution, or when I go into a church and find it filled with cartoons, some of them vile caricatures of religion itself? Is it not answered when the government goes into the Cathedral, makes trash heaps of altars and crucifixes, and pastes seals on its paintings of the Madonna and in the church offices on the typewriters, certifying that they are the property of the Government?[5]

[4] Ibid., 544.

[5] Wilfrid Parsons, *Mexican Martyrdom* (Rockford, Ill.: Tan Books and Publishers, 1987), 274.

Broken Promises

The agreement (called the *Arreglos*) that was signed in 1929 by President Emilio Portes Gil and the Catholic Church had begun with high hopes for a new chapter in Mexican church-state relations. Archbishop Ruiz had made a formal statement, days after the *Arreglos* was published, assuring Catholics that the government had recognized the Church's right to exist and had given assurances that the Church would now have adequate freedom to function in Mexican society. Yes, a change in the constitution would have been good, he admitted, but "the evils of a century cannot be cured in a day."[6] With the resumption of worship and a new era of reconciliation, he said, Catholics could work for constitutional changes in a new climate of good will. The Cristero rebels were skeptical of this promise, but they laid down their arms, and the government immediately responded with generous armistice conditions: full guarantees of protection for the lives and property of officers and men (even civilians) who supported the rebellion; payment of twenty-five pesos per rifle to soldiers who turned in their weapons, and permission for those who needed their horses to keep them; certificates of safe conduct for all officers, and permission to keep their side arms.

It looked like the revolutionary government was indeed abiding by its promises, but then worrisome signs began to appear. Former Cristero officers were being assassinated at an alarming rate: a colonel in Zacatecas, then a general in Jalisco, then a mass execution of forty-one ex-soldiers in Jalisco. The government showed little interest

---

[6] David Bailey, *¡Viva Cristo Rey!: The Cristero Rebellion and the Church-State Conflict in Mexico* (Austin: University of Texas Press, 1974), 288.

in investigating these deaths. Even more worrisome was the question of Church properties. Church services had resumed in many places, but in many others the local authorities refused to hand back the churches, rectories, seminaries, and other church buildings, and when Archbishop Ruiz complained to the minister of the interior he was given a sobering answer. "It is true," the minister said, "that the President offered this—I was present—but he did not know what he was offering. If those buildings were vacated and returned, it would stir up a swarm of enemies."[7] It was becoming increasingly clear that the anticlerical wing of the political establishment was ignoring the provisions of the *Arreglos* and of the armistice, regardless of what Portes Gil had promised.

By 1931, when the Church prepared to celebrate the four hundredth anniversary of the apparition of Our Lady of Guadalupe, all pretensions of church-state cooperation had been dropped. In June of that year, Governor Adalberto Tejeda of Veracruz (whose anticlerical reputation matched that of Garrido) approved a law limiting the number of priests in his state to one per hundred thousand inhabitants, and by way of justification he said that the Catholic Church was "the enemy of all work tending toward human redemption".[8] (The bishop immediately suspended worship in the state.) The governors of Chiapas and Yucatan followed his example by drastically reducing the numbers of priests in their states, and Congress passed a law restricting the number of priests in the Federal District. Pope Pius XI finally broke his silence in September 1932, with an encyclical that reviewed the recent history of the persecution and reminded the Mexican government

[7] Ibid., 293.
[8] Ibid., 295.

that it "had no intention of destroying the 'identity of the Church'".[9] The government was doing exactly that, the pope said, with its policy of restricting the number of priests, banishing bishops, and committing atrocities against the faithful. The encyclical attracted widespread attention in the United States, where the full text was printed by many diocesan newspapers and by the *New York Times*.[10] But when President Abelardo Rodríguez (Portes Gil's successor) saw the text, he accused the pope of fomenting a new rebellion. The Chamber of Deputies responded by demanding the expulsion of the apostolic delegate, Archbishop Ruiz; he was immediately arrested and deported to the United States. By this time, there were only 334 priests functioning in the entire country, and seventeen states (including Tabasco) did not have even one priest. By 1935, that number would be 305.[11] The Catholic Church in Mexico had practically ceased to function.

And it wasn't just limiting the number of priests. The government also took over education of the young in a way never seen before, following a call to action from the Jefe Máximo himself. In an influential speech he gave in Guadalajara in July 1934, Calles outlined a new phase of the revolution that would rid the schools of the "clerical and reactionary elements" that still controlled them in many states. "We must enter into and take possession of the minds of the children, the consciences of the young," he said, "because they do belong and should belong to the

[9] Pius XI, encyclical *Acerba Animi* (September 29, 1932), no. 7, http://w2 .vatican.va/content/pius-xi/en/encyclicals/documents/hf_p-xi_enc_2909 1932_acerba-animi.html.

[10] "Text of Encyclical on Mexico's Church Laws", *New York Times*, October 1, 1932; "Full Text of the Pope's Encyclical about Church in Mexico Received by Cable", *The Register*, Superior California edition, October 9, 1932.

[11] Jean Meyer, *The Cristero Rebellion* (London: Cambridge University Press, 1976), 2015.

Revolution."[12] That speech put the final nail in the coffin
of Catholic schools, many of which had managed to function by paying lip service to the provisions of the constitution, usually with the acquiescence of local authorities,
some of whom had their own children in those Catholic
schools. Under this new policy, called "defanaticization",
teachers had to make a commitment to teach hatred of the
Catholic religion in their classrooms. Here is an example of
what teachers had to sign, taken from the state of Yucatan:
"I declare that I am an atheist, an irreconcilable enemy of
the Catholic, Apostolic, and Roman religion, that I will
endeavor to destroy it, detaching consciences from the
bonds of any religious worship, and that I am ready to fight
the clergy anywhere and whenever it will be necessary."[13]

Out-of-control sex education programs were part of
this "defanaticization" campaign. In some places, children
were brought to ranches and stockyards to see animals
copulating, and in the classroom boys and girls had to take
their clothes off in front of each other while the teacher
explained the facts of life. Not surprisingly, the reaction
among parents was furious, in some cases even bizarre. In
Zacatecas, the daughter of a mayor refused to go to school
one morning, and when her irate father realized that it was
the disrobing in class that traumatized her, he marched over
to the school with a revolver in his hand. "My daughter
disrobes only in the presence of her mother," he told the
teacher, as he waved the revolver in her face. "You have
committed an outrage against her. But since this is your
new teaching, you should be ready to do it yourself. Take
off your clothes, and I will take off mine!"[14] The teacher

[12] Parsons, *Mexican Martyrdom*, 223.
[13] Ibid.
[14] Ibid., 260.

did not do it, of course. She screamed and fainted, but the mayor had made his point. Meanwhile, other more determined types—some old Cristero soldiers—took up guns for real and tried to organize a second Cristero rebellion, but their efforts went nowhere because Catholics were tired of fighting and the Church excommunicated them. However, their guerilla campaign did take a toll on the teachers who were "defanaticizing" the children. In three years, one hundred schoolteachers were assassinated and two hundred were wounded or mutilated (usually by cutting off their ears).[15]

In the face of this chaos, most ordinary Catholics turned to clandestine home schools as the only option, with former public school teachers doing the teaching along with religious sisters who dressed in lay clothes. They did so under penalty of law, of course, because according to the Cárdenas interpretation of the constitution (which had been amended by the Mexican Senate) even teaching religious doctrine in the home was against the law. In Mexico City alone, an estimated sixty-one thousand children were attending those home schools, all under the nose of a government that was helpless to do anything about it.[16] The situation was chaotic, and Cárdenas eventually came to the conclusion that the "defanaticization" program would have to end. In any case, he was growing tired of the needless vulgarity being displayed by the priest-baiters in his government.

Peace at Last!

Lázaro Cárdenas made another far-reaching change at this time. He broke loose from the Jefe Máximo's control and

---

[15] Meyer, Cristero Rebellion, 205.
[16] Parsons, Mexican Martyrdom, 251.

fired all the Calles loyalists in the army and in the cabinet, including Tomás Garrido Canabal, whom he forced into exile in Costa Rica. He put Calles on a plane for San Diego, California, and told him not to come back. Having asserted his independence, he then took steps to reduce the tension between the revolutionary regime and the Church, thus freeing the government to concentrate on the more important issues facing the nation. A new era of peace and common sense was on the horizon in Mexico, and a new generation of young governors, who were less ideological than their predecessors, helped usher it in.

So did Luis María Martínez, the scholarly churchman who was appointed to succeed Pascual Díaz as archbishop of Mexico City. Martínez had been a friend of Cárdenas since their youth in Michoacán, and he was able to see the president's good side: his sincere commitment to the poor and his simple lifestyle. (As president, Cárdenas cut his salary in half and refused to live at Chapultepec Castle.) Martínez encouraged his priests to work constructively with the socialist government in power, and in a much-discussed pastoral letter he called on priests to show more concern for the socioeconomic welfare of the poor.

At the same time, churches were beginning to reopen all over the country: first in Mexico City and Veracruz, then in Nayarit and Jalisco, then in Chiapas and Tabasco—even Tabasco! The Church's darkest hour was finally over, and Mexican Catholics would never again see a spasm of persecution like this. In the following decades, memories began to fade, and the anticlerical laws of the 1917 Constitution became more and more anachronistic. Government officials turned a blind eye to the proliferation of Catholic schools, many officials quietly sending their own children to those schools. Stories abounded about fast-talking nuns holding up education inspectors at the door while their colleagues rushed to turn around the pictures on the walls—pictures that had an image of our Lady on the front and an image of Benito Juárez on the back. Then in 1979, Pope John Paul II visited Mexico, drawing massive crowds of enthusiastic Catholics and charming government officials who were happy to be included in the festivities. When some commentators jokingly reminded President José López Portillo that the pontiff was breaking the law by wearing a white cassock in public, the president volunteered to pay the fifty-cent fine.

A few years later, under the presidency of Carlos Salinas de Gortari, the anachronisms of the 1917 Constitution were finally repealed. The Church was given a legal identity under the law, thus allowing her to own property again, and convents and monasteries that existed in defiance of the law were given formal recognition. Priests were also allowed to vote. Archbishop Girolamo Prigione, the pope's special envoy to Mexico at the time, summed up the seventy-year-old anomaly that was finally ending with these words: "In Mexico we have lived a paradox: that of a profoundly Catholic nation that has had to coexist with the most anticlerical constitution on the planet. By comparison, the constitution of the Soviet Union sounded like a Christmas song."[17]

What Happened to the Pivotal Players?

All those involved in the negotiations to end the Cristero War continued to be involved in the outcome of the *Arreglos*, each limited by the number of years given him. Some lived remarkably short lives.

---

[17] Tim Golden, "Mexico Ending Church Restraints after 70 Years of Official Hostility", *New York Times*, December 20, 1991.

Father John Burke

Father John Burke wasn't in Mexico City for the signing of the *Arreglos*, but he continued to follow the Mexican religion crisis, giving regular reports to the administrative committee of the U.S. bishops on the progress of the settlement. When Portes Gil's successor, Pascual Ortiz Rubio, visited Washington in December 1929, Burke and Morrow (both of whom were worried about how things were going in Mexico) met with him, explaining to him that the modus vivendi was only a temporary arrangement and that the Catholic Church in Mexico was counting on a change in the constitution. The president-elect was sympathetic but said the timing was not right. "If the Catholics will be patient for a while and wait quietly," he said, "I will be able, after two years, to secure such changes; I think they ought to be made."[18] Rubio did eventually try to make some changes, but soon found himself out of a job; the Jefe Máximo got rid of him. It probably didn't help that by then his two sons were in a Catholic college in the United States: St. Benedict's College for men in Atchison, Kansas.[19]

When Franklin D. Roosevelt became U.S. president in 1933, Catholics were more hopeful that the United States would take a stronger stand on the persecution of Mexican Catholics, but his presidency soon got trapped in an embarrassing blunder. In a speech given at an education seminar in Mexico City, Josephus Daniels, the new ambassador, embraced the education policies of Plutarco Calles,

[18] John Sheerin, *Never Look Back: The Career and Concerns of John J. Burke* (New York: Paulist Press, 1975), 157.

[19] "Sons of Rubio Have Religion among Studies: Mexican President's Boys Termed Good Fellows at Atchison", *The Register*, Superior California edition, December 14, 1930.

even quoting the words that Calles used in his famous Guadalajara speech that "we must enter and take possession of the minds of childhood, the minds of youth."[20] In effect, Daniels was giving the impression that the U.S. government supported the Cárdenas education policies, and news of his speech caused an immediate uproar in the United States. The Catholic press (including magazines like *America*, *Commonweal*, and the *Catholic World*) carried blistering editorials against Calles,[21] and the firebrand radio preacher Father Charles Coughlin told his twenty-five million listeners that for two decades American presidents had aided and abetted the rape of Mexico. Individual bishops also spoke out, in particular the independent-minded archbishop of Baltimore, Michael Curley, who said the twenty million Catholics of the United States were fed up with Roosevelt. He even attacked the administrative committee of the Catholic bishops and the "mild-mannered" priest (Burke) who was fooled by Calles. "Let our gentle, sacerdotal diplomats in this country stay at home," he said.[22] There was also action in the U.S. Congress, with resolutions in both the Senate and the House of Representatives, and the Knights of Columbus was calling on the president to act.

All sides now looked to Father John Burke for help. Pope Pius XI requested, through the U.S. apostolic delegate, that he get involved on behalf of the Holy See, while at the same time President Roosevelt (FDR) sought his advice. Burke had enjoyed the respect of five presidents, but FDR admired him most, consulting him regularly on

[20] Sheerin, *Never Look Back*, 160.

[21] For example, "The Last Turn of the Screw", *Commonweal*, August 24, 1934, is an editorial on the education policies of Plutarco Elías Calles.

[22] Sheerin, *Never Look Back*, 165.

matters of religion. It mystified the bishops of Mexico that a Catholic priest could command such respect in a Protestant nation like the United States, while they were living under conditions of such unprecedented persecution.

In his White House meetings on the subject, Father Burke briefed Roosevelt on the background to Ambassador Daniels' blunder (the Calles speech in Guadalajara). He reminded him that the Mexican government was exiling hundreds of Catholics, including bishops, priests, nuns, and laity without due process. His words got a sympathetic hearing. The president immediately talked to the Mexican ambassador about it, and shortly afterward Roosevelt put out a statement condemning all religious persecution that repeated, practically verbatim, some ideas Burke had given to him in a memo,[23] without mentioning Mexico by name. It was obvious what Roosevelt was referring to, and his statement did produce one modest result. The Mexican ambassador sent word to Father Burke that his government would be open to discussing the religious problem with a new apostolic delegate in Mexico. However, that offer went nowhere, in part because the Vatican saw no sense in appointing another apostolic delegate to Mexico without a guarantee that he would not be dismissed by the government before he unpacked his suitcase. (During the Obregón-Calles presidencies, two apostolic delegates were dismissed a couple of months after their arrival on the job.)

The end result: the issue of Mexican church-state relations remained unresolved for decades, with the Catholic

---

[23] Ibid., 166. According to an article written by Anthony F. O'Boyle, "Roosevelt, Romulo Honored by University", *Notre Dame Scholastic*, December 13, 1935, Roosevelt gave a speech at Notre Dame University later that year, telling his audience that the United States regarded religious and educational freedom as supreme among the rights of man, and that this policy was freely offered to other nations if they desired to accept it.

Church continuing to operate without any juridical status or civil rights. During those years, the Vatican had to appoint low-level officials to represent the pope in Mexico—officials who were assigned to the Church in Mexico, not the government. They had no diplomatic credentials. Finally, when President Salinas reformed the Mexican constitution in 1992, his government and the Vatican exchanged diplomats at the ambassadorial level, thus ending a church-state stand-off that had lasted 125 years, since the time of Benito Juárez, who made the formal break with Rome when he executed Emperor Maximilian.

By 1992, Father John Burke had long since gone to his reward. He died in 1936 at the age of sixty-one, and at his funeral eulogists focused on his achievements in the United States rather than his achievements in Mexico. He was, after all, the founder of what is now known at the National Conference of Catholic Bishops, arguably his greatest achievement. "We believe that the name of Monsignor Burke will be recorded in the history of the Catholic Church in the United States," *Commonweal* magazine commented, "high among the very greatest leaders of Catholic Action—on the same level of creative influence where stand such figures as Cardinal Gibbons, Archbishop Hughes and Bishop England."[24]

Dwight Morrow

Dwight Morrow's life was even shorter than that of Father Burke's. In 1930 he was elected to the U.S. Senate, representing the state of New Jersey, but died suddenly in 1931, having served less than a year. He was only fifty-eight years old. As a partner in J. P. Morgan, he died one of

---

[24] "A Great Servant of the Church", *Commonweal*, November 13, 1936, quoted in Sherrin, *Never Look Back*, 9.

the richest men in New Jersey, with an estate worth about
135 million dollars in today's money.

His early death may have hastened the demise of the
Mexican peace agreement. During a visit to Rome around
this time, Archbishop Francisco Orozco met Father
Edmund Walsh, S.J., and the two reminisced about the
Cristero War and its aftermath. What had been the guarantee that the *Arreglos* would be honored, Orozco asked
the Jesuit. His reply: "Morrow ... but Morrow died on
us."[25] Morrow's early death may also have been part of
the reason that President Portes Gil was able to claim that the
ambassador had no significant role in the negotiations that
ended the war. In his self-serving autobiography, written
three and a half decades later, Portes Gil said: "As regards
the supposed intervention of the U.S. ambassador, I deny
absolutely that there was any."[26] He had two interviews
with Morrow, Gil claimed, during which the ambassador
congratulated him for his achievements and nothing more.
What Gil conveniently forgot was that the agreement he
signed with the Church in 1929 was, almost word-for-
word, the modus vivendi that Ambassador Morrow had
drafted for his predecessor the previous year.[27]

Morrow's term in Mexico did have a happy ending for
his family. His daughter, the future Ann Morrow Lindbergh, met aviator Charles Lindbergh in 1927 while he
was on a goodwill tour in Mexico City, and the two got
married shortly afterward. The tour had been organized by
Ambassador Morrow as a way to improve relations between
the United States and Mexico. Ann Lindbergh would later
become a famous aviator herself and a well-known author.

[25] Bailey, *¡Viva Cristo Rey!*, 298.
[26] Ibid., 299.
[27] Ibid.

Archbishop Leopoldo Ruiz

Archbishop Leopoldo Ruiz led the negotiations that ended the Cristero War and had to lead the implementation of the settlement. As soon as the agreement was signed, he instructed the Cristeros to lay down their arms, but soon had to face the wrath of militant Catholics who felt betrayed by both the government and the Church. One embittered group of old Cristeros (in Michoacán, Ruiz's own state) accused him and Díaz of apostasy and formed its own schismatic community that sought refuge in a life of prayer and solitude. As it turned out, Ruiz was eventually exiled by the revolutionaries he thought he could trust and ended up running the affairs of the apostolic delegate's office from San Antonio, Texas, where his fellow bishops had lived in exile before the *Arreglos* was signed. He became a familiar name in the American Catholic press, which was reporting on the renewed persecution of the Church in Mexico with increasing horror. A description of his exile in 1932, written by Ruiz himself, appeared on the front pages of diocesan publications all over the United States. The newspaper in the Sacramento diocese ran a banner headline on the front page that said: "Delegate Tells Story of His Expulsion".[28] He finally resigned as apostolic delegate in 1937 and was allowed to return to Morelia, where he lived out the rest of his life, helping to direct the archdiocese he had run years earlier. A coadjutor bishop had been appointed by then. He died in 1941 at the age of seventy-six.

Archbishop Pascual Díaz

Archbishop Pascual Díaz lived his final years as archbishop of Mexico City, the most prestigious position in

[28] Leopold Ruiz y Flores, "Delegate Tells Story of His Expulsion", *The Register*, Superior California edition, October 16, 1932.

the Mexican hierarchy, but it was his lot not to see much of that prestige. He had no official place to live because the government did not return the episcopal palace, and renting a place was difficult because people were afraid their property would be confiscated.[29] In 1931, he was blindsided by the Chamber of Deputies when they suddenly passed a law restricting the number of priests who could function in his vast archdiocese, and he would have immediately resorted to the old weapon—suspension of worship—if Rome had not prevailed on him to hold back. Rome wanted to give the *Arreglos* a chance to work, hoping that President Ortiz Rubio would break with the Jefe Máximo and follow his own star. He never did, of course, and as church-state relations went on a downward spiral, Díaz suffered humiliation after humiliation. At one point, he and four other clergymen were arrested and thrown into a filthy jail like common criminals; among the charges leveled against him was the claim that he was carrying a machine gun in his car. He also had to suffer the hostility of the Cristeros who considered him a traitor. They never forgot his 1927 intervention that brought about the change in Vatican policy regarding the war. He died in 1936 at the age of sixty.

The National League for the Defense of Religious Liberty

The National League for the Defense of Religious Liberty (Liga Nacional Defensora de la Libertad Religiosa, LNDLR), which directed the Cristero War, was ordered by Archbishop Ruiz to drop the word "religious" from its name if it proposed to continue its involvement in politics. The directors ignored the order at first, but eventually had to obey in an effort to stay relevant. The organization

[29] Bailey, *¡Viva Cristo Rey!*, 297.

continued to function for another decade, but eventually went out of existence.[30] Some of the directors, however, continued to speak and write—and claim victory. The Cristeros, they said, had by force of arms forced the revolutionaries to accept the Church's right to exist and the de facto authority of the pope. The best known of these was Miguel Palomar y Vizcarra, the brilliant Jalisco attorney who had been made a Knight of St. Gregory at the request of Archbishop Orozco years earlier. A disciple of *Rerum Novarum*, he had been a key figure in the Catholic congresses, a leader of the Catholic party in the Jalisco legislature, and eventually one of the founders of the League. A prodigious writer and lecturer, he continued to defend the rebellion he helped direct and continued to vent his anger at all sides: the revolutionary government, the American ambassador, and the Catholic bishops.[31] He died in 1968 at the age of eighty-eight.

Who Won the Cristero War?

Looking back with the perspective of history, it can be said that neither side lost. The revolutionary regime was indeed threatened by the new Catholicism of *Rerum Novarum*, and Plutarco Calles badly miscalculated the willingness of Catholics to fight in a grassroots rebellion. Nevertheless, the stability of the government was never threatened, and the rebellion did nothing to change the antireligious provisions of the 1917 Constitution. In fact, in the 1930s, those provisions became even harsher. It

[30] The ACJM went through a similar evolution. After initially trying to keep its identity, it became absorbed by a new Catholic Action movement initiated by Archbishop Díaz.

[31] Bailey, *¡Viva Cristo Rey!*, 299.

was not until 1992, when a new generation with a less polarized view of the world came on the scene, that President Carlos Salinas abrogated the extreme elements of the constitution.

On the other hand, the Catholic Church did not lose the war either. The rebellion forced the government to talk peace eventually and admit (on paper at least) that the Catholic Church had a right to exist and was a pillar of society in Mexico. More importantly, the brutality and persecution visited on the people of Mexico only made the faith of the people stronger. To this day, the shrines of the martyrs inspire countless thousands of pilgrims, and the Basilica of Our Lady of Guadalupe in Mexico City is one of the most visited shrines on the planet. The faith that is so much admired in Mexican Catholics today can be attributed to the suffering of their grandparents and great-grandparents in the 1920s and 1930s.

The Cristeros, however, failed in their aim to overthrow the Calles government, despite their considerable success on the battlefield. At the zenith of their power, they controlled significant areas of the country, even setting up civil administrations, but that success was limited to a half dozen states and involved only the minority of Catholics who lived in the rural areas. The majority of Mexican Catholics watched the Cristero Rebellion from the sidelines—from fear, but also from ambivalence. They were loyal to the Church, despite the atheistic rants of the revolutionaries, but they were also sympathetic to the social agenda of the government. They wanted Mass on Sunday, but they wanted a government program that promised a better wage on Monday. As David Bailey puts it: "Just as many of the people were puzzled when revolutionary orators told them that the Church was an enemy of their happiness, so were they unconvinced by arguments that only a government inspired by Catholic ideals could give them prosperity and justice."[32]

With a stalemate in the war and a divided clergy, it was Rome that finally decided to end the conflict. During the final negotiations, the Holy See pushed hard for a change in the anti-Catholic laws of the Mexican constitution, but in the end Vatican officials accepted a lesser deal for a very practical reason. They wanted the churches of Mexico reopened.[33] Mexican Catholics had been deprived of the sacraments for three years, and to prolong that suspension, Rome believed, could result in serious spiritual damage, maybe even the total abandonment of the faith by the people. There was also a concern about the continued absence of the bishops from their dioceses. With nobody in charge in a diocese, church life could quickly descend into laxity and chaos. So having convinced the Mexican bishops that the deal worked out with Portes Gil was the best they would get, Rome decided to go with that deal, fully aware that it would anger the League directors and the officers on the battlefield, none of whom had been consulted.

As soon as Archbishop Ruiz announced the agreement and called on the rebels to lay down their arms, support for the Cristeros evaporated overnight. Jesús Degollado, who had replaced Enrique Gorostieta as supreme commander, had no choice but to surrender, and he did not hide his bitterness when he addressed his disappointed troops. The Cristeros had not been conquered by their enemies, he said, but had been abandoned by "those who were to have been the first to receive the worthy fruits of their sacrifices and abnegation".[34] It was an understandable

[32] Ibid., 309.
[33] Ibid., 281.
[34] Ibid., 288.

expression of anger from the supreme commander, but inevitably it lacked objectivity. The Cristeros never had a realistic chance of overthrowing the government of Mexico because the United States supported the Calles regime and had an embargo on supplying arms to rebel groups. Thoughtful Catholics in Mexico (clerical and lay) were happy to keep it that way. They did not want the Cristeros to win for two reasons: Firstly, they were concerned about the lay control of parishes that developed during the three years of the war. They worried that when the parishes returned to normal life, those lay leaders might not welcome the return of the priests, about half of whom opposed the Cristero War or waited it out on the sidelines. Secondly, while they sympathized with the Cristero fight for religious freedom, they did not sympathize with their ambition to take over the government. They feared that the Cristeros would make a bigger mess of governing than the anticlerical politicians had. Father José Garibi, secretary to Archbishop Orozco and later cardinal, put it this way in an interview with Jean Meyer: "The Cristeros were worse than the government men. What disorder! And to think that they nearly became the government. At least the federation is made up of people on the side of order. It was providential that there were Cristeros, and providential that the Cristeros ceased to exist."[35] That was also the conclusion of Archbishop Ruiz, Bishop Díaz, and the Holy See.

How the rank-and-file Cristero rebels handled the aftermath, however, was also providential. The majority of them returned to their farms and villages and resumed their former lives, but they kept the memory of the rebellion alive in their families, passing on war stories to their

[35] Meyer, *Cristero Rebellion*, 69.

children and grandchildren about what it was like to go for days without food, displaying heroic courage as they faced the machine guns of the Mexican armed forces. Those memories are alive in Mexican families to this day. When Mexican Catholics celebrate the Feast of Christ the King and join in the usual cry, *Viva Cristo Rey*, at the end of Mass, many do so with tears in their eyes because they are celebrating members of their own families who died for the faith. The sacrifices of those family members count in the eyes of God, even if they did not merit official canonization.

CHRONOLOGY

1519: Hernán Cortés and his forces land in Mexico

1524: Missionaries begin conversion of Indians to Christianity

1545: Las Casas (Protector of the Indians) becomes bishop of Chiapas

1551: The University of Mexico is founded

1767: Expulsion of the Jesuits from Latin America

1810: Father Miguel Hidalgo y Costilla launches the War of Independence

1822: Agustín de Iturbide crowned emperor of independent Mexico

1823: Antonio López de Santa Anna overthrows Iturbide

1824: Mexico's first constitution; Church privileges remain in place

1833: Antonio López de Santa Anna becomes president

1848: Treaty of Guadalupe Hidalgo

1855: Antonio López de Santa Anna overthrown after eleven terms

1857: New constitution curtailing the influence of the Catholic Church

1858–1861: War of the Reform between Liberals and Conservatives

1861: Conservatives defeated; Benito Juárez becomes president

1862: French army invades Mexico, supported by Conservatives

1864: Maximilian made emperor of Mexico, supported by Conservatives

1867: Liberals defeat Maximilian; Juárez reestablishes the republic

1876: Porfirio Díaz leads new rebellion and becomes president

1891: Pope Leo XIII issues encyclical *Rerum Novarum*

1910: Francisco Madero overthrows Porfirio after thirty-four years in power

1911: National Catholic Party founded (lasted only two years)

1913: Francisco Orozco becomes archbishop of Guadalajara (February 9)

1913: Francisco Madero overthrown; War of Generals begins (February 9)

1913: ACJM founded to involve Catholic youth in public life

1913: Diet of Zamora climaxes a Catholic social justice movement

1914: Archbishop of Guadalajara flees country; first of five exiles

1917: New anticlerical constitution issued from Querétaro

1918: Boycott in Jalisco paralyzes state economy in eight months

1920: Álvaro Obregón becomes president; constitution not implemented

1924: Plutarco Calles becomes president; constitution is implemented

1925: Calles attempts to set up his own "Mexican pope"

1926: Calles Law requires priests to register with the state (June 14)

1926: Worship suspended by bishops in Mexico (July 31)

1926: Cristero War breaks out in small isolated areas (August 1)

1927: League takes over the scattered Cristero uprising (January 1)

1927: Anacleto González Flores martyred in Guadalajara (April 1)

1927: Father Miguel Pro martyred in Mexico City (November 23)

1928: Father Toribio Romo martyred in Tequila (February 25)

1931: Archbishop Francisco Orozco exiled for the fifth time

1936: Francisco Orozco dies peacefully in Guadalajara at age seventy-one

ACKNOWLEDGMENTS

I am indebted to my namesake, Dr. James Murphy (no relation), professor emeritus of English at the University of California (UC), Davis. He was the one who encouraged me to write this book, and when I finally got something on paper his advice and guidance at every step of the way was invaluable. He was my coach. The structure of this book would have been different (more confusing) were it not for his suggestions.

Two other former UC Davis professors, Dr. Sherry Fields and Dr. Jane Beal, also read the manuscript and made helpful suggestions.

I am also indebted to Deacon Gerry Pauley of Immaculate Conception Parish, Sacramento, and his wife, Barbara. They took a special interest in the project and spent countless hours researching articles about the Cristero War in old issues of our diocesan newspaper, the *Catholic Herald*, formerly the *The Register*, Superior California edition. The newspaper clippings they put together tracked how an average U.S. diocesan newspaper covered the crisis over a ten-year period, thus providing me with a bird's-eye view of the American perspective. Their four folders of clippings were an invaluable resource.

Personal friends provided me with much-needed encouragement, in particular Bishop Jaime Soto of Sacramento, Auxiliary Bishop Tom Curry of Los Angeles, and Monsignor Albert O'Connor of Sacramento. I am indebted to numerous Mexican families from whom I

heard fascinating stories of the Cristero War, but two families stand out. During my many visits to the Lemus family in Mexico City, I had the chance to meet their aging
father who was a veteran of the Cristero War. In 1991, I
had the privilege of presiding at his funeral in the Mexican
capital. Meanwhile, the Romo family of Sacramento has
told me many stories about their famous cousin, Father
Toribio Romo, whose relic is enshrined in the altar of
our cathedral, Cathedral of the Blessed Sacrament in Sacramento; he was one of those canonized by Pope John
Paul II in 2000. About three hundred members of that
family celebrate the saint's feast every year with a Mass and
picnic in a Sacramento park, and they always include me
in those celebrations.

SELECTED BIBLIOGRAPHY

Bailey, David. *¡Viva Cristo Rey!* Austin: University of Texas Press, 1974.

Ball, Ann. *Blessed Miguel Pro*. Rockford, Ill.: Tan Books and Publishers, 1996.

Fernández, Fidel González. *Sangre y Corazón de un Pueblo*. Guadalajara: Arzobispado de Guadalajara, 2008.

Krauze, Enrique. *Mexico: Biography of Power*. New York: HarperCollins, 1998.

López-Menéndez, Marisol. *Miguel Pro: Martyrdom, Politics, and Society in Twentieth-Century Mexico*. Lanham, Md.: Lexington Books, 2016.

Meyer, Jean. *The Cristero Rebellion*. London: Cambridge University Press, 1976.

―――. *La Cristiada*. Mexico City: Editorial Cleo, 2008.

―――. *La Cristiada*. Garden City Park, N.Y.: SquareOne Publishers, 2013.

―――. *La Cruzada por Mexico*. Mexico City: Tusquets Editores México, 2008.

Meyer, Michael, William Sherman, and Susan Deeds. *The Course of Mexican History*. New York: Oxford University Press, 2007.

Rodríguez, Javier Navarro. *Tierra de Mártires*. Guadalajara: Impre-Jal, 2002.

Norman, Mrs. George. *The Life and Martyrdom of Father Michael Pro, S.J.* London: Catholic Book Club, 1938.

Parsons, Wilfrid. *Mexican Martyrdom*. Rockford, Ill.: Tan Books and Publishers, 1987. First published, New York: Macmillan, 1936.

Starr, Kevin. *Continental Ambitions: Roman Catholics in North America*. San Francisco: Ignatius Press, 2016.

Schlarman, Joseph. *Mexico: A Land of Volcanoes*. Milwaukee: Bruce Publishing, 1950.

Sheerin, John. *Never Look Back: The Career and Concerns of John J. Burke*. New York: Paulist Press, 1975.

INDEX